BRIDGE BUILDING

"The methodology of see, judge, act comes alive in the teaching and witness of Pope Francis. This simple yet prophetic approach to theology, demonstrated throughout the book, provides a bridge for understanding Catholic social thought, Vatican II, and the Ignatian and Latin American roots of Francis's teaching."

Erin Brigham, PhD
Joan and Ralph Lane Center for Catholic Social Thought and the Ignatian Tradition
University of San Francisco

"I highly recommend this remarkable book to all those teaching theology at any level in the contemporary U.S. cultural context. It masterfully addresses one of the most pressing ecclesial issues in U.S. Catholic life: overcoming the privatization of faith and the disparity between doctrines of social justice or indeed any civically engaged practice and the lived experience of the Church for most U.S. Catholics and their leaders. Bridge Building succeeds as a genuinely collaborative and cohesive collection of relevant essays by offering practical means for the U.S. Catholic faithful to realize Vatican II's call for the prophetic inculturation of Church in and for our society."

John J. Markey
Professor of Theology, Oblate School of Theology

"The book provides the debate on Jorge Mario Bergoglio's pontificate a much-needed series of studies in the concept of "bridge building"—more important than ever in a global "pontifex", bridge-builder like pope Francis. This book makes a very clear case for the importance of Francis' pontificate in connecting ecclesiological concepts such as communion and synodality with practical theology—migration, inclusion, peacebuilding, disability, and human development."

Dr. Massimo Faggioli
Professor of Historical Theology, Villanova University

BRIDGE BUILDING

BRIDGE BUILDING

Pope Francis' Practical Theological Approach

EDITED BY
THOMAS M. KELLY, PhD AND
BOB PENNINGTON, PhD

A Herder & Herder Book
THE CROSSROAD PUBLISHING COMPANY
NEW YORK

A Herder & Herder Book
The Crossroad Publishing Company
www.crossroadpublishing.com

© 2020 by Thomas M. Kelly and Bob Pennington

The text of this book is set in 10/14 Sabon LT Pro.

Composition by Rachel Dlugos
Cover design by Sophie Apel
Cover image by MaxyM/shutterstock.com

Library of Congress Cataloging-in-Publication Data
available upon request from the Library of Congress.

ISBN 978-0-8245-9806-8 paperback
ISBN 978-0-8245-0177-8 cloth
ISBN 978-0-8245-50178-5 ePub
ISBN 978-0-8245-50179-2 mobi

Books published by The Crossroad Publishing Company may be purchased at special
quantity discount rates for classes and institutional use. For information, please e-mail
sales@crossroadpublishing.com.

This book is dedicated to the life, commitments, and ministry of

Rev. Robert Pelton, CSC

In gratitude for bridges built and the inspiration for building more.

CONTENTS

Part IV: Bridge Theology: Forming Bridge Builders in the Classroom

ACKNOWLEDGMENTS

This book is the result of a chance meeting at the University of Notre Dame Center for Social Concerns in the spring of 2019. Dr. Thomas Kelly and I met after we each presented a paper at the Catholic Social Tradition Conference. We soon realized we share the same passion for practical theology, a type of theology that seeks to methodically build bridges of faith and reason in a way that aims to transform a culture of indifference and injustice through social action.

After sharing our idea with many of our colleagues, who signed on to write chapters for our project, we approached Chris Myers of Herder and Herder/Crossroad Publishing. Without his belief in our project, Dr. Kelly and I would not have been able to turn our idea into a reality.

We also want to acknowledge our gratitude to our colleagues who believed in our project and signed on to contribute chapters. Each author adds valuable insight to our project and for that Dr. Kelly and I are grateful.

We also would like to thank the ACTA Foundation for their generous support of our scholarship, which is integral to the Catholic Social Action in the Americas Conference, a bi-annual venture that began in 2018 that aims to bring together laity, theologians, and religious alike to engage in dialogue on topics such as immigration, economics, ecology, addiction, LGBTQ+, racism, and sexism in society and the Church's response.

PART I

Bridge Theology: Method and Methodology

Introduction to Bridge Theology

Thomas M. Kelly, PhD and Bob Pennington, PhD

In the middle of the past century the Catholic Church asked a fundamental question of itself—one that would determine its future in very concrete ways. The question was how to engage the "world" that the Church had seen itself as above, even separate from. In this context, a plethora of issues and controversies vexed the Church throughout the 19th and early 20th centuries: Should human beings be free to worship according to their conscience? Should "secular" sciences that begin outside of revealed truth be used to better understand the world? Are people outside our own religious community in any kind of contact with God? Can we use modern literary methods to better understand the Bible? Are all people called to holiness or only those who are ordained? Do lay people in the Catholic Church have a role beyond praying, paying, and obeying?

As basic as these questions are to our modern eyes, they had to be addressed, and how the Church would respond set the trajectory for how it would interact with the world in almost every way. This response began formally with the commencement of the Second Vatican Council in 1962. Contrary to popular wisdom at the time, the Church would surprise many and embark upon a significant reorientation of its own self-understanding, its role and purpose in the world, and its relationship to its own members

1

as well as to peoples throughout the world. The great challenge was exactly how to implement practical changes coming out of the Council.

As theologians in the United States, we have witnessed the non-reception of Vatican II in our local, regional, and national Catholic Church. Indeed, passive rejection is the story of Vatican II in the United States—in other words, many of the conclusions of Vatican II are quietly tolerated while many of its most important teachings are simply ignored. In the United States cultural context there continues to be a privatization of piety and personal spiritual life disconnected from the world in which we live. This form of faith promotes a preference for liturgy and dogma over and against a civically engaged practice of faith.

Many authors in this book have taught at Catholic universities for many years and encounter students who have never heard of the Second Vatican Council. They often think people outside of Catholicism are condemned, the world is "fallen" or not worth engaging, and Sunday Mass is the most, if not only, important religious obligation for them to fulfill. They can recite every teaching the Church promotes on sacraments or sexual issues (whether they agree or not) but know little or nothing about biblical teachings, a living wage, teachings on immigration, climate change, labor unions, interreligious dialogue, or ecumenical commitments. In short, the Catholic Church of North America has failed to communicate significant aspects of Vatican II.

As professors at Catholic colleges and universities who receive children formed by the Church across the country, what has *not* been taught in either parishes or primary and secondary Catholic educational institutions, is striking. For example, the vast majority of students come to university from Catholic schools and parishes without ever having engaged in work for justice. They have been formed and participated in an almost exclusively "charity" model of social concern. This is widespread despite the fact that *Gaudium et Spes* endorsed a justice-first model accompanied by charity. The differences in worldview between these two strategies are glaring. Those accustomed to a charity model have very different opinions about the causes of poverty as well as possible solutions. Maintaining a charity model, one that prefers one-off donations (for example, to a homeless shelter) is quite different than a justice model, which teaches and engages the causes of social problems (such as why there is so much homelessness). Thus, most Catholics remain uneducated about the social realities they encounter on a daily basis. There is also the problem of compartmentalizing "faith"—away from social reality, with a focus on individual piety.

Allow us to share a short story. A young seminarian in Omaha, Nebraska, graduated and took up a position as pastor of a church. He entered into a parish community that had a long commitment to a "lunch ministry" with people who experience homelessness in its own neighborhood. Many parishioners participated in this ministry and found it both meaningful and profoundly holy. One of the first "accomplishments" of the new pastor was to shutter this ministry in favor of an hour of adoration of the Blessed Sacrament. Adoration of the Blessed Sacrament is a wonderful manner of encountering Christ. A "lunch ministry" to homeless men and women is a wonderful manner of encountering Christ. Why are these acts of faith perceived as being in opposition to each other? An encounter with the homeless should lead us to Jesus; an encounter with the Blessed Sacrament should lead us to our neighbor. What is lacking is a *bridge* between Christian spirituality and the temporal mission of the Church to serve the Kingdom of God.

Why Pope Francis and Why Now?

Pope Francis is radical because he is traditional. He teaches from the Catholic tradition articulated at Vatican II (1962-65), teachings that are rooted in New Testament scripture. Most of the statements that have defined his papacy can be directly cross-referenced to the documents of Vatican II on everything from poverty to the importance of synodality. On March 16, 2013, the BBC announced that Pope Francis "… has said he wants 'a poor Church, for the poor' following his election as head of the world's 1.2bn Catholics on Wednesday."[1] That sounds suspiciously similar to the following statement made at Vatican II in the Dogmatic Constitution on the Church in the Modern World, *Lumen Gentium*: "Just as Christ carried out the work of redemption in poverty and oppression, so the church is called to follow the same path if it is to communicate the fruits of salvation to humanity" (LG, 8). Elsewhere, Francis says the following about priests:

---

[1] BBC World News, https://www.bbc.com/news/world-europe-21812545.

The priest who seldom goes out of himself ... misses out on the best of our people, on what can stir the depths of his priestly heart.... This is precisely the reason why some priests grow dissatisfied, lose heart and become in a sense, collectors of antiquities or novelties—instead of being shepherds living with "the smell of the sheep." This is what I am asking you—be shepherds with the smell of sheep.[2]

Again, this is quite similar to *Lumen Gentium*:

They [Priests] should be mindful that by their daily conduct and solicitude they should show the face of a truly priestly and pastoral ministry to believers and unbelievers alike, to Catholics and non-Catholics: that they are bound to bear witness before all people to truth and life, and as good shepherds seek after those (see Lk 15:4-7) who, having been baptized in the Catholic Church, have given up the practice of the sacraments, or even fallen away from the faith (LG, 28).

Perhaps it is finally now, more than 50 years after Vatican II, that we can put into practice concrete strategies for bridging old and new understandings of the Church, social ethics, interreligious dialogue, ecumenical endeavors, and so on. We are desperately in need of such "bridges" as Catholics attend weekly Mass while families are separated, and children are caged at our border. Bridges are necessary when we fail, repeatedly, to address the pastoral needs of the divorced and remarried. Bridges are necessary in a world in the midst of climate change with little or no response. Bridges are necessary for ministering to people who suffer addiction and other mental health challenges throughout our society. During our lifetime, former Catholics have become the second largest religious group in the United States. Bridges are threats to some and liberation for others—just like the Good News of Jesus.

Bridges threaten those who define themselves over and against the "other" in an absolute way. "Those" divorced and remarried people are not welcome at our Mass. "Those" immigrants who speak a different language are not welcome in our land. "Those" with a different understanding and

---

[2] Dennis Coday, https://www.ncronline.org/blogs/francis-chronicles/pope-s-quotes-smell-sheep.

experience of sexuality or gender are not like us and therefore are not welcome. Bridges as threats or bridges as freedom for—these seem to be the two dominant perspectives in the Church today. Bridges liberate those who understand Jesus and his announcement of the Kingdom of God as welcoming all, especially those who are despised, marginalized, and vulnerable.

"Bridge Theology" is an integral theological theory and practice that builds on a dominant motif of Francis' pontificate: *bridge building*. Concretely, this means a practical theology that welcomes, unites, and encourages encounters in the real world of everyday life. Francis promotes this idea in several of his public statements, including his letter to the International Conference of Catholic Theological Ethics in the World Church, Sarajevo, 26-27 July 2018. In this letter, Francis "warns of the need to build, in an environment of tension and division, new paths of closeness between peoples, cultures, religious, visions of life and political orientations." And Francis urges the Church to work to "remove the walls of division and to build bridges of fraternity everywhere in the world."[3]

Pope Francis' call for members of the Catholic Church to build bridges presents a question for theologians and educators. How can the community of Catholic scholars, who work in the cultural context of the United States, provide theological insight not only into what theological bridge building is but also how this paradigm can help form students, or seminarians, to be bridge builders in a civic context? Francis frames it this way: "Research and study ought to be integrated with personal and community life, with missionary commitment, with fraternal charity and sharing with the poor, with care of the interior life in relationship with the Lord"[4] (Pope Francis, 2014).

We believe that, to adequately respond to this question, insight is needed from a range of Catholic scholars who discuss bridge theology in terms of method and methodology, sociopolitical analysis, theological reflection, and community-engaged pedagogy.

In broad strokes, the discussion of bridge theology in this book invites readers to consider the practical theological value of *metanoia* (conversion)

[3] https://www.americamagazine.org/faith/2018/07/26/letter-pope-francis-moral-theologians-gathered-sarajevo.

[4] http://www.vatican.va/content/francesco/en/speeches/2014/april/documents/papa-francesco_20140410_universita-consortium-gregorianum.html.

and praxis (lived faith). Our authors invite readers to consider conversion toward social action that seeks to transform personal prejudices and political realities where social injustice is accepted as the cultural norm, specifically regarding the global ecological problem, the plight of migrants and refugees, and extreme global poverty. In this way the paradigm of bridge theology serves the Church by overcoming the fragmentation between some forms of theology where "an opposition between theology and pastoral ministry emerges as if they were two opposite and separate realities which have nothing to do with each other" (Pope Francis, 2015).[5]

In Part I, we describe the method and methodology that sustains bridge theology. Here we explicitly declare bridge theology as a methodological development that emerges from Vatican II in a way that people can understand. Each author explains how the method and methodology of bridge theology first requires an insertion of the theologian, minister, or layperson into a specific reality in order to listen and learn from people on the ground before moving toward sociopolitical analysis, theological reflection, and social action. Part I therefore presents various methods and methodologies as a historical development toward what can now be named bridge theology. Included in this discussion is Joseph Cardijn's See-Judge-Act methodology and its roots in Thomas Aquinas' description of the virtue of prudence, synodality as methodology, and Pope Francis' theological methodology.

In Part II, we confront and connect global injustices with theological insight and a discussion of social action. Authors will make connections to Conciliar documents such as *Lumen Gentium, Gaudium et Spes*, and Catholic figures whose theological texts help to frame the Church as a community whose mission and goal is service to "crucified people" and the Kingdom of God. Multidisciplinary efforts are emphasized, specifically in regard to topics such as migration, environmental issues/ecology, poverty, prison ministry/restorative justice, and health care.

In Part III, we demonstrate how Catholic figures have inserted themselves into reality in service to "crucified peoples" and the Kingdom of God. We explain how readers can assess the actions and practices of these figures through storytelling. Authors explain how these figures have helped the

[5] Part of a video address at the International Theological Conference of Buenos Aires (September 1–5, 2015), held on the occasion of the one hundredth anniversary of the founding of the Faculty of Theology in Buenos Aires. The fiftieth anniversary of the Second Vatican Council also took place at this meeting.

Church confront unjust realities and make connections through theological reflection. In light of this reflection, we discuss how such figures represent theological bridge building in and through their ministry. Included in this discussion are the recently beatified Rutilio Grande, Ignacio Ellacuría, and Saint Oscar Romero.

Finally, in Part IV we discuss bridge building in the context of higher education and civic action. We focus on how a pedagogy that scaffolds learning from methods and methodologies, to sociopolitical analysis, and theological reflection on prominent figures, which then forms students to be bridge builders. More specifically we present resources with pastoral practicums and academic service learning, community organizing, and so on. In this discussion, authors describe how students at St. Thomas University travel to South Florida farms to engage in service learning encounters with migrant workers in Immokalee; how students in Los Angeles use the See-Judge-Act method to advocate for the DREAM Act and immigration reform as a form of service-learning; and, finally, how students, faculty, and staff at Creighton University connect to neighborhoods in Omaha, Nebraska.

CHAPTER ONE

Pope Francis' Methodological Realism: The Bridge from the Virtue of Prudence to Practical Theology

Bob Pennington, PhD

Introduction

IN HIS LETTER TO the International Conference of Catholic Theological Ethics in the World Church (Sarajevo, 26-27 July 2018), Pope Francis writes: "Without renouncing prudence, we are called to recognize every sign and mobilize all our energy in order to remove the walls of division and to build bridges of fraternity everywhere in the world."[1] Pope Francis' call to build bridges as a theological practice is one he often repeats throughout interviews, homilies, and writings. An important question, however, is: Why does he suggest we build bridges "without renouncing prudence"?

---

[1] Pope Francis, Sarajevo, http://www.vatican.va/content/francesco/en/messages/pont-messages/2018/documents/papa-francesco_20180711_messaggio-etica-teologica.html.

In this chapter we explore how Pope Francis' remark about the virtue of prudence actually reveals a crucial insight about theological methodology. To make his insight clear we first explore the history that bridges Cardinal Joseph Cardijn's See-Judge-Act method to Thomas Aquinas' description of the virtue of prudence. We will then see how Cardijn's methodology also forms a bridge to crucial documents written by Pope John XXIII, Pope Paul VI, the authors of *Gaudium et Spes*, and the Latin American Bishops Conference at meetings in Medellín, Puebla, and Aparecida. We conclude by examining how Cardijn's methodology is used by Pope Francis to construct a practical theological realism that aims to build bridges of mercy for crucified people.

Cardijn and See-Judge-Act

Born to a Catholic working-class family in Brussels, Belgium, on November 13, 1882, Léon Joseph Cardijn matured in a time defined by the democratic revolution in France, laissez-faire capitalism, and the industrial revolution. Cardijn's youth was also the time of *Rerum Novarum*.[2] Deeply influenced by these social, political, economic, and religious developments, as well as by his contact with young factory workers, Cardijn realized his vocation was to become a priest.

When Cardijn entered the major seminary he became absorbed in the works of controversial 19th-century French "social Catholics" such as Frédéric Ozanam (founder of the St. Vincent de Paul Society), Alphonse Gratry, and Léon Ollé-Laprune.[3] In the seminary, Cardijn also learned of *Le Sillon*, the lay democratic movement and magazine organized by Marc Sagnier.[4] What is key to note is that Ollé-Laprune, his famous student Maurice Blondel, and Blondel's student Marc Sagnier all championed a philosophical methodology grounded in practical reason, the examination of

---

[2] Pope Leo XIII issued *Rerum Novarum* in 1891. The Latin title, meaning "new things," refers to the Industrial Revolution and is ultimately acknowledged as the foundation of modern Catholic social teaching as well as the cornerstone of a papal policy that is adopted by Leo's successors, who issue encyclicals on its 40th, 70th, 80th, and 100th anniversaries. For more, see Joe Holland *Modern Catholic Social Teaching: The Popes Confront the Industrial Age* (New York: Paulist Press, 2003), 144.

[3] Stefan Gigacz, *The Leaven in the Council: Joseph Cardijn and the Jocist Network at Vatican II*. Ph.D. diss., University of Divinity, Melbourne, Australia. Obtained in private email exchange with author in 2017.

[4] Gigacz, *The Leaven in the Council*.

action, and real life. Such was the methodological perspective favored by the young Cardijn.

After his ordination, Cardijn initiated a specialized Catholic action movement named *Jeunesse Ouvrière Chrétien* (Young Christian Workers) in Brussels.[5] At meetings of the Young Christian Workers, Cardijn integrated the See-Judge-Act method that he created while imprisoned by the Germans during World War I. Later in his life Cardijn explained the logic of his method: "life must be one of the essential bases of a sound theology, it is... a methodological base without which we would only be making artificial gestures, aiding and abetting the divorce... between religion and the world."[6] Cardijn suggested that this type of methodological realism, rooted in everyday life, helps the laity be "formed first of all by the discovery of facts, followed by a Christian judgment, resulting in the actions they plan, the plans they carry into effect, the responsibilities they shoulder."[7]

Ultimately, Cardijn did not want to limit theology to *theory* because he believed it detached religious faith from its civic context, specifically the economic and cultural context shaped by the industrial revolution and laissez-faire capitalism. Rather, Cardijn's goal was to teach lay people how to reflect theologically on civic, economic, and cultural realities so that they could better embody Christian practices or actions in order to transform unjust realities judged as an affront to the Christian vision of the Kingdom of God. What is crucial to note about Cardijn, and his See-Judge-Act method, is that an intellectual and theological bridge connects him to Saint Thomas Aquinas.

Philosopher David Lutz claims that while Cardijn indeed deserves credit for his development of the See-Judge-Act method, he did not create it *ex nihilo*.[8] Rather, Lutz explains that Cardijn's method is a development that bridges the Catholic intellectual tradition and pre-Christian Greek phi-

[5] Eugene Langdale, "Introduction," in *Challenge to Action: Addresses of Monsignor Joseph Cardijn* (Chicago: Fides, 1955), 7-12.

[6] Joseph Cardijn, *Laymen into Action*. Translated by Anne Heggie. London: Geoffrey Chapman LTD, 1964, 148-9.

[7] Cardijn, *Laymen*, 150.

[8] I am indebted to Dr. David Lutz for his masterful insight on the connections between Cardijn's See-Judge-Act method and Thomas Aquinas' description of the virtue of prudence. Most of what follows on this connection was discussed by Dr. Lutz at the "Lay Movements as Structures of Grace: The Legacy of Cardijn, the See-Judge-Act Method, and Catholic Action in the Americas," a conference at Mount St. Joseph University, Cincinnati, Ohio, 2018.

losophy. In *Nicomachean Ethics*, Aristotle describes *phronesis* as an intellectual virtue "concerned with practice; so that it needs knowledge both of general truths and of particular facts, but more especially the latter."[9] Contemporary philosopher Richard Kearney describes *phronesis* as "a form of practical wisdom capable of respecting the singularity of situations as well as the nascent universality of values aimed at by human actions."[10] Alasdair MacIntyre sums up Aristotle's view of *phronesis* as that which guides a person in "the right action to do in each particular time and place," which is "what ethics is all about."[11]

Aristotelian *phronesis* forms an important bridge to Saint Thomas Aquinas' description of the intellectual virtue of prudence. Aquinas' account of the virtues, which is both Aristotelian and Christian, adds an analysis of *phronesis*, or *prudentia* in Latin, that is more systematic and detailed than Aristotle's. Aquinas explains that while the moral virtues determine the ends at which we should aim, "it belongs to prudence rightly to counsel [*consiliari*], judge [*iudicare*], and command [*praecipere*] concerning the means of obtaining a due end."[12] Aquinas sometimes calls these three steps "acts of the practical reason: 'counsel'; 'judgment' about what has been counseled; and 'command.'"[13] At other times, Aquinas explains that taking counsel "belongs to discovery." The second act being "to judge what one has discovered." Finally, commanding "consists in applying to action the things counseled and judged."[14]

In addition to this insight from Aquinas himself, several scholars agree that Cardijn's See-Judge-Act method is rooted in Aquinas' description of the virtue of prudence. John N. Kotre refers to "Observe-Judge-Act" as "a formula straight from Aquinas."[15] According to Edward L. Cleary, "The methodology of See-Judge-Act (even if it owed something to Marxist praxis) came

---

[9] Aristotle, *Nicomachean Ethics* (New York: Barnes & Noble, 2004), 1141b.

[10] Richard Kearney, *On Stories* (London: Routledge, 2002), 143.

[11] Alasdair MacIntyre, *After Virtue* (Notre Dame: Notre Dame Press, 2010), 154-162.

[12] Thomas Aquinas, *Summa Theologica*, trans. Fathers of the English Dominican Province, 2nd & Rev. Ed. (London: Burns, Oates & Washbourne, 1920), IIa IIae, q. 47, a. 10.

[13] Aquinas, *Summa Theologica*, IIa IIae, q. 53, a. 4.

[14] Aquinas, *Summa Theologica*, IIa IIae, q. 47, a. 8.

[15] John N. Kotre, *Simple Gifts: The Lives of Pat and Patty Crowley* (Kansas City: Andrews McMeel, 1979), 39.

from Thomas Aquinas's teaching on prudence."[16] Terrance G. Kardong, OSB, tells us:

> Besides echoing *sapiential* pragmatism, insistence on concrete action is typical of ancient monasticism, which was much more a lifestyle than a theory. This kind of thinking lies behind Thomas Aquinas' teaching on the parts of prudence: observe, judge, act, a triad that was the heart of Jocist theory in the years after World War II.[17]

According to L. Ian MacDonald, "The work of the lay Catholic activists was inspired by the motto of Thomas Aquinas, *Voir, Juger, Agir* (Observe, Judge, Act)."[18] Tércio Bretanha Junker writes, "The 'See-Judge-Act' method... has its incipient development in Thomas Aquinas (*Summa Theologica, Treatise on Prudence and Justice,* IIa IIae q. 47 a. 8)."[19] Bernard V. Brady cites a paragraph about Cardijn's method in John XXIII's encyclical *Mater et Magistra*:

> First, one reviews the concrete situation; secondly, one forms a judgment on it in the light of these same principles; thirdly, one decides what in the circumstances can and should be done to implement these principles. These are the three stages that are usually expressed in the three terms: look, judge, act [*aspicere, iudicare, agere*].[20]

Brady then comments, "John XXIII is summarizing the characteristics of the virtue of prudence as explained by Thomas Aquinas."[21] In "Vatican II's

[16] Edward L. Cleary, *Crisis and Change: The Church in Latin America Today,* 2nd ed. (Maryknoll, NY: Orbis Books, 1985), 4.

[17] Terrence G. Kardong, *Benedict's Rule: A Translation and Commentary* (Collegeville, MN: Liturgical Press, 1996), 7.

[18] L. Ian MacDonald, *From Bourassa to Bourassa: Wilderness to Restoration,* 2nd ed. (Montreal & Kingston: McGill-Queen's University Press, 2002), 86.

[19] Tércio Bretanha Junker, *Prophetic Liturgy: Toward a Transforming Christian Praxis* (Eugene, OR: Wipf & Stock, 2014), 20.

[20] John XXIII, Encyclical Letter *Mater et Magistra,* 15 May 1961, 236. http://w2.vatican.va/content/john-xxiii/en/encyclicals/documents/hf_j-xxiii_enc_15051961_mater.html.

[21] Bernard V. Brady, *Essential Catholic Social Thought* (Maryknoll, NY: Orbis, 2008), 37.

Decree on the Apostolate of the Laity: Text and commentary," Dominican writer Francis Wendell, OP, explains:

> The See, Judge, Act method, conceived by Thomas Aquinas, activated by Cardinal Cardijn, and canonized by Pope John XXIII, is indeed a continuing process and a discovery that is invaluable to the layman. It keeps the person with his feet in the order of reality and his head and heart in the realm of faith.[22]

Finally, Thomas J. Bushlack concurs: "Aquinas defines prudence as 'right reason in action'" (*Summa Theologica* II-II 47.2). A simple way to summarize the stages of prudence is provided by the phrase "see, judge, act."[23] While the bridge between Cardijn's See-Judge-Act method and Aquinas' description of the virtue of prudence is evident, other bridges extend from Cardijn to members of the Magisterium, at Vatican Council II, and at various meetings of the Latin American Bishops.

See-Judge-Act in Rome

After decades of ministerial success with his Catholic Action Movement, Cardijn was invited to the Vatican to meet with Pope Pius XI.[24] After their meeting in March 1925, Pius XI blessed "the aim, method, and organization of the J.O.C."[25] Cardijn later wrote that Pius XI approved the movement because the Pope recognized "the Church must be rooted in the realities of life."[26]

---

[22] Peter Foote, "Laymen, Vatican II's Decree on the Apostolate of the Laity: Text and Commentary" (Chicago: Catholic Action Federations, 1966), 61. Cited in Mary Irene Zotti's *A Time of Awakening: The Young Christian Worker Story in the United States, 1938 to 1970* (Chicago: Loyola University Press, 1991), 263. In addition to Wendell, Kristien Justaert notes that the root of Cardijn's method is Thomistic. For more, see Kristien Justaert, "Cartographies of Experience: Rethinking the Method of Liberation Theology," in *Horizons*, 42.2, December 2015, 249.

[23] Thomas J. Bushlack, *Politics for a Pilgrim Church: A Thomistic Theory of Civic Virtue* (Grand Rapids, MI: Eerdmans, 2015), 114.

[24] Langdale, "Introduction," 7-12.

[25] Cardijn, *Laymen,* 35.

[26] Cardijn, *Laymen,* 35.

The first public papal reference to the See-Judge-Act method was made by Pope Pius XII in his address to the International YCW Pilgrimage to Rome on August 25, 1957:

> You want to live a profound, authentic, Christian life, not just in the secret of your consciences, but also openly, in your families, in your neighborhood, in the factory, in the workshop, in the office, and also to show your sincere and total belonging to Christ and the Church. Your solid organization, your method summed up in the well-known formula: "See, judge, act," your interventions on the local, regional, national and international levels, enables you to contribute to the extension of the Reign of God in modern society and to enable the teachings of Christianity to penetrate with all their vigor and originality.[27]

The bridge from Pius XI to Pius XII extends further to Pope John XXIII who, in his 1961 encyclical *Mater et Magistra*, states:

> Teachings in regard to social matters for the most part are put into effect in the following three stages: first, the actual situation is examined; then, the situation is evaluated carefully in relation to these teachings; then, only is it decided what can and should be done in order that the traditional norms may be adapted to circumstances of time and place. These three steps are at times expressed by the three words: observe, judge, act.[28]

What is significant about John's adoption of Cardijn's method is the claim that: "It is important for our young people to grasp this method and to practice it. Knowledge acquired in this way does not remain merely abstract, but is seen as something that must be translated into action."[29] In addition to the bridges from Cardijn to Pope Pius XI, Pius XII, and John

---

[27] For more, see http://cardijnresearch.blogspot.com/2014/10/see-judge-act-from-john-xxiii-to-pope.html.

[28] Pope John XXIII, *Mater et Magistra*, No. 236.

[29] Pope John XXIII, *Mater et Magistra*, No. 237.

XXIII, a clear bridge exists from Cardijn to *Schema XIII*, the working draft of what ultimately became *Gaudium et Spes*: The Pastoral Constitution on the Church in the Modern World. The research of Stefan Gigacz shows that: "In October 1964, after much criticism of an earlier draft of the Schema, the Central Sub-Commission adopted the See-Judge-Act method to re-draft the final version."[30] In fact:

> The Commission instructed: To the maximum extent possible each (drafting) sub-commission should: start from the facts; bring a Christian judgment in the light of the Gospel and Catholic tradition from the Fathers up to contemporary documents of the Magisterium; indicate concrete orientations for action.[31]

In other words, those in charge of drafting Schema XIII used Cardijn's See-Judge-Act method to construct the document that Pope Paul VI promulgated to conclude Vatican Council II in 1965.

Another bridge exists from Cardijn to Pope Paul VI, who appropriated the See-Judge-Act method in *Populorum Progressio* and *Octogesima Adveniens*. Fr. Allan Figueroa Deck suggests that the influence of Cardijn on Pope Paul VI is undeniable.[32] Deck adds that an examination of *Populorum Progressio* reveals that Pope Paul VI not only "put into practice" Cardijn's "observe, judge, act" method but "enthusiastically received it as a simple but powerful way to help those on the margins connect their faith with

---

[30] A copy of the original report of the Central Sub-Commission meetings that made the decision to use the See-Judge-Act method to write *Gaudium et Spes* is available at the Archives of the *Institut Catholique de Paris*. It can be found at http://www.josephcardijn.com/1964-schema-xiii-adopts-see-judge-act. The original document "Vatican II, Schema XIII, *Réunion Sous Commission Centrale*," was constructed on October 17-20, 1964.

[31] The original states, "*Méthodes de travail: 1. L'organisation interne de chaque sous-commission et ses travaux relèvent de l'autorité de son Président, 1. Dans toute la mesure du possible, chaque sous-commission devra: partir des faits; porter un jugement chrétien, à la lumière de l'Evangile et de la tradition catholique, depuis les Pères jusqu'aux documents contemporains du magistère. indiquer des orientations concrètes d'action* (aspect pastoral)." For more, see http://www.josephcardijn.com/1964-schema-xiii-adopts-see-judge-act.

[32] Allan Figueroa Deck, SJ, "Commentary on *Populorum Progressio*," in *Modern Catholic Social Teaching*, Kenneth R. Times, OFM, editor (Washington D.C., Georgetown University Press, 2005), 297.

real life."[33] And, in Paul's Apostolic Letter *Octogesima Adveniens* (1971), Cardijn's See-Judge-Act method is apparent:

> It is up to the Christian communities to analyze with objectivity the situation which is proper to their own country, to shed on it the light of the Gospel's unalterable words and to draw principles of reflection, norms of judgment and directives for action from the social teaching of the Church.[34]

See-Judge-Act in Latin America

A bridge from Cardijn's See-Judge-Act method also extends to Latin America. This is evident in documents created at meetings of the *Consejo Episcopal Latinoamericano* (CELAM) in Medellín, Colombia (1968); Puebla, Mexico (1979); and, Aparecida, Brazil (2007).

The Second General Conference of Latin American Bishops took place between August 24 and September 6, 1968, in Medellín, Colombia. The *Justice, Peace,* and *Poverty* documents show that the bishops drew inspiration from Cardijn's See-Judge-Act methodology. For example, each of the final documents is divided into three sections. Part I in each of the documents is titled either: Pertinent Facts; The Latin American Situation and Peace; or The Latin American Scene. Part II of each document is titled either: Doctrinal Basis; Doctrinal Reflection; or Doctrinal Motivation. And Part III of each document is titled either: Projection for Social Pastoral Planning; Pastoral Conclusions; or Pastoral Orientation. In other words, each document first "sees" reality, then "judges" it from the position of Christian doctrine, in order to prepare pastoral plans for "action." If there is any doubt that there is a bridge from the bishops at Medellín to Cardijn, a brief look at the concluding "Message to the Peoples of Latin America" clearly shows the influence of the See-Judge-Act method. For example, the bishops wrote that

---

[33] Allan Figueroa Deck, SJ, "Commentary," 299.

[34] Pope Paul VI, *Octogesima Adveniens*, No. 4. http://w2.vatican.va/content/paul-vi/en/apost_letters/documents/hf_p-vi_apl_19710514_octogesima-adveniens.html.

the new historical era "requires clarity in order to see, lucidity in order to diagnose, and solidarity in order to act."[35]

The Third General Conference of Latin American bishops took place in 1979 at Puebla, Mexico. Ernesto Valiente claims that the bishops who wrote the Puebla document, like those who constructed the Medellín documents, drew inspiration from Cardijn's See-Judge-Act method.[36] The use of Cardijn's methodology was made most explicit, however, at the Fifth General Conference at Aparecida, Brazil, in 2007. Valiente explains that before the 2007 meeting 22 national episcopal conferences critiqued the preparatory document that ignored Cardijn's See-Judge-Act method in favor of an ahistorical Christology.[37] As a result, a task force from CELAM crafted a working "synthesis document" that reinstated the See-Judge-Act method. In Part I, "The Life of Our People Today," the bishops state "in continuity with previous general conferences of Latin American Bishops, this document utilizes the See-Judge-Act method."[38] The bishops explain that with Cardijn's method the Church is able to *see* Latin America reality and *judge* it according to Jesus Christ in order to *enact* the spreading of the Kingdom of God.[39] They explain that the method has been successful in enabling "us to combine systematically, a faithful perspective for viewing reality; incorporating criterions from faith and reason for discerning and appraising it critically; and accordingly acting as missionary disciples of Jesus Christ."[40] What is noteworthy is that at Aparecida, Cardinal Jorge Bergoglio was elected by the other bishops to chair the committee charged with drafting the final document. Why does this matter? Because the man who explicitly used the See-Judge-Act method to construct the Aparecida document became the first pope to appeal to Cardijn's method since Pope Paul VI.

---

[35] General Conference of the Bishops of Latin America and the Caribbean, Message to the Peoples of Latin America, 574. In *Renewing the Earth: Catholic Documents on Peace, Justice and Liberation,* edited by David J. O'Brien and Thomas A. Shannon (Garden City, New York: Image Books, 1977).

[36] O. Ernesto Valiente, "The Reception of Vatican II in Latin America," in *Theological Studies,* no. 73 (2012), 812.

[37] Valiente, "The Reception of Vatican II in Latin America," 819.

[38] General Conference of the Bishops of Latin America and the Caribbean. *The Aparecida Document:* V. (Lexington, 2014), No. 19.

[39] General Conference of the Bishops of Latin America and the Caribbean, *Aparecida,* No. 19.

[40] General Conference of the Bishops of Latin America and the Caribbean, *Aparecida,* No. 19.

Pope Francis and See-Judge-Act

In continuity with the methodological preferences of Pope John XXIII, Pope Paul VI, CELAM, and liberation theologians, Pope Francis appropriates Cardijn's prudence-based See-Judge-Act method. For example, in *Laudato Si*, Pope Francis clearly uses the See-Judge-Act method to review (see) the best scientific research today, then consider (judge) principles from Judeo-Christian tradition, and, in light of this theological consideration (judgment), advance proposals for dialogue and action (act), on both a local and global level.[41] In other words, Francis' methodological process in *Laudato Si* represents Cardijn's method that prioritizes an empirical assessment of reality (Step 1) in order to change reality (Step 3) through critical theological reflection as a mediatory step (Step 2). Francis justifies this methodological approach by invoking a phrase he has uttered more than once: "Realities are more important than ideas."[42]

A crucial aspect of Pope Francis' appropriation of Cardijn's See-Judge-Act method is that his methodology demonstrates a practical theological realism focused by an analogical Christology rooted in the gospel of Matthew 25. As Francis makes clear in the final Aparecida document, the poor give us an opportunity to encounter Christ himself (Matt 25:37-40).[43] For example: "The suffering faces of the poor" and the "suffering face of Christ" are connected because as Jesus said: "Whatever you did for one of these least brothers of mine, you did for me" (Matt 25:40).[44] And "the poor and those who suffer actually evangelize us" because their suffering represents Jesus' suffering on the cross.[45] In other words, the suffering faces of street people in large cities, migrants, sick people, addicts, and the imprisoned become the face of Jesus on the Cross.[46] And, by using

[41] Pope Francis, *Laudato Si*, 15. Accessed January 15, 2015, Vatican.va.

[42] Pope Francis, *Laudato Si*, No. 110 and 201, a point he first made in *Evangelii Gaudium*, 231. With this statement Francis shows he is much more aligned with an Aristotelian approach as opposed to the Platonic approach favored by his predecessor, Benedict XVI. Later, in No. 116, Francis states, "The time has come to pay renewed attention to reality."

[43] General Conference of the Bishops of Latin America and the Caribbean, *Aparecida*, 88.

[44] General Conference of the Bishops of Latin America and the Caribbean, *Aparecida*, 125n178.

[45] General Conference of the Bishops of Latin America and the Caribbean, *Aparecida*, 88.

[46] General Conference of the Bishops of Latin America and the Caribbean, *Aparecida*, 126, 129-132.

practical theological reflection to consider how the "crucified of history" provide an analog to understand "Jesus' reality as the crucified one,"[47] a methodology grounded in prudence is able to provide people with a lens to see "the crucified in history" as a place where the practice of mercy, the *bonum morale* (ethical virtue) of the Christian tradition, is made real in Christian praxis.[48]

In *Evangelii Gaudium*, Francis develops his practical theological realism throughout the document. For example, he argues: "When we read the Gospel we find a clear indication" that we should aid "not so much our friends and wealthy neighbors, but above all the poor and the sick, those who are usually despised and overlooked, 'those who cannot repay you'" (LK 14:14).[49] Francis provides additional warrants for his claim about the Church's ethical option for mercy toward the poor with examples from various doctors, saints, and the Magisterium of the Church. Francis invokes the words of John Chrysostom to remind Christians in the present that early Christians believed: "Not to share one's wealth with the poor is to steal from them and to take away their livelihood."[50] Francis also invokes the work of Pope John XIII, who emphasized the human rights of the poor.[51] Francis also calls attention to the bishops of Brazil who listened to the cry of the poor and responded by proclaiming:

> We wish to take up daily the joys and hopes, the difficulties and sorrows of the Brazilian people, especially of those living in the barrios and the countryside—landless, homeless, lacking food and health care—to the detriment of their rights. Seeing their poverty, hearing their cries and knowing their sufferings, we are scandalized because we know there is enough food for everyone and that hunger is the result of a poor distribution of goods and income.[52]

---

[47] Sobrino, *Jesus in Latin America*, 148.

[48] Sobrino, *Jesus in Latin America*, 140-141, 144-145, 156.

[49] Pope Francis, *Evangelii Gaudium*, 42.

[50] Pope Francis, *Evangelii Gaudium*, 50n55.

[51] Pope Francis, *Evangelii Gaudium*, 140n154.

[52] Pope Francis, *Evangelii Gaudium*, 141n158.

Francis does not end with verbal posturing and quotations of documents from the Bible, fathers, doctors, bishops, or past popes of the Church. Rather, Francis invokes his own lived experience and encounters with the poor. Francis says: "I can say that the most beautiful and natural expressions of joy which I have seen in my life were in poor people who had little to hold on to."[53] Speaking from my own personal experience as a mission worker in the Dominican Republic, I concur with Francis' statement that the poor embody an ineffable beauty and joy. Like Francis, I believe that the poor have much to teach us and, therefore, we need to listen to the poor and embrace the wisdom that God wishes to communicate through them.[54] Such learning entails appreciating the poor in their goodness, listening to their experience of life, their culture, and their ways of living the faith.[55]

What is most significant about Francis' ethical concern for the poor is that it shows his approach to theologizing is defined by a practical theological realism that sees the Church not only existing in history but as a Church that aims, in a concrete way, to change historical reality.[56] For Pope Francis the foundation of this realism is found in the gospel,[57] which helps Christians see that reality is the place where people are crucified, and, therefore, must be the place where Christians put theory into practice in order to take people down from their cross.[58]

Another key aspect of his appropriation of Cardijn's See-Judge-Act method is made apparent in his address to volunteers at World Youth Day 2016 in Krakow, Poland. Pope Francis states:

In the Gospel mystery of the Visitation (cf. Lk 1:39-45)... we can see an icon of all Christian volunteer work. I would take three attitudes shown by Mary and leave them to you as an aid to interpreting the experience of these days and an inspiration for your future commitment to service. These three attitudes are listening, deciding and acting.[59]

[53] Pope Francis, *Evangelii Gaudium*, 14.

[54] Pope Francis, *Evangelii Gaudium*, 145.

[55] Pope Francis, *Evangelii Gaudium*, 146.

[56] Pope Francis, *Evangelii Gaudium*, 86-88.

[57] Pope Francis, *Evangelii Gaudium*, 71.

[58] Pope Francis, *Evangelii Gaudium*, 163.

[59] For more, see http://cardijnresearch.blogspot.com/2016/08/look-decide-act-with-mary-and-pope.html.

Pope Francis clearly reconfigures Cardijn's See-Judge-Act methodology in the form of Listen-Decide-Act. What is crucial about Francis' adaptation of Cardijn's See-Judge-Act method is that it champions an approach that begins with listening.[60] Since his first encyclical *Evangelii Gaudium*, Francis has urged Christians to listen to others, especially young people and the elderly.[61] Francis claims that listening to others includes those who gather empirical data and generate science in fields such as anthropology, sociology, and economics, among others.[62] What this suggests is that the skill of listening to the wisdom of others, a technique that is part and parcel of ethnographic approaches, is an integral part of Pope Francis' appropriation of Cardijn's method.

Conclusion

Clearly, a methodological bridge connects Cardijn's See-Judge-Act method to Thomas Aquinas' description of the virtue of prudence. Cardijn's method also forms a bridge to various members of the Magisterium and the creation of documents crucial to Vatican II and Catholic social teaching. Cardijn's method further acts as a bridge to Pope Francis' practical theology grounded in a methodological realism that emphasizes listening and the practice of mercy toward those who are crucified by unjust realities across the globe. The practice of listening is also a key feature of synodality, a process recently championed by Francis as a way of communal discernment, where all members of the church are listened to, instead of a more centralized decision-making process that the Church practiced in the past.

---

[60] Pope Francis, *Address of the Holy Father, Tauron Area, Kraków, Sunday, 31 July 2016*. http://w2.vatican.va/content/francesco/en/speeches/2016/july/documents/papafrancesco_20160731_polonia-volontari-gmg.html.

[61] Pope Francis, *Evangelii Gaudium*, accessed January 15, 2015, Vatican.va, 84.

[62] Pope Francis, *Evangelii Gaudium*, 100n110, 101n111.

CHAPTER TWO

Synodality as Bridge Building for Global Catholicism

BRYAN FROEHLE, PHD

In It Together

SYNODALITY IS ABOUT WALKING together.[1] As such, it builds from an understanding of a Church guided by the Holy Spirit in which the understanding of church, *ekklesia*, refers to an "assembling" rather than a perfect society (*societas perfecta*). Synodality is at once an ancient and newly emerging way of proceeding within global Catholicism that transcends centralization and control in favor of collaboration. It is not about a different way of making decisions so much as it is making them through collective discernment. Any reflection on synodality as methodology must therefore be informed by resources within spirituality, missiology, and practical theology.[2] Synodality is not a replacement or addition to collegiality, which refers to the relationship between bishops as sacramentally understood symbols of unity within their particular churches. Rather, synodality is the active work

---

[1] See the International Theological Commission, *Synodality in the Life and Mission of the Church*, 3.

[2] For a discussion of Catholic approaches to practical theology, see Kathleen A. Cahalan and Bryan Froehle, "A Developing Discipline: The Catholic Voice in Practical Theology." In Claire E. Wolfteich, ed., *Invitation to Practical Theology: Catholic Voices and Visions* (Mahwah: Paulist, 2014).

that builds up the Church at all levels and engages all, by entering into the divine mystery to understand what God is doing. A synodal church reflects the practical wisdom of bridge building that is more horizontal than vertical. Synodality is therefore comfortable embracing difference while living into a unity that is not imposed but instead grows from collectively and humbly pursuing the Spirit of God in the world today.

From Centralization to Collegiality to Synodality

The Catholic Church is more globally extensive than truly globalized. Catholic dioceses have extended far beyond Europe for over half a millennium. Yet the highest levels of Catholic leadership remained European even as the number of Catholic dioceses outside Europe grew throughout the 20th century and the majority of the Catholic population located far from the world's second smallest continent.[3] More than that: Catholic ecclesial life tended toward uniformity, even unanimity, following the lead of the center. This did not so much change as consolidate in new ways after the Second Vatican Council ended in 1965. A truly globalized Church, embedded in the local, in communion globally, would not come about magically just by opening the windows.[4] The "coming of the world Church" turned out to be a bit delayed.[5]

Becoming a truly global Church required more than simple shifts in demographics or even the aspirations of advisors and popes. Such a transformation required struggle and even disagreement. Global Catholicism developed in fits and starts, in movements backwards as well as forward, probing and prodding a variety of paths, sometimes quite haltingly. The post-conciliar Church was seemingly more familiar with "griefs and anxieties" than "joys and hopes." Church leadership after Vatican II reflected a new collegiality among bishops, initiated during the ecumenical council itself, as they

---

[3] Though the European continent became the Christian homeland for contingent historical reasons by the early modern era, Catholic Christianity had always been present outside the narrow confines of Europe. See Dale T. Irvin and Scott W. Sunquist, *History of the World Christian Movement: Earliest Christianity to 1453* (Maryknoll: Orbis, 2001).

[4] "I want to throw open the windows of the Church so that we can see out and the people can see in," is the phrase John XXIII used at the opening of the Second Vatican Council.

[5] See Walbert Buhlman, OFM Cap, *The Coming of the Third Church: An Analysis of the Present and Future of the Church* (Maryknoll: Orbis, 1977), originally published in German a few years before.

joined together with the successor of Peter in new forms of action such as episcopal conferences and synods of bishops. Yet these developments were nonetheless controlled and halting in their own way from the start during the papacy of Paul VI (1963-1978), particularly in the aftermath of the global cultural shocks of 1968. Tensions regarding power, authority, and the role of the center could not be worked out all at once. Succeeding papacies and global Catholic conversations continued along a path of containment and centered on European and North Atlantic conversations and concerns, even while building on new developments and new concerns.

John Paul II, the second-longest-serving pope in two millennia of Bishops of Rome, will surely be remembered for his leadership in ending the Soviet empire that divided the European continent. Yet this struggle was itself closely correlated with efforts to check ecclesial shifts in Latin America and elsewhere, moves that recentralized forms of action and practice, placing concerns of the center over the realities of the local, particular churches. Similarly, Benedict XVI will be remembered for his focus on European questions, including a theological and philosophical preoccupation with the declining salience of religious commitment within Europe. Yet during this time it became clearer that a focus on concerns identified with a small peninsula jutting from the vast Afro-Asian landmass was short-circuiting responses to ecclesial realities around the world.

All this emerged from a fear and resistance to fragmentation. Both John Paul II and Benedict XVI, and the college of bishops they appointed around the world, reacted to fragmentation within the Church through the exercise of centralized authority. Yet this same strong centralized authority inevitably protected bad actors, as sexual abuse and financial mismanagement scandals have demonstrated. But the crisis itself was in the models of governance and underlying understandings of "church." A model of control, centralization, and containment is built on fear—a fear with origins in the long 19th century of the Church and the needs and stresses of that time. Whatever its origins, however, it could not reflect the possibilities of a truly global Church in the dawn of the third millennium. The day had come not for a fortress Church but for a bridge-building Church.[6]

---

[6] Bridge building is the concept behind the ancient Roman term taken on by the popes: pontifex. The pontiff, the pope, as the servant of the servants of God, *servus servorum dei*, has a vocation as the bridge-builder-in-chief, the model bridge-builder, a vocation to which all Christians are called as reconcilers (2 Cor 5:18) and ambassadors of God's mission of reconciliation (2 Cor 5:20).

After Benedict, Francis. The consensus of the cardinal electors in 2013 that resulted in the first non-European pope came about when the centralizing approach had reached a ceiling. A new path was needed. Benedict's resignation was provoked by the scandals tied to those who had flourished under the centralizing approach that had characterized his papacy as well as his leadership in the papacy of John Paul. Benedict's successor emphasized the peripheries in language and action from the start, but the reality was hardly that of flipping a switch. Change is organic even in tumultuous moments; leaders and thinkers deeply committed to resisting fragmentation through centralization and containment continued, as did the pope emeritus.

The centralization option was never the only response to the globalization of ecclesial reality. Popes Benedict XVI, John Paul II, and Paul VI had always gestured toward other modalities, as various bishops, religious orders, Catholic movements, and various other ecclesial leaders and thinkers did as well. They often themselves embodied more than simply an instinct of centralization. From the earliest centuries, religious life in the Catholic Church had provided a horizontality that complemented the verticality of hierarchy.

The very nature of Catholic life itself, after all, is multidimensional. Sacramentality brings a "both/and," and multiple modalities are always near the surface. The very structures that Paul VI had created after the Council—such as the Synod of Bishops, for all its emphasis on centralized papal leadership, nonetheless could naturally grow into a space for synodality under Francis—just as the diocesan structures of synod and pastoral council found in the carefully created 1983 Code of Canon Law, carried within themselves the possibilities of synodality.[7]

It is said that the Church thinks in centuries, and that an ecumenical council takes a century to implement, for the same reason: a Church marked by sacred, sacramental bonds is less a machine than an organism. Change happens generationally, as members are born and die, and new life takes the place of what had gone before. Following the *communio* ecclesiology of *Lumen Gentium*, the Church is about relationship. Bridge building is thus at the heart of ecclesial

---

[7] Consider Acts 15:1-35 in light of Gal 2:1-19. The initial experience of the Jerusalem Council, the "paradigm for synods celebrated by the Church" (*Synodality in the Life*, 20), narrated in the Letter to the Galatians, became the unfolding of the larger working of the Spirit in the Acts of the Apostles written a generation later. Salvation history must be seen in the light of its unfolding: one must interpret it in light of a "fusion of horizons." See Hans-Georg Gadamer, *Truth and Method* (New York: Bloomsbury, 2013), 386.

action. If bridge building is the method, synodality is the methodology, the theological theory of this way of proceeding that is so central to the life of the Church.

The resignation of Benedict XVI marked an exhaustion of the centralization strategy. Collegiality—that is, the bonds of bishops appointed by the Holy See acting together with the Holy See—had become another means of centralization. While this was intended to short-circuit fragmentation and stem palpable ecclesial weakness in the European and North Atlantic heartland of the Church, centralization only hastened fragmentation and weakness. New developments would need to be consistent not with the mechanical response of centralization but with a turn to the sacramentality of ecclesiality.

A now-global Church had emerged. Existing ecclesial practices of centralization had been tried and found wanting. In response, the logic of sacramentality points toward horizonality more than verticality: an ecclesiology of communion, about bridge building more than control and containing. Benedict's successor took the name "Francis" as a reference to the saint who embraced the poor and who responded to the vision of San Damiano: rebuild my Church. This very task is more practical than conceptual, less structural than communal. In institutional power dynamics, one faction competes with another, some power base emerges, and so it goes. This is the political science model of the Church based on an underlying hermeneutic of fear and an institutionally oriented ecclesiology.

Yet this is not the core logic of Church, which is "in Christ like a sacrament or as a sign and instrument both of a very closely knit union with God and of the unity of the whole human race."[8] When understood sacramentally rather than institutionally,[9] the logic shifts from a fear of fragmentation and contestation to a deep listening of the Holy Spirit in the midst of the assembly (*ekklesia*). This Spirit-focused ecclesiology yields practices of synodality, of discernment rather than contestation and control. Such practices include "encounter and engagement, contemplation and service, receptive solitude and life in community, cheerful sobriety and the struggle for justice."[10]

---

[8] *Lumen Gentium*, 1. See https://www.vatican.va/archive/hist_councils/ii_vatican_council/documents/vat-ii_const_19641121_lumen-gentium_en.html.

[9] See Avery Dulles, *Models of the Church*, and his concern regarding the inadequacy of the institutional model of the church when taken by itself.

[10] *Querida Amazonia*, 77. See http://www.vatican.va/content/francesco/en/apost_exhortations/documents/papa-francesco_esortazione-ap_20200202_querida-amazonia.html.

It should be no surprise that the first pope of the "global south" embraced the method of "See-Judge-Act" as given ecclesial voice by Catholic Action movements associated with Cardinal Joseph Cardijn. This method, named by the ordinary magisterium in a 1961 encyclical of John XXIII, was embodied in movements and theological practices originating in Latin American church councils and liberation theologies, the theology of struggle in the Philippines, and the pastoral circle coming out of the Tangaza school in Kenya. Whether referred to as the "hermeneutic circle" or "pastoral circle" or some other term, they are methods of collaboration rather than contestation, even when they have led to dramatic witness in the midst of death-dealing conflict.

Methodology

The underlying methodology is oriented to the Holy Spirit and focused on both discernment and witness. It reflects the pivot marked in the Pact of the Catacombs of November 16, 1965, a few days before the promulgation of the *Decree on the Apostolate of the Laity* (November 18) and a few weeks before that of the *Pastoral Constitution of the Church in the Modern World* (December 7), approved just before the Council ended on December 8, 1965. That latter document notably embraced discernment of the signs of the times, adopting a problem-driven rather than precept-driven approach, engaging experience in the light of tradition and culture. As such, it is a core document for bridge-building theology.[11] Rather than resolving difference through centralized authority, difference, even fragmentation, is normal and acceptable, provided all are in relationship.

> To carry out such a task, the Church has always had the duty of scrutinizing the signs of the times and of interpreting them in the light of the Gospel.... Triggered by the intelligence and creative energies of human beings, these changes recoil upon them, upon their decisions and desires, both individual and collective, and upon their manner of thinking and acting with respect to things and to people. Hence, we can already speak of a true cultural and social transformation, one which has repercussions on humanity's religious life as well. As happens in any crisis of growth,

---

[11] Massimo Faggioli, *Catholicism and Citizenship: Political Cultures of the Church in the Twenty-First Century* (Collegeville: Liturgical Press, 2017).

this transformation has brought serious difficulties in its wake.... The People of God believes that it is led by the Lord's Spirit, Who fills the earth. Motivated by this faith, it labors to decipher authentic signs of God's presence and purpose in the happenings, needs and desires in which this People has a part along with other men of our age. For faith throws a new light on everything, manifests God's design for man's total vocation, and thus directs the mind to solutions which are fully human.[12]

This approach built upon mid-20th-century developments in missiology, practical theology, moral theology, theological anthropology, ecclesiology, systematic theology, and more. In turn, this insight enshrined in the conciliar documents and the developments in doctrine of which it is a part spurred further developments.

These developments flow from the synthesis of spiritual theology and forms of practical theology, which in the Catholic context involved moral theology and missiology in very particular ways, together with developments in philosophy, including hermeneutics (theories of understanding). Together they might all be called a bridge theology, for which the method is practical and rooted in the method of pastoral circles. The methodology itself is that of synodality.[13]

Synodality

"Synod" means "a way together," implying a common walk, even echoing one of the first names for Christians, followers of the Way. In the *Code of Canon Law* as revised after the Council and released in 1983, the synodal process was given new language and a new impetus for individual dioceses. It was often tied in some way to the work of the Diocesan Pastoral Council,[14] which is itself an innovation designed to bring together not just priests or religious or lay people, but a wisdom group that in some way represents

---

[12] *Gaudium et Spes,* 4 and 11.

[13] See Massimo Faggioli, "From Collegiality to Synodality: Pope Francis's Post-Vatican II Reform," *Commonweal,* November 23, 2018. "Francis's emphasis on synodality bridges the gap between his Vatican II theological culture and the new horizon of post-conciliar global Catholicism. It is a bridge that he cannot cross alone." See https://www.commonwealmagazine.org/collegiality-synodality.

[14] See Bryan Froehle, et al., *Diocesan and Eparchial Pastoral Councils: A National Profile* (Washington: Center for Applied Research in the Apostolate and the National Conference of Catholic Bishops, 1998).

priests, religious, and all those who make up a diocese. In this way, it mimics the parish pastoral council, meant to provide something similar for the parish pastor. Many other consultative bodies emerged, some of ancient origin, others with newer innovations.

As Pope Francis put it in 2015:

> "A synodal Church is like a standard lifted up among the nations (cf. Is 11:12) in a world which—while calling for participation, solidarity and transparency in public administration—often consigns the fate of entire peoples to the grasp of small but powerful groups. As a Church which 'journeys together' with men and women, sharing the travails of history, let us cherish the dream that a rediscovery of the inviolable dignity of peoples and of the function of authority as service will also be able to help civil society to be built up in justice and fraternity, and thus bring about a more beautiful and humane world for coming generations."[15]

Synodality and the Synod of Bishops

The major image of the synod on the global-historical stage was that of the Synod of Bishops. It was envisioned as a way of continuing the conversations of the Second Vatican Council by convening selected bishops from around the world in much fewer numbers and around a tightly defined, focused domain. However, the function of this design of the synod as launched after the Council by Paul VI, is as an advisory body to the pope, who is to offer the final word of the synod at a time well after its conclusion. Until the time of Pope Francis, the action of the synod of bishops was thus controlled, even scripted, and all the more so under Pope John Paul II. The possibility of fragmentation, even difference from the predetermined papal agenda, was largely suppressed through the exercise of centralized authority.

---

[15] "Ceremony Commemorating the 50th Anniversary of the Institution of the Synod of Bishops," Address of His Holiness Pope Francis, Paul VI Audience Hall, Saturday, 17 October 2015, final paragraph. See http://www.vatican.va/content/francesco/en/speeches/2015/october/documents/papa-francesco_20151017_50-anniversario-sinodo.html.

Bishops have a particular role in a sacramental Church—the fullness of orders and principle of apostolic succession mean that diocesan bishops embody in some way a sign and symbol of unity and relationship, both within their local church and in communion with the Bishop of the city of Peter and Paul. Bishops, therefore, are naturally networked to practice synodality with the Bishop of Rome.

Bridge Theology as Fundamental Ecclesiology

Bridge theology is thus as much practical-ecclesiological as systematic-theological, firmly rooted in discipleship and pastoral concerns. Bridge theology suggests that the key principle is not hierarchy but network. Hierarchy implies a vertical model, akin to a pyramid, from the people who "pay, pray, and obey" at the bottom and those who command and control at the top. Yet, as a flat hierarchy, the Catholic Church is a poor expression of the classic hierarchical model. That is, each of the diocesan bishops[16] of the world is in communion with the pope, and thus, their dioceses[17] are in communion with other dioceses of the Church Catholic. This model misses the relationship a diocese might have with other dioceses, not in the form of an "archdiocese" to a "diocese," which is in any case quite limited, but of dioceses with each other in general, and bishops with each other in general, and the role of mediating organizations such as Bishops' Conferences. This flat hierarchy model, with all roads from all dioceses and their diocesan bishops leading to Rome, reflects a certain understanding of the Catholic Church, albeit a seriously inadequate one.

A more adequate ecclesiology is that of bridge theology, which in turn builds on methods and models that emerged in the 20th century and that have come into their own in the early 21st century through a complex historical process of reception and appropriation. This process is by no means complete—and that is itself the point of "bridging theology," which is surely

---

[16] Or eparchs, as the ordinaries of eparchies, the equivalent of a diocese for the 23 Eastern churches within the Catholic Church, are termed within *the Code of Canon Law of Eastern Churches* (1991). There are some 2,886 Catholic dioceses or the equivalent of the Western church in the world, and some 250 eparchies of the 23 different Eastern churches in full communion with the Catholic Church.

[17] Or eparchies, the equivalent term for a diocese.

here to stay as an authentic, deeply rooted, and organic development within global Catholicism.

This theological paradigm has a public theological element that recognizes that the public and the personal are two sides of the same coin. A true *diakonia* (service) of the community requires personal faith and ongoing conversion within a person and between persons, simultaneously demanding the conversion and engagement of broader societal elements and institutions.[18] In this sense it is ecclesiological in light of the model of the Church as a community of disciples.[19]

Bridge theology is thus neither purely academic nor pastoral, but both. As the "circle method" offers an integrated methodology that is necessarily both "hermeneutical" and "pastoral," bridge theology reflects a similar "both/and" approach.[20] It reflects the rich intellectual tradition of Catholic Christianity and those formed in its institutions of higher education and formation programs together with strong horizontal connections to the pastoral life.

Bridging Is How Theology Is Done

If "spirituality" might be seen as relatively more intrinsic to a person, and the spiritual is part of human experience, "religion" is that domain of practices that is more extrinsic.[21] Theology, however, is the interactive space for

---

[18] International Theological Commission, *Synodality in the Life and Mission of the Church* (2018), 119: "The Church's synodal life presents itself, in particular, as *diakonia* in the promotion of a social, economical and political life of all peoples under the banner of justice, solidarity and peace. God, in Christ, redeems not only the individual person, but also the social relations existing between them."

[19] Avery Dulles, SJ, *Models of the Church*, expanded edition (New York: Image, 1991).

[20] Bryan Froehle and Karla Koll, "World Christian Revitalization: Consultation Methodology and the Circle Method." Pages 181-203 in Karla Koll, ed., *Christian Revitalization in Central America and the Caribbean* (Wilmore: First Fruits, 2019); Bryan Froehle and Agbonkhianmeghe E. Orobator, SJ, "The Circle Method." Pages 40-55 in Philomena Njeri Mwaura and J. Steven O'Malley, eds., *African Urban Christian Identity: Emerging Patterns* (Nairobi: Acton, 2015). See also Frans Wijsen, "The Practical-theological Spiral: Bridging Theology in the West and the Rest of the World." Pages 108-216 in Frans Wijsen, Peter Henriot, SJ, and Rodrigo Mejia, SJ, *The Pastoral Circle Revisited: A Critical Quest for Truth and Transformation* (Maryknoll: Orbis, 2005).

[21] Thus creed, code, cult, and even "community" have an origin outside the person, but general "spiritual" feelings or orientations, however expressed, are innate to the person's nature and originate or have receptors inside a person.

"God-talk," where the formal theological conversation takes place among those engaging in theological scholarship to one degree or another. This formal theological conversation, however, is integrated with "popular theology," the everyday theology of ordinary people.[22] What grandmothers share in work and deed with their grandchildren, or what people discuss about faith with co-workers, is not entirely separate from formal theology. Often popular theological conversations have a relatively direct relationship with formally trained theologians through books people have read or conversation partners they have engaged. In other opportunities, ordinary theologians have heard those who were formally trained by formally trained theologians—for example, in studies for the ministerial priesthood or lay ecclesial ministry or formation for religious life. The methods of bridge theology are those of practical theology—praxis, reflective action that flows from reflection on action and action upon reflection—is at the heart of the wisdom and insights that connect intellectual work with that of ordinary communities of faith. This is not about the ideal, or based on a kind of metaphysics of perfection. Rather, bridge theology is about the messiness of everyday life and ordinary communities of faith, linking them together in concrete everyday life, not to produce some sort of inaccessible perfection but to cooperation with God in God's mission in the world as it is.

Bridge theology is not an "either/or" theology but a "both/and" theology. It does not itself create fragmentation because it refuses to see fragmentation. Rather than denying difference, however, bridge theology embraces it. Difference is not to be feared but to be bridged; this is what bridge theology does in its approach to method itself. Pluralism does not violate a supposed universality and uniformity of the Catholic Church, because universal in the sense of uniformity is not what it means to be "catholic," a word that is derived from "holos," meaning "whole" or "wholistic." "Cata" means "according to"—to be "catholic" is to be "according to the whole." Starting from the long, loving gaze of Christ for the Church, for those who

---

[22] As noted in *Querida Amazonia*, 78: "More than forty years ago, the bishops of the Peruvian Amazon pointed out that in many of the groups present in that region, those to be evangelized, shaped by a varied and changing culture, have been 'initially evangelized.' As a result, they possess 'certain features of popular Catholicism that, perhaps originally introduced by pastoral workers, are now something that the people have made their own, even changing their meaning and handing them down from generation to generation.' Let us not be quick to describe as superstition or paganism certain religious practices that arise spontaneously from the life of peoples."

follow the way of the Gospel, bridge theology melds apparently dialectically defined "either/or" type differences, such as the "sacred" and the "secular," into one. Bridge theology understands that much of the social imaginary of the past several centuries, first in Europe and then increasingly around the world, have broken human life and action into separate spheres—a political sphere, an economic sphere, a family sphere, a religious sphere. *Rather than seeing these separate "spheres," bridge theology focuses on the relationships that connect them, seeing them as intersecting, even superimposed one on another, rather than as truly separate one from another.*

Possibilities of This Paradigm

How can bridge theology help form Catholics today, especially those who specifically study bridge theology? Students and others who engage bridge theology and its practical theological approach to method and methodology, including the importance of the ongoing, Gospel-based process of conversion (metanoia), come to see that the public is the personal is the public, and that action and reflection are one. This means new responsibilities to engage the major issues of the day such as the environment and climate change, migrants and refugees, and global poverty and integral human development. One of the greatest possibilities for this emerging "bridging" discourse in theology is to help transcend divisions and fragmentation in the Church by fearing, not difference, but the loss that occurs when difference is not engaged.

Bridge theology is a methodological development that emerged from Vatican II but was present from the birth of the Church itself and in the ways of proceeding and language developed over the centuries. Bridge theology as such requires an insertion of the theologian, minister, or layperson into a specific reality in order to listen and learn from people on the ground before moving toward sociopolitical analysis, theological reflection, and action. As suggested above, the historical development of what may properly be termed bridge theology includes Joseph Cardijn's See-Judge-Act approach, Joe Holland and Peter Henriot's pastoral circle methodology, Jose Luis Segundo's hermeneutic circle, and many more. The most adequate theological theory of such methods is synodality, and the work of bridge building itself is deeply informed by decades of conversations around method in practical theology and allied disciplines.

Bridge Building as a Work of Practical Theology

Bridge building needs tools to ground theological insight and pastoral action. Such methods reflect the relationship of ministry to the Church and come from an understanding of the nature of the Church. One of the most helpful typologies to understand the nature of the Church is Avery Dulles' classic six types: Church as institution; communion (mystical body); sacrament (presence of Christ in the world); herald (evangelizer, proclaimer); servant; and community of disciples. According to Dulles, the Church may be any of these models, and typically combines elements of more than one, but it may not be only institutional in nature without abandoning the Gospel. This is because the Church does not exist for itself or by itself, but rather as an expression of the mission of God. "It is not that the church has a mission; rather the mission has a church." This reveals that God is mission itself.[23] Thus, bridge theology has rich conversation partners in ecclesiology and missiology, and related developments in contextual theologies, including Latinx theologies developed in North America and Latin American theology more generally. All of these conversations, in turn, have a method that reflects developments in contemporary practical theology since the Council.

According to James and Evelyn Whitehead, the three most important elements of context are (1) Scripture and the Christian tradition, (2) the surrounding culture and institutional factors, and (3) personal experience. These three must be integrated to avoid major dangers: that of idolatry (Scripture with individual experience); hubris (experience with culture); and the Ivory Tower (culture with Scripture and tradition). These Catholic conversations grew from a deep philosophical and methodological grounding, reflecting the conceptual framing of synodality itself, but soon came to be part of a wider theological conversation with all Christians, reflecting the vocation of the synodal Church itself as always ecumenical.[24] Methods vary with each particular pastoral problem or concern, but all are grounded within the core tasks of practical theology, each of which can be identified with a question. "What is

---

[23] This theological position is deeply embedded in *Ad Gentes*, 2, and *Lumen Gentium*, 2-4. See Stephen B. Bevans, SVD, and Roger P. Schroeder, SVD, *Constants in Context: A Theology of Mission for Today* (Maryknoll: Orbis, 2004). See also Stephen Bevans, "Protestant Influences on Catholic Mission Thinking," *Verbum SVD* 58:2-3 (2017), 150-162. As Bevans notes, the origin of the focus on *missio dei* in Catholic circles is within conversations that had been emerging within other Christian contexts.

[24] *Synodality in the Life*, 117.

going on?" represents a descriptive-empirical task. "Why is this going on?" represents an interpretive task. "What ought to be going on?" represents a normative task. "How might we respond?" represents a pragmatic task.[25]

These four tasks resemble but are not the same as the three that James and Evelyn Whitehead describe: attending; asserting (refining in the crucible); and responding (or acting). The Whiteheads' work reflects the See-Judge-Act process that goes back to Joseph Cardijn and indeed all the way to Aristotle and similar ancient reflections on the human process of knowing.[26] The "four tasks" draw on and adapt a fourfold understanding of fundamental practical theology (practice as theory-laden), descriptive theology (hermeneutics and methodology), systematic theology and theological ethics, and strategic practical theology.[27]

What these approaches have in common are methods that are more or less analogous and, more importantly, a methodology that rejects a top-down, purely deductive, propositional approach and instead bridges the whole person and the whole community in the whole context. For this reason, these methods cannot become "cookbooks" or step-by-step instructions. In so doing, they miss the complexities of ministry and the nuances of God's action. For this reason, the term "movement" is more helpful than "step," which implies an always-linear progression.

Holland and Henriot's work on a four-movement approach to social analysis provides an ecclesial-theological frame. Together with Frans Wijsen's revision of this approach, it may be read in light of the three movement See-Judge-Act approach and that of the Whiteheads as an extension of the second of the three movements.[28] These can be correlated, though not entirely aligned, with the four movement-based approaches of Don Browning and Richard Osmer, and with the further development of additional movements given by Thomas

[25] Richard Osmer, *Practical Theology* (Grand Rapids: Eerdmans), 4.

[26] Many would relate this in turn to the work of the philosopher Bernard Lonergan, SJ. See John Haughey, SJ, *Where is Knowing Going? The Horizons of the Knowing Subject* (Washington: Georgetown University Press, 2009).

[27] See Don Browning, *Fundamental Practical Theology* (Minneapolis: Fortress, 1995).

[28] See Joe Holland and Peter Henriot, SJ, *Social Analysis*, revised and enlarged edition (Maryknoll: Orbis, 1983). See also Frans Wijsen, "The Practical-theological Spiral: Bridging Theology in the West and the Rest of the World." Pages 108-216 in Frans Wijsen, Peter Henriot, SJ, and Rodrigo Mejia, SJ, *The Pastoral Circle Revisited: A Critical Quest for Truth and Transformation* (Maryknoll: Orbis, 2005). Holland and Henriot adapt methods that originated in philosophy and theology for those in pastoral settings, as did James D. and Evelyn Eaton Whitehead, *Method in Ministry*, revised edition (Sheed and Ward, 1995).

Groome for religious education and ministry on the one hand, and Johannes van der Ven for empirical theological research on the other.[29] Through all this, one might identify outlines of a kind of "common-denominator approach" embracing four "movements"; labeled with paired terms, they avoid any reductionist implication that might be suggested by any single term.

The circle method as such reflects common movements in bridge theology and synodality. The paired titles for these four movements are "identifying-inserting," "assessing-analyzing," "correlating-confronting," and "empowering-extending." This approach engages Paul Tillich and David Tracy's correlation method, including the critical praxis correlation method of Rebecca Chopp, all of which are featured primarily, but not exclusively, in the third movement of "correlating-confronting."[30]

Further, this process can be related to the Appreciative Inquiry cycle of discover, dream, design, and deliver.[31] This cycle of organizational development starts first with the definition of topic and related parameters before entering the circle of discover, dream, design, and deliver.

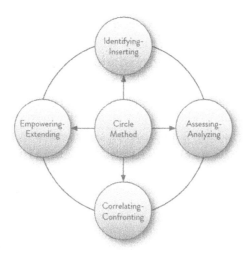

[29] Thomas Groome, *Sharing Faith: A Comprehensive Approach to Religious Education and Pastoral Ministry, The Way of Shared Praxis* (Eugene: Wipf and Stock, 1999). See also Johannes van der Ven, *Practical Theology: An Empirical Approach* (Leuven: Peeters, 1998).

[30] Paul Tillich, *Systematic Theology*, Volume 1 (Chicago: University of Chicago Press, 1973); David Tracy, *Blessed Rage for Order: The New Pluralism in Theology* (Chicago: University of Chicago Press, 1975); Rebecca Chopp, *The Praxis of Suffering* (Eugene: Wipf and Stock, 2007).

[31] David L. Cooperrider and Diana Whitney, *Appreciative Inquiry: A Positive Revolution in Change* (San Francisco: Berrett-Koehler, 2005).

All of these movements are embedded in each of these movements, and all are best experienced in a "circle" of conversation so as to better attend to the guidance of the Holy Spirit. Each of the movements may be associated with particular types of questions, as shown below.

Movement Actions	Movement Questions
Identifying-Inserting	What is the setting, including geographic, social, cultural, and other factors? What organization(s) and organizational stories are most related to the situation, including their origins, developments, and structures? What people and personal profiles are most related to the situation, including leaders, members, insiders, and outsiders? What understandings of God, God's action, and Christian renewal are most involved?
Assessing-Analyzing	What is going on within this case overall, particularly from a "bird's-eye" view? What specific difficulties and opportunities does the organization and people face, and how have they acted? How might observers analyze or theorize about the situation and actions undertaken? Where can divine action most readily be seen in this situation?

Correlating-Confronting	What theological/biblical concepts, stories, or meanings can be related to this case?
	What personal, church, or other experiences can be related to this case?
	How does this situation challenge or expand specific understandings of theological/biblical truth or experience?
	What deeper understanding of theological/biblical truths seems to be emerging from exploring this case?
Empowering-Extending	How does this new insight deepen energy for Christian renewal?
	What are the next steps for leaders and scholars?
	What could limit leaders and scholars in these next steps?
	What new cases will need to be considered?

Bridging Ministry and Discipleship

There are six distinct, central ways of bridging flow from discipleship and furthering the life of discipleship, which is ultimately what bridge building is about: participating ever more authentically in the ministry of reconciliation, the ministry of teaching and healing of Jesus.[32]

- *Following.* "Ministers are teachers who help disciples learn the path of discipleship, its joys and its risks. Teaching, evangelization, and catechesis arise from being a follower."

[32] Kathleen Cahalan, *Introducing the Practice of Ministry* (Collegeville: Liturgical, 2010), 58.

- *Worshipping.* "Ministers preside over the community's prayer and worship in order that the community's worship might unify the community as one body. Leading worship and prayer arise from the call to be a worshipper."

- *Witnessing.* "Ministers are the Church's witness through the ministry of preaching. The ministry of preaching arises from disciples' call to give witness and testimony."

- *Caring.* "Ministers accompany disciples as a spiritual guide, offering care, healing, and guidance, particularly in time of pain and suffering. Pastoral care arises from the call to practice neighbor love and forgiveness of self and others."

- *Prophesying.* "Likewise, to be a neighbor to the stranger and outcast, to be a prophet regarding the poor and the alien, requires leaders who can help the community discern, organize, and call forth prophetic responses to the cries of the poor. Social ministry and outreach arise from the call to be a prophetic neighbor."

- *Stewarding.* "Ministers lead by administering and governing the community's resources, which arises from the demands of stewardship."

Bridge building is at the heart of Christian practice rooted in the earliest expression of the faith. This was expressed in the same Greek language in which the New Testament was written: *marturia,* witnessing (including elements of *kerygma,* proclamation/preaching, and *didache,* teaching/s); *koinonia,* community (common ground, fellowship); *diakonia,* service; and *leiturgia,* worship (the people's work, *laos,* people and *ergon,* work). Synodality is the theological understanding of the fusion of horizons embodied by practical theological method. It takes place in the discerning of God's action in the world. These dynamics are at the heart of an ongoing birthing of an ever more truly global, truly catholic Church.

The Work of a Synodal Church: Bridging, Not Amalgamating

A synodal Church builds bridges. Bridge building is Church building. It is synodality in practice, as in *Querida Amazonia.* Catholic does not mean universal or uniformity by universality. A "universal part," for example, is everywhere and anywhere the same. The word instead means something very different: according to (*cata*) the whole (*holos*). To be catholic, then, is to respect the whole without forcing it always and everywhere into a single thing. These dynamics are at the heart of an emerging ecclesial reality ever more truly global, ever more truly catholic. To be Catholic requires bridge building!

In the midst of what is surely a change of epochs rather than a mere epoch of change, the Catholic Church is becoming its future by being what it always must be: a bridge builder. The path trod together ("synod") is not easy, but others have been tried and found wanting. Today's global Catholic Church cannot be a perfect society or a counter culturally prophetic critique of social life from the outside. It is rather a bridge builder across cultures and contexts, gathering and discerning, acting neither with haste nor with undue delay. In an emerging ecclesial reality where the periphery is the center and the center is the periphery, the path forward is clear. Such a path is shaped more by emerging practices than by defined concluding formulae—bridge building.

CHAPTER THREE

From Social Unity to the Pastoral Activity of the People of God— The Contribution of the Conference of *Medellín*

RAFAEL LUCIANI[1], PHD
TRANSLATED BY THOMAS M. KELLY, PHD

Introduction

MEDELLÍN—THE SECOND GENERAL CONFERENCE of Latin American and Caribbean Bishops—signified the passage from a reflective Church to an adult Church, today converted into a *Source Church*. The way in which *Medellín* positioned the Church involved a methodological advance with respect to the Second Vatican Council. Not only did it assume the method of See-Judge-Act from the Catholic Worker Youth of Joseph Cardijn, inspired by the theology of the signs of the times of *Gaudium et Spes*, but it was also

---

[1] Venezuelan layperson, PhD in Theology from the Pontifical Gregorian University of Rome. Theology Expert of CELAM (Consejo Episcopal Latinoamericano) and CLAR (Conferencia Latinoamericana de Religiosos/as).

41

concerned, specifically, with "proposing lines of pastoral action, in order to transform, in the direction of the Kingdom of God and the liberation of the poor, the realities pierced by structures of sin, and by the cry and hope of the little ones."[2]

In one of the position papers presented during the Conference, Bishop Samuel Ruiz of Chiapas clearly determined the way forward given what was at stake: "We must change our conception and attitude of a Church located outside the world, in front of the world and against the world. The Church is the People of God committed in history: the church; the Church is in the world."[3] With this vision, the bishops at *Medellín* were promoting a new discourse with a social and adult Christian subject that led them to commit to the changes demanded by society. Not surprisingly, the Conference insisted that:

> ... it is not enough to reflect, achieve a greater vision and speak; it is necessary to act.... This assembly was invited to make decisions and establish projects, only if we were willing to execute them as our personal commitment, even at the cost of sacrifice (*Introduction*, 3).

Medellín was inaugurating a new *way of proceeding*, one that would require the need to reform structures and convert mentalities and overcome sole doctrinarian conservative pastoral models. We will expose here some key notions proposed by *Medellín* in order to achieve a connatural union between the identity and ecclesial mission of the Church as *People of God*—its action and pastoral presence in the midst of the world—and the experience of a historical and relational understanding of salvation. In terms of a bridge theology, this contribution will help to value the qualitative leap that represents the inductive methodology in theological method, faithful to the novelty of *Gaudium et Spes* and its unique reception in Latin America.

[2] J.O. Beozzo, "Medellín: Inspiração e raízes," *Revista Eclesiástica Brasileira* 232 (1998), 828.

[3] G.S. Ruiz, "La evangelización en América Latina" in *La Iglesia en la actual transformación de América Latina a la luz del Concilio. Ponencias*, CELAM (ed.), Consejo Episcopal Latinoamericano, Bogotá 1968, 167.

The Need to Reform Structures and Convert Mentalities

With the decision to start from social analysis and a commitment to society's transformation, the participants at *Medellín* did not limit themselves to describing what was happening on the continent, but began by scrutinizing the causes that produced underdevelopment and inequality in the region. In doing so, they placed themselves on the side of the victims, of those who have been left out of any possibility of enjoying comprehensive social benefits, and acted as Christian citizens called to "defend, according to the evangelical mandate, the rights of the poor and oppressed" (*Document on Peace*, 22). A new horizon was also opened from which to define the identity and mission of the Church. It was not a matter of determining a new place of pastoral action or thinking about the survival of the ecclesiastical structure, but of accepting the emergence of an absolute newness that would affect the way of being an institution by facing, prophetically, that "ecclesial identity today is solidarity with the poor and insignificant, through them we enter into the Lord who points us the way to the Father."[4] For Gustavo Gutiérrez, the underlying question resonated in the environment:

> ... What demands are presented to the Church as a universal sacrament of salvation in a world marked by poverty and injustice?... This means walking on the path of poverty (*Ad Gentes* 5). That is what *Medellín* calls a poor Church, a Church that must commit itself to the poor and to poverty in order to be a sacrament of salvation.[5]

The movement that occurred was not mild. It meant moving from a Church that responded to the poor mainly through charitable assistance (*Pastoral Care of the Elites*, 5) to another way of serving them that was committed to training them and promoting them as subjects and agents of their own life in society and in the Christian sphere (*Peace*, 14). It meant a Church that could not be defined by honorific and hierarchical relations (*Poverty of the Church*, 12), often distant from the reality that people live (*Justice*, 18), but from now on should be present as a servant (*Poverty of the Church*, 18) in the light of

[4] G. Gutiérrez, *Densidad del presente*, CEP, Lima 1996, 109.

[5] Ibid., 150-151.

community experience and fraternal treatment of the People of God (*Pastoral Care of the Elites*, 10). All this implied discerning the pastoral dimension of the Church, to overcome all forms of clericalisms (*Document on Priests*, 4), and moralizing attitudes that exclude (*Pastoral Care of the Elites*, 17).

An Inductive Pastoral Approach to Reality

Therefore, at *Medellín* the Church committed itself to overcoming the model of "a conservative pastoral approach based in sacramentality with little emphasis on the previous approach" (*Popular Pastoral Care*, 1). This prior approach changed to a way of proceeding that is "authentically poor, missionary and paschal, detached from all temporal power and boldly committed to the liberation of all people" (*Document on Youth*, 15). It was a transformation that implied a genuine conversion of the Church to constantly:

> ... seek a re-conversion and an education of our people in the faith at ever deeper and more mature levels, following the criteria of a dynamic pastoral approach in line with the nature of the faith, impelling believers towards both the personal and communal dimensions of their reality (*Document on Popular Pastoral Practice*, 7).

This must happen, not only with individuals but with communities (*Document on Lay Movements*, 13), by calling for "justice, solidarity, witness, commitment, effort and victory for the complete fulfillment of the saving mission entrusted by Christ" (*Poverty of the Church*, 7).

To achieve this, the assembly practiced an authentic act of Christian discernment *in situ* and together, based on a sociographic study of Latin American reality. This inductive approach to reality is described by José Camps:

> Unlike the Second Vatican Council, and extending beyond its method, the *Medellín* assembly did not want to deliberate from the beginning on ready-made schemes. To take accurate knowledge of the problems of the continent as a starting point, the Conference began its work by hearing an impressive "Sociographic vision of Latin America," by the Brazilian sociologist Alfonso Gregory, secretary for the Latin America

Federation of Centers of Socio-religious Studies. From the overwhelming set of facts and figures on the demographic, economic, social and religious situation in Latin America, Fr. Gregory himself drew the conclusions that would mark deeply the work of the assembly: the increasing marginality of the majority of the population with respect to the privileged minorities, and especially the marginality of the continent in the world context, which creates a situation of institutional violence, which cannot fail to provoke a counter-violence by reaction.

The discernment involved how to carry out the necessary transformations, both in social reality and in Church institutions.

The Commitment to Integral Human Development

The "Position Paper" of Marcos McGrath to the assembly raised "change" as the main sign of the times of the Latin American era, following the call of the *Gaudium et Spes* to channel the disappointment with a modernity that had failed to provide for the welfare and development of all people. McGrath called for nonviolence, and thus proposed the path of human promotion to generate the transformation of structures from within.[6]

Medellín understood the notion of change in three dimensions: "structural change, transformation of attitudes and conversion of hearts" (*Peace*, 14). It warned that the change in the mentality of the elites was fundamental in this entire process by expressing that "it is convenient to examine first of all their attitudes, mentalities and their function in social change" (*Pastoral Theology for Elites*, 3). They, together with all the People of God, should assume their historical responsibility through actions and words addressed to the most needy and marginalized (*Education,* 1).

---

[6] "In Latin America, these attitudes are mainly defined around the social problem—called 'human promotion,' 'development,' 'revolution,' etc. Obviously, for us, the urgent task of changing unfair structures referred to in conciliar documents, encyclical documents and many pastoral letters is considered. This will be seen concretely when the field of human promotion is covered." M. McGrath, "Los signos de los tiempos en América Latina hoy," in *La Iglesia en la actual transformación de América Latina a la luz del Concilio. Ponencias,* CELAM (ed.), Consejo Episcopal Latinoamericano, Bogotá 1968, 82.

The language of *Medellín* was not narrative or declarative, but performative, that is, relational. It invited people to *do* what was *said*, to put into practice what was asked of others in the framework of a holistic project of liberation and integral development of all human beings. This represents a case of a bridge theology, assuming the novel path of the inductive method of *Gaudium et Spes* and moving forward towards a commitment to transform reality from a collaboration of individuals, intermediary associations, and members of the ecclesial, political, and economic sectors.[7] This common effort characterized the bishops' way of proceeding at the Conference, assumed that their commitment to the transformation of the continent was derived from their status as Christians, and was their response to God's call to reject the sinful situation caused by injustice and inequality.[8] Throughout the Conference, it was clear that there was a need for a common and joint effort of all people if any change in society were to be produced.

A Common Effort from Below and Within

It is significant that *Medellín* defines the process of change in proportion to integral human development and calls it *socialization*, that is, a common action between different actors through a process of transformation and reconstitution of the social fabric. In this way, it avoids change only by the elites while the majority (the base) acts passively and merely receives:

> Socialization, understood as a sociocultural process of increasing the personalization and solidarity of believers, leads us to believe that all sectors of society, and in this case, mainly the economic (and) social sectors, must overcome the challenges to justice and fraternity, and various antagonisms, to become agents of national and continental development (*Justice*, 13).

---

[7] "We must strongly empathize with the message of Christ to understand that the Kingdom of God will not have reached maturity where there is no integral development. Therefore, in our pastoral service we will look for ways to embody the love of the Lord in the Church today." J. Landázuri Ricketts, "Discurso inaugural," in *La Iglesia en la actual transformación de América Latina a la luz del Concilio. Ponencias*, CELAM (ed.), Consejo Episcopal Latinoamericano, Bogotá 1968, 19.

[8] "When talking about a situation of injustice we refer to those realities that express a situation of sin; this does not mean ignoring that, sometimes, the misery in our countries can have natural causes that are difficult to overcome" (*Peace*, 1).

The reconstitution of the Latin American sociocultural fabric should be launched by a Church that accompanies society through actions in favor of a participatory society composed of personalized subjects in solidarity. This society will practice "the requirement that the faith poses in its commitment to human realities" (*Liturgy*, 5; *Lay Movements*, 10). It is necessary to understand this relationship between faith and life because it is essential for understanding the ecclesial identity and mission of *Medellín*. These are the terms through which the institution is called to "inspire, encourage and urge a new order of justice that incorporates all people in the management of their own communities" (*Justice*, 16).

There was talk of action that should begin from the base and involve pastoral collaboration in "the creation of mechanisms for participation and legitimate representation of the population, or if necessary, the creation of new forms" at the level of "the municipal and communal organizations" (*Justice*, 16). This ecclesial way of proceeding was characterized by starting from below and "from within" (*Peace*, 15), and not from above or from outside, or by ideological imposition. Therefore, bishops could affirm that "no sector should exclusively reserve political, cultural, economic and spiritual leadership. Those who have the power of decision-making must exercise it in communion with the wishes and options of the community" (*Message to the peoples of Latin America*).

Such an organizational model was the expression of a local and regional reception of the Church as the People of God (*Lumen Gentium*, 13) and does not respond to economic-political ideologies or theories that give "primacy to capital" or favor the "totalitarian concentration of state power." Thus, it was necessary for any socialization process to create distance and distinguish itself both from a "liberal capitalist system" and from "Marxist socialism" because:

> Both systems militate against the dignity of the human person. One takes for granted the primacy of capital, its power and its discriminatory use of profit-making. The other, although it ideologically supports a kind of humanism, is more concerned with collective humanity, and in practice becomes a totalitarian concentration of state power (*Justice*, 10).

The *Medellín* proposal was an alternative because it was not ideological. Rather, it was inspired by the principle of incarnational solidarity lived by Jesus himself, through which historical reality was considered a "theological place and irruption of God" (*Pastoral Care of the Elites*, 13). From the incarnational solidarity of the Church, the ecclesial community could discern its mission "in the light of the Gospel" (*Justice*, 3), namely, discovering the saving passage of God through our history and with it "his presence that wants to save people whole, soul and body" (*Introduction*, 5). Anthropology, Christology, and soteriology were thus united in a life-giving theology of the historical and the temporal, or as McGrath said, in "the relationship between the theology of creation and the theology of development, and the relationship of both to the theology of redemption."[9] Because of this "profound unity that exists between the saving project of God, carried out in Christ, and the aspirations of humanity" (*Catechesis*, 4), it was possible to affirm that there is an indissoluble unity "between salvation history and human history; between the Church, the People of God, and temporary communities; between the revealing action of God and the experience of human beings" (*Catechesis*, 4). The theological key is the correlation established "between the revealing action of God and the experience of humanity" (*Catechesis*, 4), that is, in the "ability to faithfully listen to the Word of God" (*Formation of the Clergy*, 9) by means of language and human facts (*Dei Verbum*, 2) through which God truly communicates Self.

It's a new way of proceeding that implies hearing the Word of God *contextually*, that is, in a specific sociocultural context that becomes the theological place of its reception and update. By doing so, a bridge theology can be appreciated, capable of connecting both the mentalities of individuals and the social structures from an inductive methodology that recognizes the authoritative character of the concrete reality of the people as *locus theologicus*. Cardinal Landazuri Ricketts explains it:

> Know how to listen, also, to the voice of the world. Well, maybe we are used to a "clerical" view of the world. Sometimes it occurs in us almost spontaneously, mistrust, distrust, fear, before what is called, I do not know very exactly, "the profane" and, nevertheless, the Word

---

[9] McGrath, "Los signos," 90.

of God became human and dwells among us giving meaning to every-thing that exists and is realized by humans. Therefore, whenever we listen to human beings we listen to Christ; whenever we care about human beings, we care about Christ. And to the extent that we meet human beings, learning and knowing how to encounter them, we en-counter the same Lord.[10]

The real presence of God is heard and discerned in our midst. God commu-nicates Self, here and now, tangibly, through human actions.[11] This disposi-tion to listen to God and to discern His real presence in the world is the basis of the principle of the Church always reforming itself.

The Church's Capacity to Reform in Service to Social Change

Medellín was very clear in recognizing that "any review of ecclesial struc-tures, insofar as they can be reformed, must be done to meet the demands of specific historical situations, but also with eyes fixed on the nature of the Church" (*Pastoral Activity*, 5). It is a reform or adaptation of structures whose purpose is the formation of pastoral action and citizen formation where faith and life go together (*Pastoral Care of the Elites*, 21). Its final purpose is constituting *people as subjects*, training them integrally so they become "agents of their own integral development" (*Education*, 3, 16). Through this formation, they can avoid being social and ecclesial objects of external and colonizing ideologies. Consequently, any personalization process generated must start from genuine fraternal cohesion (*Introduction*, 4), with no coercion. All reforms revise "first, attitudes, mentalities and functions based on social change, which then inform manifestations of their faith" (*Pastoral Care of the Elites*, 3).

The words of Avelar Brandão Vilela, president of CELAM, and of Mon-signor Eduardo F. Pironio, general secretary, in the introduction to the po-sition papers (presentations), emphasized the need to understand that there

---

[10] Landazuri Ricketts, "Discurso inaugural," 47.

[11] "Christ, actively present in our history, anticipates his eschatological gesture not only in man's impatient yearning for his total redemption, but also in those conquests that, as predictive signs, man is achieving through an activity carried out in love" (*Introduction*, 5).

is no before and after between actions in favor of social change and manifestations of faith, because faith is not *a priori* to human action. Salvation operates in history as liberation from ignorance, oppression, misery, hunger, and death—that is, as a first fruit of what life in the Kingdom will be:

> The idea of integral salvation encompasses the totality of human beings (soul and body, individual and society, time and eternity), the entire world and its things. This salvation—which the Church offers as a sign and instrument—demands the total liberation of humanity from the servitude of sin and its consequences (ignorance, oppression, misery, hunger and death) and the incorporation of a new life with grace, the beginning and spark of eternity. The Kingdom of God is already present among us and marches, intimately united with human progress; towards the consummate fullness of eschatology.[12]

Along these same lines, Cardinal Pironio exposed in his position paper that salvation is the full development of human values, which means "complete liberation, overcoming all misfortune, redemption from sin and its consequences (hunger and misery, disease, ignorance, etc.)."[13] Following Paul VI, Pironio recalled that "the human being is called to be human, to 'do more, learn more, and have more so that they might increase their personal worth'"*(Populorum Progressio*, 6). The architects of their own destiny, human beings have a specific mission in time and a divine call to which they correspond. In God's plan, every person is born to seek self-fulfillment, for every human life is called to some task by God"[14] (*Populorum Progressio*, 15). All dehumanizing conditions inhibit full development and result from situations of sin that must be overcome because they impede the salvific presence of God among us.

---

[12] D.A. Brandão Vilela, E.F. Pironio, "Palabras de presentación," in *La Iglesia en la actual transformación de América Latina a la luz del Concilio. Ponencias*, CELAM (ed.), Consejo Episcopal Latinoamericano, Bogotá 1968, 10-11.

[13] E.F. Pironio, "Interpretación cristiana de los signos de los tiempos hoy en América Latina," in *La Iglesia en la actual transformación de América Latina a la luz del Concilio. Ponencias*, CELAM (ed.), Consejo Episcopal Latinoamericano, Bogotá 1968, 115.

[14] Ibid., 110.

In this sense, Monsignor Eugenio de Araujo Sales says, "a human community, which fails to provide for everyone's harmonious growth, is cruelly unjust."[15] The discernment about the true meaning of what this collaborative effort implies must be directed to first train the poor as authors of their own future and never as passive recipients. With this, *Medellín* proposed a new theology of historical creation that discovered in the human being the "co-creator and manager with God of his destiny" (*Pastoral Practice*, 12). Such a vision is required to articulate the social and the pastoral presence of the Church in the World.

Articulation of the Social and Pastoral Dimensions of the Church: "We Are Saved Not Individually, but as a Community"

Common social action constitutes the Church as a sign of the "Kingdom of Justice" and not of itself. She is the "servant of Yahweh" called to denounce the inequity of the world for her salvation. By acting and serving together, the Church not only contributes to the transformation of the world but also realizes its catholicity and communion through a radiant unity (in diversity), freedom and charity:

> (Through collaborative action) it becomes a sign of the fellowship that allows and consolidates sincere dialogue. This requires, first, that mutual esteem, respect and harmony be promoted within the Church, recognizing all legitimate diversities, to open, with ever increasing fertility, the dialogue between all those who make up the People of God, both pastors and other faithful. The bonds of the union of the faithful are much stronger than the reasons for division between them. There is unity in what is necessary, freedom in doubt, love in everything (*Document on Social Media*, 22).

It should be stressed that *Medellín* does not understand social or ecclesial changes to be the result of the sum of individual actions. Solidarity and communal

---

[15] E. de Aráujo Sales, "La Iglesia en América Latina y la promoción humana," in *La Iglesia en la actual transformación de América Latina a la luz del Concilio. Ponencias*, CELAM (ed.), Consejo Episcopal Latinoamericano, Bogotá 1968, 130.

cohesion are generated socially, that is, through shared processes and not individually, and also together, in the pastoral work of the Church that enables
us to be subjects and makes us a community. The *Concluding Document* of
Medellín emphasizes that overcoming individualistic or collectivist mentalities is fundamental: "According to the will of God, men and women must be
sanctified and saved not individually, but as a community" (*Popular Pastoral
Theology*, 7). The understanding of human existence and Christian salvation
in its *communal* character are criteria that permeate the entire final text in a
more substantive and cultural way than it is often framed. A few days after
the Conference, Jorge Mejía wrote:

> The issue of community permeates the entire document in one way or
> another. The fact is even more remarkable because each section was
> drafted by a different commission with its own concerns and optics,
> and without any communication with others. Conversely, I am not
> aware that instructions for the commissions mentioned the issue of
> communities. Therefore, it is clear this arises from a deep perception,
> not even reflected, but indisputably present in multiple experiences of
> study and pastoral work. One could also say, at the risk of seeing only
> a human effort, that the Spirit of the Lord is the safest guide here. [16]

Three ways that *Medellín* grants a primacy to the community character and
nature of social and ecclesial work are: the reception and deepening of the
model of the People of God from Vatican II (*Lay Movements*, 7); the realization of the Church's evangelizing mission through its pastoral and liberat-
ing work (*Justice*, 6; *Education*, 9); and the implementation of a historical
and relational understanding of salvation (*Justice*, 4). This affirms that "for
the Christians, the communal way of life is of particular importance, as a
testimony of love and unity" (*Catechesis*, 10). When considering the state
of the community as inherent to the identity of the Church, the notion of
credibility is linked to the figure of its witness in society.

The ecclesiology and the soteriology of community witness emerges
from a continual practice of horizontal relationships based on the dignity of

---

[16] J. Mejía, "Crónica de la vida de la Iglesia. Medellín y las comunidades de base," *Criterio*
1558 (1968), 805.

all as sons and daughters of God (*Pastoral Practice*, 6), of the communion that exists between the baptized (*Pastoral Practice*, 7), of participation in the common priesthood of the faithful (*Priests*, 16), and the cooperation of all in the common work (*Lay Movements*, 7). From this desired equality, a full diversity of charisms, services, and functions follows, because it is recognized that "in the bosom of the People of God, which is the Church, there is a unity of mission and diversity of charisms, services and functions" (*Lay Movements*, 7). This "gives in the Church, at all levels, a sense of authority, with a character of service, exempt from authoritarianism" (*Youth*, 15). All communities facilitate personal and communal relationships and encourage the connection between faith and human development.

Personal and Community Witness

Members of the Church have greater credibility when they witness to their own faith in the midst of the world through the demonstration of a transparent community capable of accommodating and promoting social development. This is how pastoral action becomes the way to proceed and reflects a Church in service to the formation of small communities which are concrete signs that announce the anticipation of redemption (*Education*, 9) in its varied and multiple forms:

- "small grassroots social communities" to avoid the hegemony of the dominant power groups (*Justice*, 20)

- "grassroots organizations" that will claim rights (*Peace*, 27)

- families as "communities of faith" (*Family and Demography*, 19)

- "educational communities" that promote awareness and liberation (*Education*, 15, 19)

- strong "youth communities" in the organization of youth ministry (*Youth*, 6)

- "ecclesial communities" that ensure the ordering of parishes (*Pastoral Practice*, 13)

- performance of work in "teams or communities of faith" (*Lay Movements*, 12)

- "the basic Christian community as the first and fundamental ecclesial community" (*Pastoral Practice*, 10)

For *Medellín*, the need for the Church to inspire confidence is, at the same time, a credibility problem in the lifestyle of its members and in the way in which the Church responds to the signs of the times. The form of witnessing is expressed in two senses in the following texts:

> This evangelization must be carried out through personal and community witness that is expressed, in a special way, in the context of normal commitments. The evangelization we have been talking about must explain the values of justice and collaboration, found in the aspirations of our peoples, in an eschatological perspective. Evangelization requires the Church as a sign of this (*Pastoral Care of the Elites*, 13).

> We want our lifestyle to be modest; our dress, simple; our institutions functional, without ostentation. We ask priests and the faithful to treat us in a manner consistent with our mission as pastors. We want to renounce honorary titles from another era (*Poverty of the Church*, 12).

> We encourage those who are called to share the fate of the poor, living with them and even working with their hands (*Poverty of the Church*, 15).

In these lines, we see how the Church mediates the salvation that is signified and communicated in its own historical witness, not outside of it, but mediated through the building of a society free from dehumanizing structures and relationships.[17] It is, therefore, the struggle for the dignity of the poor that determines this social dimension of the Church. As an institution, it is

---

[17] "Somehow, the history of salvation has to do with salvation in history; but, on the other hand, it implies that the salvation announced by the Church in history must announce it from the very history of salvation and not from other instances outside it." I. Ellacuría, *Conversión de la Iglesia al Reino de Dios*, Sal Terrae, Santander 1984, 220.

not and cannot be the subject of faith (*credere in ecclesiam*), without being
the object of faith (*credere ecclesiam*). The Church is a sacramental sign, not
for itself but for the Mystery (*res significata*) that grounds it and enables it
to be the means of salvation.

The mission of the Church through its pastoral presence can only be understood in its incarnation (*Catechesis*, 6) in a variety of different socio-cul-
tural contexts and mentalities (*Catechesis*, 8) and in the firm resolve to build
a more human world (*Poverty of the Church*, 18). It is a perspective that
allows us to delve into the Vatican II principle of the pastoral nature of doctrine that provoked "new forms of faith" and helps us "discover a new way
of being present in contemporary forms of expression and communication
in a secularized society" (*Catechesis*, 3). This perspective is possible due to
the Latin American reception of the novel inductive methodology of *Gaudium et Spes*, which concedes an authoritative character to the manifestation
of the Word in the words and gestures of the people and their cultures. In
doing so, a bridge theology can be clearly identified as an inherent condition
of the theological method, and not simply as a secondary and optative element of the doing of theology.

It must be emphasized that it is not possible to separate pastoral action from social processes. An example comes to mind when talking about
the centrality of the family. It is clear that it is "necessary to consider the
doctrine of the Church to establish pastoral activity that will lead the Latin
American family to preserve or acquire the fundamental values that enable
it to fulfill its mission. Among these, we want to point out three especially:
the family—forming family, faith educator, and promoter of development"
(*Family*, 4). Doctrine and pastoral activity are in a reciprocal relationship, a
continuous feedback loop, at the service of the evangelizing mission of the
Church. This will generate processes of personalization (*Justice*, 13) and
the creation of free subjects (*Education*, 8) in society. Otherwise, we simply
perpetuate religious indoctrination or theological abstraction.

Applying the principle of the pastoral connection with doctrine means
the *Medellín* proposal does not promote merely an alternative social program. The bishops are recognizing the "supernatural dimension that is part
of the same development, which determines the fullness of the Christian
life" (*Education*, 7). Therefore, the Church can say the "pastoral mission
is essentially a service of inspiration and education of the consciences of

believers helping them perceive the responsibilities of their faith in both their personal and social lives" (*Justice*, 3). It is a service rooted in the centrality of the Word that encompasses both its organizing power and its ability to gather small communities of Christian life in suitable places for the integration of social and Church life (*Pastoral Practice*, 7).[18]

Thus, the community constitutes the core of the primary care of all pastoral activity in the Church. Otherwise doctrine would become abstract ideology, with no roots in history and no relation to the concrete life of people; in short, we would have a Christianity without an incarnation in the social realities of peoples and their cultures.

"A New Way of Being a Church, Not a New Church"

The inseparable unity between the mission of the Church and human development was the place to start building this new way of being Church. Cecilio de Lora's testimony is valuable in recalling that "this prophetic intuition generates a new way of being a Church, not a new Church."[19] This newness is found in the understanding of "the grassroots Christian community as the initial cell of ecclesial structuring and focus of evangelization, and now a fundamental factor for human promotion and development" (*Pastoral Practice*, 10). This means that:

> The Church of Latin America wants to build upon small communities, the so-called Christian base communities. These communities emerge in *Medellín* not as a mere pastoral methodology, but as *the Church itself in progress.*[20]

These communities do not represent a discontinuity with the ecclesial model prior to *Medellín* but "establish a new synthesis and underline essential aspects that were not explained before or were not lived out sufficiently or were diluted in the ecclesial experience." They appear "not by reciprocal

---

[18] "En nuestra misión pastoral confiaremos ante todo en la fuerza de la Palabra de Dios," *Pobreza de la Iglesia*, 14.

[19] C. de Lora, "Del Concilio a Medellín hoy", *Horizonte* 24 (2011), 1239.

[20] A. Cadavid Duque, "Actualidad de Medellín para la Iglesia latinoamericana y del Caribe," *Medellín* 135 (2008), 510.

exclusion but by intensification," making the relationship between faith and life tangible.[21] As José Marins clarifies with great precision:

> The Christian base community is a community in a theological sense and not merely a sociological sense. It is ecclesial because it lives out all the basic elements of the Church-community: faith-prophecy, worship-hope, love-liberation, apostolic succession. She is, then, a unique community: a socialization of the mystery of God and the realization of humanity; vitally connected with the other levels of the Church (diocesan and universal).[22]

Medellín recognized the "inadequacy of the traditional structure in many parishes to provide a community experience" (*Pastoral Practice*, 4). Unlike the traditional parish, these communities are "more flexible pastoral structures, more adapted to the real environments that often—at least in cities—are more functional than territorial."[23] However, when making a proposal that starts from the base upwards, the newness of Christianity is captured. It cannot be defined as a religion in the classical sense: temple, priest, and sacrifice. It is at the base where the interpersonal relationship with others occurs. It is there that the true strength and prophetic sense of the gospel is revealed. However, after giving primacy to the individual and their private religion as a result of a reduction of the religious to sacramental ritual, the founding reality of the community has been relativized.

The creation of interpersonal relationships of identity and belonging are characteristic of the social processes that initiated Christianity. These types of relationships are perhaps one of the core elements lacking today in many parishes and pastoral models, making impossible the enablement of real communities. In his presentation on the Church in Latin America, Monsignor Eugenio de Araujo Sales wisely points out:

---

[21] J. Marins, T.M. Trevisan, C. Chanona, *Comunidades eclesiales de base. Origen, contenido, perspectivas*, Paulinas, Bogotá 1977, 30.

[22] Ibid., 43.

[23] Ronaldo Muñoz observes "the need to move from the current structuring in parishes to networks of grassroots communities, with itinerant ministers working within pastoral planning." R. Muñoz, *Nueva conciencia de la Iglesia en América Latina*, Sígueme, Salamanca 1974, 368.

We will strongly encourage the transformation of Latin America when parishes become lived examples of the authentic formation of human-Christian communities. Not only by administering the sacraments or preparing the truths of the Gospel; not only by preaching the *Kerygma* as the announcement of traditional truths accepted as supernatural, but also by awakening in these people the sense of their own dignity, the force of their rights, and an awareness of their value. These communities will encourage them to demand from politicians, technicians, businessmen, and all those who occupy key positions a respect for the human person and their inalienable prerogatives. There will be a revolution in Latin America and a genuine experience of the Universal Declaration of the Rights of Humanity, whose second anniversary we commemorate. Not through violence, but by acting with the force of justice. Parishes will not only be the focus of spiritual life, but centers of integral human formation.[24]

Therefore, *Medellín* calls for an ecclesial conversion, a change that demands a theological-pastoral reform "that encourages a genuine sense of community" (*Pastoral Practice*, 35). The community dimension is not something added or optional to the Christian experience. It is actually the most important and creative spirit of an ongoing historical event. Therefore, its recovery is indispensable for Christianity to be attractive again and for the Church to be credible in our society.

Conclusion

The path that the *Medellín* Conference proposed marked a qualitative leap in the way of being Church, advancing the inductive methodology[25] of the Signs of the Times of *Gaudium et Spes*, and bringing together the social and the pastoral dimensions of the Church, inviting us to think:

[24] E. de Aráujo Sales, "La Iglesia en América Latina y la promoción humana," in *La Iglesia en la actual transformación de América Latina a la luz del Concilio. Ponencias,* CELAM (ed.), Consejo Episcopal Latinoamericano, Bogotá 1968, 135.

[25] Cf. C. Schickendantz, "Un enfoque empírico-teológico. En el método, el secreto de Medellín," *Teología y Vida* 58 (2017), 421-445.

... first of all in the very life of the Church as a community among people; that they think first of the Spirit, the options and the structural channels of human relations so that we can integrate the internal life of the Church with social solidarity.[26]

Only then is it possible to speak of an authentic birth of a Church. This is a great challenge. As explained by Ronaldo Muñoz:

The Church as an institutional body cannot offer to history its own form of unity if it does not live by gathering that unity and communal spirit in the very foundations of society. It must live by entering into the complex and changing fabric of human relations that constitutes our society in crisis. In this light, we understand the growing importance that grassroots Christian communities have in the renewal of the Latin American Church, in all environments, and especially in the popular media and among youth.[27]

The spirit of this unique Conference continues to live in the authentic and lasting process of Church reform today and the call for personal and ecclesial conversions that begin from the base, becoming friends of the poor, and working together with them, to build a more humane and just world, as a Church that is both poor and for the poor.

---

[26] R. Muñoz, *Nueva conciencia de la Iglesia en América Latina*, Sígueme, Salamanca 1974, 362.

[27] Ibid., 366.

CHAPTER FOUR

Bridge Building with Social Analysis and Theology: A Path Toward Reconciliation and Peacebuilding

MARIA CIMPERMAN, RSCJ, PhD

BUILDING A BRIDGE OFFERS an opportunity to see with new eyes why the bridge is needed, where it is needed, and how to together create paths that serve all, particularly those in most need.

Pope Francis consistently, and even insistently, asks us to build bridges. I offer a few such examples. In his conversation with young Italians in Krakow, Poland, on July 27, 2016, during World Youth Days, he said:

> Peace builds bridges, whereas hatred is the builder of walls. You must decide, in life: either I will make bridges or I will make walls. Walls divide and hatred grows: when there is division, hatred grows. Bridges unite, and when there is a bridge hatred can go away, because I can hear the other and speak with the other. When you shake the hand of a friend, of a person, you make a human bridge. You make a bridge. Instead, when you strike someone, when you insult another person, you build a wall. Hatred always grows with walls. At times, it may happen

that you want to make a bridge and you offer your hand, but the other party does not take it; these are the humiliations that we must suffer in life in order to do good. But always make bridges. And you have come here: you were stopped and sent home, then you took a risk on the bridge to try again: this is the right attitude, always. Is there a difficulty that prevents me from doing something? Go back and then go ahead, return and move on. This is what we must do: make bridges. Do not fall to the ground, do not say, "Oh, I can't," no: always look for a way of building bridges. You are there, with your hands, make bridges, all of you! Take each other by the hand. I want to see lots of human bridges.... This is the plan for life: make bridges, human bridges.[1]

In his opening address during the 2019 World Youth Days in Panama, Pope Francis cited the wisdom of Pope Benedict XVI, that "True love does not eliminate legitimate differences, but harmonizes them in a superior unity," and then continued with the warning that:

On the other hand, we know that the father of lies, the devil, always prefers people who are divided and quarrelling. He is the master of division, and he is afraid of people who have learned to work together. This is a criterion for distinguishing people: those who build bridges and those who build walls. The builders of walls seek to sow fear and make people afraid. But you want to be bridge builders![2]

Francis then offered a call and response to the thousands of young people present: "What do you want to be?"
The young people answered: *"Bridge builders!"*
Francis replied, "You have learned well; I like that!"[3]

---

[1] Pope Francis, Live Video Link-Up with Italian Youth Present at World Youth Day gathered in St. John Paul II Shrine, "Dialogue of the Holy Father with Italian Young People, Kraków, Poland, 27 July 2016. Found at: http://www.vatican.va/content/francesco/en/speeches/2016/july/documents/papa-francesco_20160727_polonia-dialogo-giovani-italiani.html.

[2] Pope Francis, Pope Francis' Apostolic Journey to Panama on the Occasion of the 34th World Youth Day, Welcome Ceremony and Opening of World Youth Day, Campo Santa Maria la Antigua—Cinta Costera, Panama, 24 January 2019. Found at: http://www.vatican.va/content/francesco/en/speeches/2019/january/documents/papa-francesco_20190124_panama-apertura-gmg.html.

[3] Ibid., Apostolic Journey to Panama.

Francis doesn't limit his evocations of bridge building to youth, either. He consistently seeks this in his interactions with the people of God. After his visit to Morocco, in his General Audience in St Peter's Square on April 3, 2019, he drew on the theme of the trip, "Servant of Hope," and said that "to serve hope in our day is to build bridges between cultures, and it was a joy and honor for me to be able to do this in the noble Kingdom of Morocco, meeting both its people and its political leaders."[4] Showing that building bridges happens as we find a common goal, Francis shared that both King Mohammed and he "reiterated the essential role religions have in defending human dignity, promoting peace and justice, and in caring for creation, our common home."[5]

My own intersection with the call to build bridges came at the July 26-29, 2018, Catholic Theological Ethics in the World Church (CTEWC) conference I attended in Sarajevo. The theme of this gathering of 500 Catholic ethicists from over 80 countries was "A Critical Time for Bridge-Building, Catholic Theological Ethics Today." Pope Francis sent a message to the theologians gathered. In it he wrote:

> The theme of your meeting is one to which I myself have often called attention: the need to build bridges, not walls…. Without renouncing prudence, we are called to recognize every sign and mobilize all our energy in order to remove the walls of division and to build bridges of fraternity everywhere in the world.[6]

This image was striking because a day earlier I had gone, with other colleagues, on a tour to the city of Mostar in Bosnia Herzegovina and viewed a rebuilt Stari Most, also known as Mostar Bridge. The original bridge was a 16th-century Ottoman bridge that was blown up in 1993 during the Croatian-Bosnian war in the Balkans. Some claim it was destroyed because of its strategic importance, but many others felt it was a deliberate effort to destroy a

---

[4] Pope Francis, General Audience (3 April 2019), https://www.vaticannews.va/en/pope/news/2019-04/pope-at-audience-building-bridges-through-hope.html.

[5] Ibid.

[6] Pope Francis, Pope's Message for International Conference of Catholic Theological Ethics in the World Church in Sarajevo, 26 July 2018, https://zenit.org/articles/popes-message-for-international-conference-of-catholic-theological-ethics-in-the-world-church-in-sarajevo/.

cultural icon. Years after the war ended, with funds from many organizations including UNESCO and the World Bank, the bridge was reconstructed, even using some of the same stones as the original.

Reconstructed in 2004, the Mostar Bridge we saw was magnificent and beautiful. Yet for me and for some of us on the tour, it was also strikingly clear that rebuilding a bridge doesn't necessarily build peace. It was important to rebuild the bridge. Yet something more was needed, and that was evident for me in some of the tension I felt in the air. When asked about the journey to reconciliation in her country, our tour guide, an engaging woman in her mid thirties who lived in Mostar with her husband and their young child, simply stated that it was enough for her that the violence had ended. "We need to get on with our lives," she said. It is true. The war had ceased with the Dayton Peace Accords, but it was a war that many argue had simply stopped. On November 21, 1995, the Dayton Peace Accords were agreed upon by the presidents of Bosnia, Croatia, and Serbia, which stopped the war in Bosnia and outlined a General Framework Agreement for Peace in Bosnia and Herzegovina.[7] The war had ceased, a bridge was reconstructed, but there was no guarantee the tensions wouldn't simmer into another conflagration. My own interest and work in reconciliation and peacebuilding tells me that rebuilding bridges destroyed by intentional human violence requires time and space going through some of the rubble of destruction in order to create a bridge more likely to prevent further violence and actually build relationships.

In his letter to the CTEWC, Pope Francis made specific requests and suggestions for the theologians—build bridges among yourselves and create networks so that you may serve others:

> With regard to the question of how theological ethics can make its own specific contribution, I find insightful your proposal to create a network between persons on the various continents who, with different modalities and expressions, can devote themselves to ethical reflection in a theological key in an effort to find therein new and effective resources. With such resources, suitable analyses can be carried out, but more importantly, energies can be mobilized for a praxis that

---

[7] The formal agreement was signed on 14 December 1995 in Paris.

is compassionate and attentive to tragic human situations and concerned with accompanying them with merciful care. To create such a network, it is urgent first to build bridges among yourselves, to share ideas and programmes, and to develop forms of closeness. Needless to say, this does not mean striving for uniformity of viewpoints, but rather seeking with sincerity and good will a convergence of purposes, in dialogical openness and the discussion of differing perspectives.[8]

Pope Francis is calling and inviting us to consider what bridge building can look like, offering us some elements such as networking, responses to cries, creating together. This is part of our vocational call to service. As a theologian and ethicist working with both theory and praxis, the call is to build on what Pope Francis is asking for and offer some further specifics on how we might go about this more particularly in our classrooms, parishes, communities and well beyond. Our call is both global and local.

Delving more deeply into what bridge theology and/or an ethic of bridge building entails may serve as a meeting point between theologian practitioners, people of faith, and people of good will. All have contributions to offer. The metaphor of bridge building and bridge theology is compelling and, like all metaphors/images, there is more than meets the eye. My desire is to contribute to this work toward constructing bridge theology, contributing a few key elements and then entering into dialogue with other contributors and practitioners. My basic premise is the following:

Bridges are meant to help us cross over seeming impasses or challenges, and therefore it is important to know the realities (social analysis) around us that call for building bridges. The pastoral spiral process is one lens from which to consider the realities around us. Acknowledging that bridge building at its core is the work of God's grace and asks for our participation, we must begin with an understanding of bridge theology or the ethic of bridge building grounded in the mystical-prophetic call. Four key ingredients or areas that contribute toward (constructing) a theology of bridge building that are imbedded in this essay are the mystical-prophetic, virtue ethics, the moral imagination, and a preferential option for the poor. Yet bridge building does more than help us cross over; bridges help us continue on the way, to move toward a destination. One call of our time is that of reconciliation

---

[8] Pope Francis, Message for CTEWC.

and peacebuilding. Grounded in the realities of our time, we will in the course of this essay briefly consider ways in which bridge building is also a path toward reconciliation and peacebuilding.

I begin our "ethical reflection in an ethical key" with how we might read the realities around us (social analysis/pastoral spiral) and bring to it four key dimensions for living and writing bridge theology—grounded in the mystical-prophetic, virtue ethics, religious imagination, and a preferential option for the poor and vulnerable. There are others, but these are key.

Bridges are built for a reason. They serve a purpose. They respond to a need. To build a bridge across an impasse requires persons working together. Bridges are not built singlehandedly. It matters whether the impasse is because a bridge has been destroyed (literally, due to mistrust or violence of any kind) or because no one has found a way across (a bridge of understanding). The process of social analysis or, more accurately, using the pastoral spiral,[9] assists with bridge building at the level of experience, social analysis, faith reflection, and action. We shall look at these, but first a few words about entering into the pastoral spiral process for bridge building.

People begin a bridge-building process such as this because of the recognition that a quick solution is not possible. A bridge is not built in a day. Second, for people to come together means that they do want a bridge, a way forward from the impasse. This must be recognized as a gift and grace, for not everyone is willing. Third, this process asks for sufficient self-knowledge to recognize one's own bias. There is no unbiased analysis. Key is naming your bias with your deepest values. Also important is a willingness to come openly to the table with these values and be willing to share one's values and hear and recognize the significant values of others. This is another space where we come with open hands so people can see us and see what we value and what that means. By holding our values with open hands and coming with eyes open, we also allow others to ask questions of our values as we do the same. All of this means there is some flexibility rather than rigidity—important for bridges as well.

---

[9] I certainly acknowledge the use of a pastoral circle instead of a pastoral spiral. However, I have found that a spiral more adequately names the process in significant social issues. Rarely do we attend to all the areas in action, but instead prioritize actions, act, assess, and then go to the next layer of the process. For the work on the pastoral circle, I am indebted to groundbreaking work of Joe Holland and Peter Henriot, SJ, *Social Analysis: Linking Faith and Justice* (Maryknoll, NY: Orbis, 1983).

With these three understandings (of time, desire, and values) people come together and offer their experience of what happened that requires bridge building. Narratives are key here and so is listening. A space of safety must exist so that diverse perspectives have room to be heard. Respect is essential. At the place of experience, one usually hears feelings as well as facts.

Sometimes it takes a lot of deep listening before those present can begin to look outward toward the chasm before them or the horizon beckoning forward beyond the abyss. Once persons sense that their experiences have value, there is a greater willingness to see the values of others. In addition, in building a bridge, the persons must not only acknowledge a problem but now begin to look toward a way to build a different future than the present. One's deepest values may remain, but even these values must be held open to be seen by others, with affirmation and perhaps also questioning. Looking forward toward a future beyond the impasse, we can move to social analysis. Yet before we do so, a few words about what it will take to sustain both the pastoral spiral process and the bridge building we seek.

Bridge theology is a process that will ask for dialogue, collaboration, time, and delving into difficult topics, issues, and realities. Looking at the areas of reconciliation and peacebuilding needed in light of histories and realities such as racism, sexism, violence against indigenous persons, and clergy sexual abuse, to name only a few, to build bridges will require sustained effort. Grounding in the mystical-prophetic call will be key for any such efforts. Amidst our efforts we must remember that bridge building is also God's work in us, among us and through us. While Pope Francis wrote this to members of consecrated life, all of us embarking on the call to bridge theology need these core dimensions of the mystical-prophetic life:

Prophets receive from God the ability to scrutinize the times in which they live and to interpret events; they are like sentinels who keep watch in the night and sense the coming of the dawn. Prophets know God and they know the men and women who are their brothers and sisters. They are able to discern and denounce the evil of sin and injustice. Because they are free, they are beholden to no one but God, and they have no interest other than God. Prophets tend to be on the side of the poor and powerless, for they know that God himself is on their side.[10]

This is a call to all believers. Five signs that one is growing in the mystical prophetic vocation are that individuals (and groups) (1) know God; (2) cultivate interior freedom; (3) read the signs of the times with a critical and creative fidelity to the gospel vision of the Reign of God, denouncing injustice and announcing the gospel vision; (4) live in closeness to and solidarity with the powerless, oppressed, and marginalized; and (5) invite all to bring their gifts to participate in the vision of the reign of God.[11] We see here the necessary combination of deep reliance on God (a spirituality) and actively denouncing the injustice of those crying out and offering a vision of the reign of God. Engaging in bridge building calls one equally to silence and meditation/contemplative practices, waiting on God for insight as well as communal engagement of all persons and gifts to create the bridge needed. Spirituality and strategy, personal and communal discernment, are all in movement yet held lightly in order to sense and respond to the movement of the Spirit. Recent work and ministry in the area of reconciliation and peacebuilding makes me keenly aware that, in addition to any theory, there is an art and spirituality that must come together when one wants to build bridges where they have been torn down. It is this stance that can hold the painful and/or hope-filled spaces that long for building bridges together and that require time and space.

On the journey of bridge building, when we open ourselves to the mystical-prophetic, our encounters are transformative. We open ourselves to encounter the God of Mystery by looking beyond the familiar or comfortable voices to those calling for more from us, calling to us with refrains resonant of the gospel calls to justice, peace, liberation, and mercy. These become mystical encounters. Filipino theologian Antonio Pernia, reminds us:

> Mysticism is built on the conviction that God is not like us, that God always has an "other face,"—the unfamiliar, mysterious face of God,

---

[10] Pope Francis, *Apostolic Letter to All Consecrated People on the Occasion of the Year of Consecrated Life*, November 21, 2014, #2.

[11] This is from my work in this area, to be found in Maria Cimperman, *Religious Life for the 21st Century: Creating Communities of Hope on a Global Scale* (Maryknoll, NY: Orbis, 2020).

the face of God that is revealed to us when we come face to face with the one who is different from us, namely, the poor, the stranger, the foreigner, the refugee, the migrant, the displaced people, the unwed mother, the single parent, the one affected with HIV-AIDS, the faith-seeker, the unbeliever, the non-Christian.[12]

We come to see that the encounter with the other is not first our gift, but rather a gift of God to us for the sake of God's mission. The call, then, is to listen and hear. Peruvian liberation theologian Gustavo Gutiérrez aptly notes: "[W]orking in this world of the poor and becoming familiar with it, I came to realize, together with others, the first thing to do is listen."[13] This also means that we intentionally get close so the other can choose to reveal God's message of flourishing for all to us.

Pernia reminds us what is possible when we open ourselves to such encounters with the other:

Gazing at God's face, we acquire the heart and the eyes of God, so that we begin to gaze at the world with the eyes of God. When we do so, we see the world differently, we see the world in a new way— enemies become friends, separating walls become open doors, strangers become brothers or sisters, borders become bridges, diversity leads not to differences and conflict but to harmony and unity. So, mysticism, which arises out of mission, leads back to mission.[14]

We are all transformed when we see and hear from the periphery. Mysticism and prophecy converge as our hearts become as wide as the world, our common home.

---

[12] Antonio M. Pernia, SVD, "Interculturality and Leadership in Consecrated Life: The Theological Significance of Interculturality," This presentation was offered at the Center for the Study of Consecrated Life (CSCL) Conference (November 2018) at Catholic Theological Union (Chicago). The essay is published in *Engaging Our Diversity: Interculturality and Consecrated Life Today*. Eds. Maria Cimperman, RSCJ, and Roger Schroeder, SVD (Maryknoll, NY: Orbis, 2020).

[13] Jennie Weiss Block and Michael Griffin, eds., *In the Company of the Poor: Conversations with Dr. Paul Farmer and Fr. Gustavo Gutiérrez* (Maryknoll, NY: Orbis, 2013), 166.

[14] Pernia, "Interculturality and Leadership in Consecrated Life," 10.

In all of this, the life of virtue is needed. A virtue is a disposition and practice toward becoming a certain kind of moral person. Virtues help us see our growing edges as gifts, freeing us to continue to practice and open ourselves. Virtue ethics asks, Who are you? Who do you wish to become? How shall you get there?[15] If one desires to become a bridge builder, then one needs to cultivate the virtue of bridge building. Bridge building requires both a particular attitude and practices. Building a bridge, whether for the first time or after one was destroyed, requires, for example, an interior disposition that sees the other as partner in the building as well as a lot of practice and creativity. With this grounding in the mystical-prophetic life, a grace we do also ask for, we now consider the social analysis needed for bridge building.

Social analysis considers the political, socioeconomic, cultural, religious, and environmental realities around an issue; looking for insight; seeking data and possible common entry points for building, linking, and networking. What are the political and socioeconomic issues around this impasse? Is there a history underneath it? What are the cultural factors that contributed to the impasse that are necessary to understand in order to go forward? What gifts of culture can help rebuild or build anew? What do religious traditions, teachings, and practices offer for understanding and for going forward? Religious analysis particularly asks for the resources of our traditions to offer their wisdom. Often Catholic social teaching intersects other areas of analysis, creating spaces where bridge building can begin across many disciplines and works.

In all of these areas, we must seek out the persons, institutions, and authorities involved. Bridge theology will engage all areas of analysis and also continually seek out any needed voices missing from the table of deliberation. Persons needed are those most adversely affected by the impasse and issues. The poor, vulnerable, and marginalized must be included, given an equal seat at the table. We also look for those with particular expertise around an area. Social analysis gives depth of data from which to see what is needed to be repaired or addressed in order to cross an impasse. This analysis, as we have seen above, is always in service of creating the bridges, the ways forward that encompass all the skills needed to construct the bridge.

---

[15] On the virtues, I'm grateful for the work of Alasdair MacIntyre in *After Virtue: A Study in Moral Theory*, 3rd edition (Notre Dame, IN: University of Notre Dame Press, 2007), and James F. Keenan in numerous writings, including *Jesus and Virtue Ethics: Building Bridges between New Testament Studies and Moral Theology* (New York: Sheed & Ward, 2002).

After analysis comes faith reflection, reflection through one's highest values and in light of things learned thus far.[16] While analysis is done through our values (i.e., what kind of economic system is just, what cultural values affirm those on the margins, etc.) and discussions about the values so that we can find understanding, faith reflection requires time and space for experience and analysis to work its way through us, sifting and sorting elements most important for going forward to action. It is a sacred creative space, where new ideas and even new bridge designs may come forth. Too often we people of good will can become impatient here and desire to "just do something." This is where the mystical dimension of seeing asks us to listen, wait, and allow the creative Spirit to move us. This time requires both solitude (even contemplative walking) and time with others to begin naming ideas that emerge. Those who cultivate the virtue of bridge building must submit to the rigors of this kind of reflective walking, perhaps even with the question of "I wonder... I wonder what would happen if... "[17]

The moral or religious imagination is a key ingredient here.[18] The work of Mennonite scholar John Paul Lederach is particularly helpful. He tells us that if we are to see what new is possible, we must cultivate the moral imagination. He defines moral imagination as the "capacity to imagine something rooted in the challenges of the real world yet capable of giving birth to that which does not yet exist."[19] According to Lederach, this includes cultivating, through practice, the following capacities:[20]

- *The capacity to imagine ourselves in a web of relationships that includes our enemies.* What we can even begin to imagine has a better chance of happening than what is impossible. This is God's work, helping us go from impossible to imaginable. Still, we need to pray for openness here.

---

[16] While I am using the four steps in order, it is to be noted that the steps can get repeated. Sometimes faith reflection tells me that I need some further information, or action steps require more time spent listening before movement.

[17] My work with this process has consistently found that those who cultivate this art of contemplative walking and practice this type of deep listening find that the insights and ideas that emerge are solid contributions toward what must happen next.

[18] Certainly the moral or religious imagination is helpful at any stage, but at this stage in bridge building it has ingredients that will shape the format of what comes next.

[19] John Paul Lederach, *The Moral Imagination: The Art and Soul of Building Peace* (New York: Oxford University Press, 2005), ix.

[20] Ibid., 5.

- *The ability to sustain a paradoxical curiosity that embraces complexity without reliance on dualistic polarity.* To be curious about someone's actions or responses means there is room for the other to offer me something I do not have—for example, an understanding that eludes me. I can even refrain from saying "I'm right and you're wrong," and try instead to see wisdom from another perspective. This is different than dismissing a topic with the oft-used refrain, "It's complicated." We instead look into the complexity for the strains of truth. If I can see something from another's perspective, I can communicate my ideas toward a goal we may actually have in common. For example, if people can see that all parties want a better future for their children, all might be able to see ways forward differently. Bridge theology absolutely requires the capacity to see complexity and diversity as gifts.

- *The fundamental belief in and pursuit of the creative act.* Bridge builders must believe that something new (beyond the impasse or conflict) can emerge. The work of bridge building seeks what cannot yet be imagined: a way over, through. This is why creating spaces and times for silence as well as sharing can open up ideas. Creativity is one of the signs of the Spirit.

- *Acceptance of the inherent risk of stepping into the mystery of the unknown that lies beyond the far-too-familiar landscape of violence.*[21] Any time we try to find another way, we risk failure. We also risk success. There is always a risk in reaching out for the new, but its beauty may take us beyond the boundaries of what we have experienced. This is the work of bridge theology and also the work of peacebuilding.

Faith/values reflection is an especially sacred space in bridge building. It is where ideas emerge that have heretofore been unarticulated or where new insights from group members build one upon another. The insights may culminate in a style or location or use of material or combination of individuals and groups that offer a bridge to a place to which it has until this time (or in a long time) not been possible to go. This is the art that goes with the spirituality mentioned earlier. Theology at its best engages the depth and breadth of our tradition, opens itself to the wisdom of other traditions, and

[21] Ibid., 5, 39, 62-63.

engages our imaginative capacities rooted in hope and faith. It may take time, and here again the mystic's discipline of attentive waiting assists us. It is here that the prophetic call to denounce injustice and announce Good News awaits insights and proposals to measure. From communal discernment we know that if all are valued in this process, wisdom can emerge from anyone in the group.

Once an insight emerges, and it will, building bridges means that you begin to create what you see. This is a time for prototyping and experimenting—a period of *ad experimentum*. This is where risking happens on a workable scale. Bridge building and bridge theology do not wait until all the details are completed. Instead this is a living theology, and continual reflection and assessment determines whether the bridge is being built properly for the needs articulated earlier. Just as people create living, dynamic networks, so does bridge building exist in a dynamic evolving manner. It is natural and to be expected that this process will also take lots of turns, for it is the human condition working alongside the Spirit.

Once the prototype is working, your directions for action are clearer. Bridge building must ultimately build a bridge, one that is usable! What is this to serve? What theology serves—the reign of God, proclaiming the message of love of Jesus Christ.

There are ways to assess the direction of the bridge building in the beginning and in an ongoing way. How does this bridge impact those most impacted and in need of healing? Will this offer the poor, marginalized, and vulnerable a bridge to welcome and inclusion in the common good?[22] How is the earth impacted? One must regularly ask, does this bridge address the key issues that created the need? Are we avoiding anything? Are there organic ballasts and buttresses of any sort that would assist? What ongoing conversations are needed to either continue to build together or keep the bridge working well and even open or expand it? Recognizing that bridge building is not linear but dynamic and evolving, what serves for the initial needs may open up further needs or desires. The work of reconciliation in our world, Church, and society requires just this kind of bridge theology.

As networks and partnerships grow, so much is possible, and we actually move more toward peacebuilding. Peacebuilding, according to scholar

---

[22] "Common good" here being that which promotes the full flourishing of each and all, including the earth.

Sulak Sivaraksa "refers to the entire range of long-term approaches to developing peaceful communities and societies based on principles of coexistence, tolerance, justice, and equal opportunity."[23] Bridge theology can help create the bridges and conditions that build peace so that impasses due to violence are few and far between and eventually eliminated. Bridge theology can contribute to peacebuilding by practicing, teaching, and continually learning how to build bridges as all work together and offer what is necessary for contributing to the building of the reign of God. All will be students, learners, teachers, and seekers. The work is difficult, costly, and for the long haul. The paschal mystery meets us here and reminds us that Love accompanies us. So, let us go—build bridges!

---

[23] Sulak Sivaraksa, *Conflict, Culture, Change: Engaged Buddhism in a Globalizing World* (Boston: Wisdom, 2005), 9.

PART II

Bridge Theology and Social Analysis

Becoming Islands of Mercy in a Sea of Indifference: Migration, Social Sin, and Conversion

KRISTIN E. HEYER, PhD

POPE FRANCIS' GESTURES OF solidarity with migrants have been central to his papacy, from his repentance in the "graveyard of wrecks" of Lampedusa to his lived example in returning from Lesbos with refugee families.[1] His bridge-building theology is evident in his written reflections on migration as well. His theological and pastoral emphases are well suited to addressing systemic and ideological barriers to justice for immigrants; he underscores structures of injustice that treat migrants like pawns on a chessboard and joins repentance from harmful idolatries with a recognition of our fundamental relatedness in light of the harm borders wreak. His emphasis on social sin reflects his theology of bridge building, in that it widens the scope of migration ethics beyond dominant "crisis management" approaches to help receiving communities recognize their complicity in pushing, pulling,

---

[1] Portions of this chapter are adapted from Kristin E. Heyer, *Kinship Across Borders: A Christian Ethic of Immigration* (Washington, DC: Georgetown University Press, 2012); Heyer, "Internalized Borders: Immigration Ethics in an Age of Trump," *Theological Studies* (March 2018); "'An Echo in their Hearts': The Church in Our Modern World," *New Theology Review* (March 2016); Pope Francis and the Challenge to Prioritize Poverty, Eds. David DeCosse, Mike Duffy, and Erin Brigham (San Francisco: Lane Center Series, 2015).

and punishing forced migrants. His focus on the ideological dimensions of sin and the affective dimensions of conversion highlights the inadequacy of standard human rights approaches; rather his words and example help pierce indifference with the shock of recognition and the "gift of tears." Finally, his bridge theology is evident in his efforts to invite those who disagree on polarizing social issues or are tempted to retreat to the realm of theoretical analysis to a praxis of encounter. This chapter explores each of the ways Pope Francis' bridge theology shapes his migration ethic and summons Christians to reject complicity and inhospitality alike.

Lampedusa: Justice for a Graveyard of Wrecks

The pope's focus on the humanity of migrants offers a countersign to prevailing virulent nationalism and media portrayals that scapegoat and demonize those on the move. During his first official trip outside Rome after his election, Pope Francis celebrated mass on the Italian island that was a safe haven for migrants seeking passage from North Africa to Europe. Prior to making any public statement, he made the sign of the cross and tossed a wreath of flowers into the sea, commemorating the estimated 20,000 African immigrants who had died over the previous 25 years trying to reach a new life in Europe. The pope celebrated mass within sight of the "graveyard of wrecks," where fishing boats carrying migrants and asylum seekers end up after they drift ashore. Other reminders that Lampedusa is synonymous with dangerous attempts to reach Europe abounded: the altar was built over a small boat; the pastoral staff, the lectern, and even the chalice were carved from the wood of shipwrecked boats. Francis lamented in his homily our disorientation in sin and indifference to the plight of these vulnerable brothers and sisters, recalling immemorial temptations to power and its consequences, "Adam, where are you?" and then "Cain, where is your brother?" These are questions addressed to each of us. "How many times do those who seek [a better place for their families] not find understanding... not find welcome... not find solidarity!" He concluded by petitioning the Lord for the grace to weep over our indifference, to weep over the cruelty in the world, in ourselves, and even in those who anonymously make socioeconomic decisions that open the way to tragedies like this.[2] Amid the pope's admission that even he remains "disoriented," he did not merely condemn "the world" for this indifference and its consequences, but repented: "Forgive us Lord!" whether for being closed in on our own well-being in a way that leads to anesthesia of the heart, or in making global decisions creating situations that lead to these tragedies.[3]

Elements of Pope Francis' visit to Lampedusa after the deaths of Eritrean migrants "visited him like a thorn to the heart," connecting this repentance from harmful idolatries with a summons to remember our fundamental relatedness in light of the harm borders wreak.[4] Attentiveness to this reality demands that the global community resist a "crisis management" approach to migration flows in favor of honest, contextual assessments of what enduring patterns the crises reveal. Underscoring these operative attitudes fueling harmful policies and lethal inaction illuminates the depth of resistance to a Christian ethic marked by justice for immigrants or accompaniment of those on other peripheries. By contrast, dehumanizing rhetoric and policies targeting asylum seekers perpetuate the myth that responsibility for irregular migration lies with border crossers alone, denying the consequences of our interconnectedness.

Roberto Goizueta's reflections on our need for such anesthetizing distractions highlight the origins and function of the "soap bubbles of indifference" Pope Francis decries. He notes that for most privileged communities, our fear and self-loathing cause us to avoid the wounds of others—we turn the channel when three-year-old Alan Kurdi is washed ashore in Turkey or glaze over at statistics of the human costs of forced migration. Those "settled" ultimately fear not their "invasion" or even the claims they make on us, but "our weak, fragile, vulnerable, wounded selves." Goizueta writes, "We avoid risking the act of solidarity, or companionship with the victims of history, not because we hate them but because we hate

[2] Cindy Wooden, "Pope Calls for Repentance over Treatment of Migrants," *Catholic News Service*, July 8, 2013, http://www.catholicnews.com/services/ englishnews/2013/pope-calls-for-repentance-over-treatment-of-migrants.cfm.

[3] Pope on Lampedusa: "The Globalization of Indifference," Vatican Radio (July 8, 2013), http://www.vatican.va/content/francesco/en/homilies/2013/documents/papa-francesco_20130708_omelia-lampedusa.html

[4] For a reflection on migration and the Eucharist in light of Lampedusa, see Dan Groody, "Cup of Suffering, Chalice of Salvation: Refugees, Lampedusa and the Eucharist," *Theological Studies* 78.4 (2017), 960-87.

ourselves."⁵ The many idols of security that dominate our newsfeeds today—evident not only in ICE tactics and detention privatization but also
military expansion and lethal injections—reflect his insight that:

> ... our ultimate powerlessness in the face of death is what drives us to
> construct personal identities, social institutions, ideologies and belief
> systems that can make us feel invulnerable and ultimately invincible
> ... we construct a world that will shield us from [the] terrifying truth
> [that our lives are ultimately not in our control].⁶

Thus his insights on the function of idols of invulnerability illuminate the
depth and lure of exclusionary dynamics at work in our communities and
world today.

A bridge theology that insists on connecting patterns of insulation with
those of displacement challenges dominant narratives about immigrants
by attending to concrete experiences rather than stereotypes. At his border
mass in Ciudad Juárez, Pope Francis bade listeners to measure the impact of
forced migration not in numbers or statistics but with concrete names and
stories, evoking a counter narrative to those dominating the airwaves:

> They are the brothers and sisters of those expelled by poverty and
> violence, by drug trafficking and criminal organizations. Being faced
> with so many legal vacuums, they get caught up in a web that ensnares
> and always destroys the poorest. Not only do they suffer poverty, but
> they must also endure these forms of violence. Injustice is radicalized
> in the young; they are "cannon fodder", persecuted and threatened
> when they try to flee the spiral of violence and the hell of drugs, not to
> mention the tragic predicament of the many women whose lives have
> been unjustly taken.⁷

⁵ Roberto S. Goizueta, "From Calvary to Galilee," *America* (April 17, 2006), http://www.
americamagazine.org/issue/569/article/calvary-galilee.

⁶ Ibid., "To the Poor, the Sick, and the Suffering," in *Vatican II: A Universal Call to Holiness*,
ed. Anthony Ciorra and Michael W. Higgins (Mahwah: Paulist Press, 2012), 73.

⁷ Pope Francis, "No Border Can Stop Us from Being One Family," *Vatican Radio*, February 18,
2016, http://en.radiovaticana.va/news/2016/02/18/pope_francis__%E2%80%98no_border_
can_stop_us_from_being_one_family%E2%80%99/1209507

Probing these complex realities behind deceptive sound bites further expands consideration beyond individuals who cross borders to consider the global contexts that compel migration.

The Catholic social tradition recognizes the right of sovereign nations to control their borders, but the right is *not* understood to be absolute. In the case of blatant human rights violations, the right to state sovereignty is relativized by the tradition's primary commitment to protecting human dignity. Whereas limits may be set, the tradition emphasizes that powerful nations have a stronger obligation to accommodate refugee flows and that the right to asylum must not be denied when people's lives are genuinely threatened in their homeland. In situations where individuals face war, pervasive gang violence, or desperate poverty, the tradition supports the right to migrate so that they can live free from credible fears of violence or the inability to feed their children. In the United States, we face record numbers of forcibly displaced persons together with nearly unprecedented resistance to our international commitment to resettle refugees. Whereas the number of refugees worldwide has reached the highest levels since World War II, for Fiscal Year 2020 President Donald Trump lowered the refugee admissions ceiling to its lowest number since the program's creation in 1980 (18,000).[8] In the case of underlying conditions propelling asylees from Central America's Northern Triangle countries to the United States, such as the world's highest murder rates, deaths linked to drug trafficking and organized crime, and endemic poverty, the value of securing borders has to be weighed against these rights of asylum seekers to seek protection and the demands of social justice.

Pope Francis emphasized on Lampedusa these histories of relationship between countries of origin and receiving countries, which are relevant in generating particular duties of reception. Typically established communities and migrants are "bound together by history, politics and economics even before the act of migration bridges the distance of geography."[9] Dynamics of employer recruitment tend to be shaped by prior bonds impacted by colonialism, military invasions, or economic ties: the ongoing legacy of 19th- and 20th-century

[8] Jens Manuel Krogstad, "Key Facts about Refugees to the U.S.," *Pew Research Center's Fact Tank* (October 7, 2019), https://www.pewresearch.org/fact-tank/2019/10/07/key-facts-about-refugees-to-the-u-s/.

[9] Silas W. Allard, "Who Am I? Who Are You? Who are We? Law, Religion, and Approaches to an Ethic of Migration," *Journal of Law and Religion* 30 (2015), 325, https://doi.org/10.1017/jlr.2015.6.

U.S. foreign policy, expansionism and neoliberal economic strategies—with attendant narratives—have generated migration flows from Latin America to the United States, for example.[10] Understanding immigration dynamics as related to unjust international political and economic divides also requires nations to share accountability in the wake of the Westphalian model's partial eclipse and to convert from opportunistic patterns of interdependence. More structural analyses suggest that migration policy should consider receiving countries' economic and political complicity in generating migrant flows rather than perpetuating scapegoating. Saskia Sassen has linked deeper dynamics of debt servicing and extraction to new migratory flows, illuminating their complex origins given "predatory" forms of advanced capitalism, opaque transnational networks, and a global governance system geared to aiding corporations.[11]

Given such systemic culpability, some have proposed an "instability tax" be levied upon private and governmental entities that destabilize migrant and refugee-producing regions—whether hedge funds profiting off of commodity-trading in African minerals or weapons manufacturers profiting from selling arms to the Middle East, or multinationals who profit from degrading or destabilizing poor nations.[12] Drawing on the Kew Gardens principles, David Hollenbach has proposed norms that help account for histories of relationship and complicity. In light of moral proximity to harm, he suggests countries that have gained economically from their colonies or with histories of military involvement in another nation "have special obligations to people in flight from that nation."[13] Existing economic relationships also confer relative duties, such that guest workers who "contribute through their work to the life and well-being of the society they have entered" should be welcomed as citizens.[14] Reducing immigration challenges solely to blaming

[10] Miguel De La Torre, *The U.S. Immigration Crisis: Toward an Ethics of Place* (Eugene, OR: Cascade, 2016), 151-52.

[11] See Saskia Sassen, "Three Emergent Migrations: An Epochal Change," *SUR File on Migration and Human Rights* 13 (2016), 29–41, https://papers.ssrn.com/sol3/papers.cfm?abstract_id=2838267; Sassen, "A Massive Loss of Habitat: New Drivers for Migration," *Sociology of Development* 2 (2016), 211.

[12] Ian Almond, "The Migrant Crisis: Time for an Instability Tax?" *Political Theology Today* (September 22, 2015), http://www.politicaltheology.com/blog/the-migrant-crisis-time-for-an-instability-tax/.

[13] David Hollenbach, "Borders and Duties to the Displaced: Ethical Perspectives on the Refugee Protection System," *Journal on Migration and Human Security* 4 (2016), 153.

[14] Hollenbach, "A Future Beyond Borders: Re-imagining the Nation State and the Church," in

those who cross borders completely eclipses transnational actors responsible for violent conflict, economic instability, or climate change from view, much less blame. Steps toward recontextualizing migration patterns in light of an honest appraisal of a nation's history of interventions in other countries and destabilizing international practices reflect the pope's bridging of migrant, origin, and destiny and could yield a more just policy framework. Pope Francis' employment of social sin further helps reframe migration ethics and praxis in these terms.

Social Sin: Bridging Insulating Ideologies and Structural Injustice

Pope Francis has repeatedly demonstrated how, for a Church as field hospital, healing the wounds must extend beyond encountering those in need with compassion and justice to healing global indifference. On Lampedusa he lamented the pervasive idolatry that facilitates migrants' deaths and robs us of the ability to weep, a theme he revisited in Manila and then Juárez, insisting "only eyes cleansed by tears can see clearly."[15] The pope's reflections and symbolism underscore the multidimensional task of repentance from complicity in injustice. In his 2015 Lenten message, summoning listeners to "become islands of mercy in a sea of indifference," Pope Francis signaled how challenging economic inequalities must extend beyond meeting needs and crafting policies to healing social sin. Identifying and countering structural injustices and the ideologies that legitimate them constitute a key contribution to a bridge theology, for they help connect those of us contributing to forces pushing and pulling migrants to those whom our actions, however unwittingly, impact. Various levels of social sin intersect in complex manners: pervasive, internalized ideologies make us susceptible to myths; operative understandings influence our actions or inaction. When bias hides or skews values, it becomes more difficult to choose authentic values over those that prevail in society, a tendency already present because of original sin.[16]

Agnes Brazal and María Teresa Dávila, eds., *Living With(out) Borders: Catholic Theological Ethics on the Migrations of Peoples* (Maryknoll, NY: Orbis, 2016), 232.

[15] Francis, "No Border Can Stop Us from Being One Family."

[16] For a more in-depth discussion of strands of social sin in the Catholic theological tradition and the concept's implications for immigration ethics, see Heyer, "Social Sin and Immigration: Good Fences Make Bad Neighbors," *Theological Studies* 71.2 (June 2010), 410-36.

Such intersections with respect to the global economy have been of particular concern to Pope Francis. Warning that our "economy of exclusion and inequality kills," he has rightly challenged not only the reductive market ethos dominating trade and migration policies but also its desensitizing effects:

> The culture of prosperity deadens us; we are thrilled if the market offers us something new to purchase; and in the meantime all those lives stunted for lack of opportunity seem a mere spectacle; they fail to move us.[17]

The elevation of wealth and influence to absolute status can become an authentic bondage. Idolatries focused on *having* over *being* can impede pursuit of the common good as much as nationalistic ones; they shape loyalties, frame questions, and inform votes and spending practices.

Hence distinct elements of social sin—dehumanizing trends, unjust structures and harmful ideologies—shape complex dynamics at play in perpetuating inequalities. In terms of immigration, the primacy of deterrence has institutionalized security concerns rather than concerns for human rights or family unity in United States immigration laws; the nation's economic interests have been institutionalized in uneven free trade agreements. When concerns about our identity get distorted by xenophobia and fear, anti-immigrant sentiment and ethnic-based hate crimes surge. At a more subtle level, a consumerist ideology shapes citizens' willingness to underpay or mistreat migrant laborers either directly or indirectly through demand for inexpensive goods and services. These interconnected attitudes and institutions produce the blindness that lulls us into equating "law-abiding" with "just" or into apathetic acceptance.

Neoliberal globalization's operative priorities are often internalized in ways that shape the perceptions and actions of the dominant culture. Whether in fatalistic understandings of the "price of progress" or the "neutrality" of the market system, these more ideological currents of globalization configure our coordinates for what becomes conceivable.[18] Bishop Robert McElroy

---

[17] Pope Francis, *Evangelii Gaudium* (November 24, 2013), no. 54.

[18] Timothy Jarvis Gorringe, "Invoking: Globalization and Power," in *The Blackwell Companion to Christian Ethics*, ed. Stanley Hauerwas and Samuel Wells (Malden, MA: Blackwell Publishing Ltd, 2004), 353.

has noted the tendency in United States culture to understand the freedom of the markets as a categorical imperative rather than an instrumental good that can blind us to the gospel's demands. George Soros terms United States society's dominant belief system "market fundamentalism"; others refer to a "gospel of consumption" driving certain modes of globalization. Various commitments to growth at all costs can become authentic bondage that contributes to a willful ignorance of unwanted wisdom. In Pope Francis' words, "An economic system centered on the god of money also needs to plunder nature in order to maintain the frenetic pace of consumption inherent in it."[19]

These entrenched, intertwined patterns of social sin require repentance from idolatries that marginalize and disempower those beyond our immediate spheres of concern and borders. From repentance and conscientization we are called to become bridges of interdependence in solidarity. In contrast to a narrative of the self-made person, a Christian understanding of ourselves as freely "gifted" can motivate actions that enact gratuity in response. Such conversion can occur through personal encounters and relationships that provoke new perspectives and receptivity. At the broader systemic level, nations must understand themselves as collectively responsible for the shared challenges posed by the migrant deaths Pope Francis commemorated on Lampedusa, which only continue to mount.

Pope John Paul II proposed solidarity as the key virtue demanded in a globalized era of de facto interdependence: "the social face of Christian love."[20] Hollenbach proposes institutional solidarity as a necessary means of moving patterns of global interdependence from ones marked by domination and oppression to ones marked by equality and reciprocity. Institutional solidarity demands the development of structures that offer marginalized persons a genuine voice in the decisions and policies that impact their lives.[21] Much of the planet experiences marginalization, or at least "economic development takes place over their heads."[22] A meaningful recovery of the

---

[19] Francis X. Rocca, "Pope Urges Activists to Struggle Against 'Structural Causes' of Poverty," *Catholic News Service*, http://www.catholicnews.com/data/stories/cns/1404449.htm.

[20] John Paul II, *Solicitudo rei socialis,* no. 40.

[21] Hollenbach, "The Life of the Human Community," *America* (November 4, 2002), 7.

[22] Pope John Paul II, *Centesimus Annus,* in *Catholic Social Thought: The Documentary Heritage,* ed. David J O'Brien and Thomas A. Shannon (Maryknoll, NY: Orbis, 1998), no. 33, 463.

sense that persons who are poor, or on the move, are *agents* rather than beneficiaries of charitable assistance or paternalist reforms remains essential.
Hence, institutional solidarity demands inclusion at the decision-making
table, structures of institutional accountability and transparency, and empowered participation (subsidiarity).[23]

In light of the depth and lure of sinful resistance to the steep challenge
global solidarity imparts, two additional dimensions of solidarity are required: incarnational and conflictual solidarities. Given the grip of egotism,
some observers have described the reception of recent Catholic teaching
on solidarity as superficial or nonexistent. Incarnational solidarity departs
from valuable intellectual and institutional dimensions of solidarity to im-
merse our bodies and expend precious energy in practices of concrete accompaniment in the real world. Christine Firer Hinze's evocative metaphors
for the reach of consumerism reflect the dynamics of social sin: a culture
whose "kudzu-like values and practices so crowd the landscape of daily
lives that solidarity finds precious little ground in which to take root."[24] She
highlights consumerist culture's use of seduction and misdirection to:

> ... lay a soothing, obfuscating mantle over systemic injustices that
> solidarity would expose, [as] its participants are fitted with Oz-like
> lenses, fed a stream of distractions and novelties, and situated in a
> 24/7 schedule of work-spend-consume that virtually ensures they will
> "pay no attention" to the suffering multitudes behind the curtain.[25]

Given the interconnection between unjust international structures in need of
reform and these pervasive ideologies, an "incarnational" solidarity such as
Hinze has proposed complements the institutional solidarity advanced above.

Promoting solidarity among institutions and persons cannot bypass
conflict and loss. Liberation theologians and social ethicists have noted

---

[23] Hollenbach, *The Common Good & Christian Ethics* (Cambridge, UK: Cambridge University Press, 2002), 225.

[24] Christine Firer Hinze, "Straining Toward Solidarity in a Suffering World: *Gaudium et spes* 'After Forty Years'," in *Vatican II: Forty Years Later, College Theology Society Annual Volume 51,* ed. William Madges (2005), 180.

[25] Ibid., 181-82.

magisterial Catholicism's tendency to prioritize unity, harmony, and synthesis in ways that circumvent necessary conflict. Without confronting issues of economic and political power and engaging grassroots mobilization, work toward and implementation of changes to the status quo will remain stunted. Therefore contesting inequalities also requires a tolerance for disagreement and may entail lament or righteous anger—in short, the recalcitrance of the privileged may demand a more "conflictual solidarity" as well.[26]

Hence Pope Francis' attention to intertwined structures and ideologies reminds us that naming the reality of sin helps shed light on the practices and attitudes that harm migrants—and so many other victims of "a throwaway culture." Eliciting conversion from patterns of unjust complicity toward solidarity calls communities beyond intermittent outreach or legislative campaigns. It is now possible to turn to the concrete, sustained forms of praxis Francis' bridge theology invites.

Praxis: Islands of Mercy amid Indifference and Isolation

In words and example, Pope Francis has "signaled a turn away from the doctrinal and institutional concerns of his immediate predecessors and pointed instead to his passionate insistence on the Church's loving engagement with the poor who make up most of the world's population."[27] Francis' initial embrace of a poor Church for the poor has become a continuous refrain, reverberating in his charge to the Church as field hospital and summons, rooted in the Gospel, to a revolution of tenderness. In *Evangelii Gaudium* Francis warns against the danger of dwelling in the realm of ideas and rhetoric alone, insisting on the priority of reality:

> We want to enter fully into the fabric of society, sharing the lives of all, listening to their concerns, helping them materially and spiritually in their needs, rejoicing with those who rejoice, weeping with those

[26] For further development of conflictual solidarity, see Bryan Massingale, "*Vox Victimarum, Vox Dei*: Macolm X as a Neglected 'Classic' for Catholic Theological Reflection," *Proceedings of The Catholic Theological Society of America* 65 (2010), 63-88.

[27] Eamon Duffy, "Who Is the Pope?," *The New York Review of Books,* February 19, 2015, http://www.nybooks.com/ articles/2015/02/19/who-is-pope-francis/.

who weep; arm in arm with others, we are committed to building a new world (no. 269).

Hence a praxis of justice and mercy for migrants must be not only mindful of the dynamics of social sin and complicity but concretely grounded in practical encounters across difference.

This commitment to bridge building for the common good swims against significant cultural tides beyond anti-immigrant sentiment, each of which hardens resistance to communitarian claims. The all-American credo that we pull up our bootstraps and make our own fate is as entrenched as it is incompatible with the reality that we share each other's fate. The Catholic conception of the common good radically challenges a culture that prioritizes economic efficiency over solidarity with the weak and marginalized, or narrow national interest over global concern, a culture in which "good fences make good neighbors" due to isolationist fears significantly hinders bridges toward common goods. Fear of the other is easily mass-marketed; mutual understanding across differences is more difficult to realize.

Pope Francis' attention to building bridges rather than walls offer us one path forward. His own dialogue with the "existential extremities" and expressed preference for a street-bound over a risk-averse and "self-referential" Church provide an apt orientation. Christian immigration ethics is fraught with risks; its "subversive hospitality" risks making conversation partners uncomfortable (whether in terms of racial dimensions of inhospitality, disrupting privilege, or naming sin) and risks accusations of eroding respect for rule of law. Preoccupation with safeguarding against such risks impedes a culture of encounter and ongoing conversion by the suffering and resilience of those at various borders.

In one sense President Trump's migration rhetoric and policies are consistent with a "growing tendency to replace collaboration for the international common good with pursuit of an illusory understanding of national self-interest," due to cultural backlash against unfamiliar intrusions or responses to economic suffering.[28] Beyond manipulative narratives, senses of real and perceived loss—and accompanying grief and resentment—foster receptivity to exclusionary rhetoric and measures. Part of the path forward requires us

---

[28] Hollenbach, "The Glory of God and the Global Common Good: Solidarity in a Turbulent World," *CTSA Proceedings* 72 (2017), 51-5.

to address not only nativism and debasing rhetoric but also deeply seated fears. In *There Goes the Neighborhood*, Ali Noorani captures the unexpected nature of the challenge immigrant activists faced in recent legislative battles: most waged a political battle, attempting to change minds with data, and neglected to appreciate that the country was having a cultural debate about identity and values.[29] This first-generation Pakistani-American raised in Santa Cruz, California, builds bridges through his encounters with Baptist peach farmers in South Carolina, sheriffs in Utah, and businessmen in Texas seeking to forge common ground. He writes, "...we need to be able to meet people where they are but not leave them there." Given the deepening tribalization of partisanship, the need to rebuild public trust and a shared sense of community cannot be underestimated or bypassed.[30]

To become islands of mercy in a sea of indifference, Christian leaders must forge common ground across difference and yet be unafraid to condemn destructive policies and practices that harm children, separate families, and roll back historic protections. A bridge-building hospitality that welcomes the least may also entail prophetic resistance: think of Bishop McElroy insisting "we must all be disruptors" at the U.S. Regional World Meeting of Popular Movements in 2017:

> We must disrupt those who portray refugees as enemies rather than our brothers and sisters in terrible need. We must disrupt those who train us to see Muslim men and women and children as sources of fear rather than as children of God.[31]

Or Cardinal Joseph Tobin accompanying a New Jersey grandfather to his ICE hearing that same year. We might think of religious institutions offering sanctuary in their classrooms or parish halls.

Preaching and advocacy should frame our complicity in generating migration flows rather than treating this as an unexpected "crisis" or "invasion." For example, it should expose how consumers directly benefit from

---

[29] Ali Noorani, *There Goes the Neighborhood: How Communities Overcome Prejudice and Meet the Challenge of American Immigration* (Amherst, NY: Prometheus Books, 2017), 23–25.

[30] Ibid., 23–25.

[31] Bishop Robert McElroy, "Message to Participants in the US Regional Meeting of Popular Movements," (February 16-19, 2017), http://cms.usccb.org/about/justice-peace-and-human-development/upload/BishopMcElroyUSWMPMEnglish.pdf.

underpaying for goods and services and politicians benefit from unfounded scapegoating. In drawing attention to relevant history and complicity in this way, Catholic leaders can appropriately frame a response to refugees in terms of human rights and restorative justice, not optional largesse. In particular, they should remind people in the pews that the Catholic social tradition makes a preferential option for the vulnerable, not a preferential option for the innocent. Catholic communities can also humanize the perceived "onslaught" of refugees with parish-based outreach programs, testimony sharing, and educational programming. They have an opportunity to connect biblical journeys of migration with those undertaken by desperate asylum seekers today.

Catholic parishes are one of the few places that minister to people on all sides of the immigration issue. In terms of recommendations for fostering difficult dialogues on this topic, the following practical recommendations are offered for consideration:

1. Guard against xenophobic rhetoric, scapegoating, and conspiracy theorizing. Reasonable people can disagree about border policies without demonizing immigrants or one another. Counteract myths about immigrants and refugees while remembering that our own "deep stories" can tempt us to select facts, too. Be mindful that migrants may be in particular need of allies to amplify their voices amid climates of increased fear and intimidation.

2. Break through not only "soap bubbles" of indifference but also insulating echo chambers. Risk difficult conversations with family members and colleagues with whom you disagree and try to identify common values. Too often we "agree to disagree" and remain confirmed in our perspectives by selective news and social media feeds, avoiding underlying differences at the root of immigration disputes. Participate in parish or other community programming that takes you outside of your typical social circles or comfort zone.

3. Avoid amnesia at national and personal levels alike. Be curious about your own immigration family histories and how they have shaped your attitudes regarding the current situation. Invite others to do the same. Investigate how your present habits—purchasing, eating, childcare, voting

practices—impact the well-being of migrants and make a change. Pressure your elected officials and goods/service providers to do the same.

In the southern Mediterranean, Pope Francis shared in the grief and anguish of forced migrants—moved by the humanity of the Eritreans he met and provoked by the inhumanity of those numb to their plight. May we too repent of our complicity and move out of our comfort zones to "become islands of mercy in a sea of indifference."

CHAPTER SIX

A Bridge Over Troubled Assumptions: Conversion and Action for Disability Inclusion

MARY JO IOZZIO, PHD

> *... here appears a portrait of the Church that sees those in difficulty [e.g., people with disability and those who are poor, rejected, or otherwise oppressed], that does not close her eyes, that knows how to look humanity in the face* in order to create meaningful relationships, bridges of friendship and solidarity in place of barriers *[emphasis added]*.
>
> —*Pope Francis, General Audience, 7 August 2019*[1]

TRAVELERS OVER THE MILLENNIA have depended on bridges built of stone and dirt, wood and rope, boulders and rocks, brick and mortar, iron and steel to cross rivers and streams and, with architectural technologies developed in Ancient Rome, over ravines and some stretches of oceans, seas, and lakes both great and small. I suspect more often than not that bridges have provided offers and the potentials to unite peoples and cultures

---

[1] Pope Francis, "General Audience" (Wednesday, 7 August 2019), http://www.vatican.va/content/francesco/en/audiences/2019/documents/papa-francesco_20190807_udienza-generale.html.

into friendship and solidarity alongside opportunities to barter and trade goods. But, as history reveals, bridges have also been used by one party to invade and ravage the party on the other side with the obvious tragic consequences of death, disabling injuries, and subjugation of the conquered by the conquerors.

Contrary to the agenda of those who have used and those who still use bridges to attack, plunder, and rape, Pope Francis invites the contemporary Church to think about constructive uses of both literal and figurative bridges. Others, increasingly aware of an unstable contemporary geopolitical climate, also look to bridges as material and emblematic metaphor.

> Around the globe, it seems, fear is dividing us—by color, creed, and sexuality—and destroying the diversity that every species, including human beings, needs to survive and thrive. Bridges, structures that join rather than separate, provide an apt and hopeful portent of infrastructure's civic and human potential. They express the fundamental bonds that exist between all human beings, connections that now more than ever must be protected.[2]

Clearly, the literal bridges include some of the most beautifully dramatic engineering feats of public works for the common good, such as London's Tower Bridge over the River Thames, New York City's Brooklyn Bridge over the East River, Iran's Si-o-se Pol over the River Zayanderud, Japan's Akashi Kaikyo over the Akashi Strait, and Bosnia and Herzegovina's Stari Most over the River Neretva.

When presented with rightly ordered intention, the figurative bridges can be as equally compelling in their majesty as those bridges named above and many others. As part of the figurative building, Pope Francis teaches that bridging is the work of the Church, a work that is at its root the Good News preached with words and in concrete actions that bear witness to the divinity of Jesus. A recent example is found in Pope Francis' reflection on Acts 3, in the words and deeds proclaimed by Peter and John to a man at the Beautiful Gate:

---

[2] See, for example, Judith Dupre, "Foreword," in *Bridges: A History of the World's Most Spectacular Spans* (New York: Black Dog & Leventhal, rev. ed. 2017).

Today we find ourselves... before a miracle which is the first account of healing in the Book of the Acts of the Apostles.... Peter and John go to pray at the Temple.... And at the Temple—they see a beggar, a man paralyzed from birth.... The lame man, the paradigm of society's many excluded and rejected, is there begging for alms.

... In meeting the Apostles, that beggar does not find money, but he finds the Name that saves [us]: Jesus Christ, the Nazarene.... And here appears a portrait of the Church that sees those in difficulty [e.g., people with disability and those who are poor, rejected, or otherwise oppressed], that does not close her eyes, that knows how to look humanity in the face in order to create meaningful relationships, bridges of friendship and solidarity in place of barriers.[3]

The Apostles have neither silver nor gold and yet they give to this ordinarily ignored and stigmatized man something greater: their attention, not a monetary gesture (which, no doubt, would have been welcome) but a relationship with him in the name of Jesus. The key is that they actually look at this man, their gaze offers genuine recognition of him as a member of the human family, a child of God, and potentially a disciple. This recognition is located in the explicit way that they invite "him *to look at them in a different way, to receive a different gift,*" not necessarily the healing that follows their words (no doubt also welcomed) but friendship. They:

... have established a relationship because this is the way that God loves to [be manifest], in *relationships*, always in dialogue, always in apparitions, always with the heart's inspiration: they are God's relationships with us.[4]

Unlike this experience of the man at the Beautiful Gate, people with disability have long been ignored by the nondisabled and powerful. Literal and figurative bridges can be of help to people with disability and the nondisabled alike to further progress on matters of "the look versus the stare" in theological,

[3] Pope Francis, "General Audience" (Wednesday, 7 August 2019).
[4] Ibid.

ethical, and ecclesial communities. The time of literal action with and for people with disability in all arenas of human commerce is at hand. Some of these bridges cross hierarchical divides, some cross national or continental divides, others cross gender divides, still others cross cultural divides—all with the purpose of bringing peoples together in common cause and, in the best scenarios, affirming relationships as Pope Francis and many others have encouraged. Nevertheless, a bridge over troubled assumptions impedes people with disability in their crossing. While some progress has been gained in the Church's practical and theological approaches to disability inclusion, some bricks and hoists and many girders of the bridge are faulty, some bridges remain yet to be built, and still others have yet to be conceived. Much of this unfinished work is stalled by failures among the powerful to recognize the potentials of full participation—inclusion—that people with disability and their families and friends yearn to have realized in their crossing.

In what follows I explore first the general subject of access in the ways that the Church and other powerful institutions in historical practice and theology have assumed that people with disability of many kinds can get their faith, education, and community formation within the exclusive privacy of their homes or the institutions where they may live. Second, I consider the isolating effect of staring or the representation of disability as a negative experience by the dominant nondisabled and counter the general understanding of lack or want with an assertion of self-determination. And third, I offer a bridge from near-complete exclusion over the troubled assumptions of the past to a condition where all are welcome in God's own house, in each of our hearts, and all places where the faithful gather.

Historical Practice and Experience: *Conversion* Requires Awareness of the Past

Assumptions are difficult to recognize, because they form part of the "common knowledge" about the ways cultures function. Mostly unexamined or unquestioned, culture is reinforced through generations until the time when newcomers—bridge-crossing travelers, immigrants, and refugees—arrive not knowing these assumptions and confront the cultural expectations of a new place and its standard operating principles. Such questioning can, but not necessarily will, lead to a reappraisal by the dominant/receiving culture of its assumptions about the "other" somewhat unlike them in their midst; these "others" also arrive with their own assumptions about themselves and about the peoples and cultures in new and foreign places. From better or worse assumptions, both parties—resident and sojourner alike—understand the common good of sustainable life and human flourishing. These historically conditioned assumptions about the common good require *conversion* for all to thrive. By *conversion* here I mean a turning toward the other and away from our own past.

God's own design for Earth's global community is human flourishing inclusive of the implications of support for that flourishing in all of creation. As Pope Francis has reminded us, *care for our common home* extends beyond the human community to all life.[5] If the Church cooperates with God's designs, it is necessary for every community to establish solidarity with and inclusion of all God's people. This is particularly true of those on the margins and the many others who have been denigrated by the imperial powers of capitalist gain: those persons presumed to be a "less than desirable" presence in God's house.[6] The Church cannot afford to do otherwise than to include them as well.

Awareness of this work requires moving beyond simple accommodations to affirmation and advocacy for people with disability, peoples both marginalized and denigrated with impunity across time and place. I begin with acceptance of liberationist insights regarding God's concern for people on the margins, outside the Church, and others deemed less than desirable in God's house and the human commons. Liberation theologies confront and question the meaning of "the poor" and find that God's preferential option applies as well to people with disability, among others, who are often poor and otherwise marginalized on account of their vulnerability and their lack of advocates. These theologies illuminate how God is the champion of those who are oppressed and marginalized.[7] While some progress in engaging the

---

[5] Pope Francis, *Laudato Si': Encyclical Letter on Care for Our Common Home* (Rome: Libreria Editrice Citta Vaticana, 2015), esp. §25, http://www.vatican.va/content/francesco/en/encyclicals/documents/papa-francesco_20150524_enciclica-laudato-si.html.

[6] See Council for World Mission, *Mission in the Context of Empire: Theology Statement 2010* (Singapore, SI: CWM Ltd., 2010), http://cwmission.org/missiontoolkit/wp-content/uploads/2013/12/Theology-Statement-2010-Published-text.pdf.

[7] Among others, see Gustavo Gutiérrez, *A Theology of Liberation: History, Politics, and Salvation* (Maryknoll, NY: Orbis Books, 1973, 1988 rev). Leonardo Boff and Clodovis Boff, *Introducing Liberation Theology* (Maryknoll, NY: Orbis Books, 1986); and Jon Sobrino, *Spirituality of Liberation: Toward Political Holiness* (Maryknoll, NY: Orbis Books, 1988).

preferential option has been made on behalf of people with disability and others,[8] history reveals that many people with disability have long been refused their places in their communities of birth and of worship as well. In this way of being refused, unfortunately, people with disability have in the past and still typify those who are marginalized in the contemporary world. Refusal on the part of Christian communities in particular is nothing less than scandalous in a tradition that holds humankind as God's own image and likeness and creation as a sacred trust. Justice demands that people with disability and others who are marginalized receive their due as persons made in the image and likeness of God, and that they will readily have unimpeded access to all the conditions necessary for their flourishing, as St. Paul reminds us (1 Cor 12:12-27), as members of the Body of Christ.

Bridges offer a metaphor for the initiatives of accommodation and inclusion desired by most people with disability and their families and friends. This metaphor can be used to expose both literal and figurative successes and failures to accommodate and include. "Bridges are interesting structures as they blend two important notions, the simplicity of connecting two points, and the complexity of the engineering necessary to make the connection."[9] For example, outside of vehicle transport, bridges are often, but not always, accessible to people with physical, sensory, and developmental impairments who use wheelchairs or other assistive devices to negotiate public and private spaces;[10] further, bridges present solutions to the current state of separation and exclusion of people with disability from the communities and cultures of their birth or in which they would like to belong. The antidote to exclusion can be bridged by considerations for infrastructure in advance of any project.[11]

---

[8] For example, the marginalization of women, people who have been racialized, and those who are lesbian, gay, bisexual, transgender, queer, and intersexed. Among others, see Kimberley W. Crenshaw, "Demarginalizing the Intersection of Race and Sex: A Black Feminist Critique of Antidiscrimination Doctrine. Feminist Theory and Antiracist Politics," in K.T. Bartlett and R. Kennedy, *Feminist Legal Theory: Readings in Law and Gender* (San Francisco: Westview Press, 1991), 57-80; Valerie Purdie-Vaughns and Richard P. Eibach, "Intersectional Invisibility: The Distinctive Advantages and Disadvantages of Multiple Subordinate-Group Identities," *Sex Roles* 59 (2008): 377-391; and Alison Kafer, *Feminist, Queer, Crip* (Bloomington: Indiana University Press, 2013).

[9] Al Condeluci, *Cultural Shifting* (St. Augustine, FL: TRN Press, 2002), 35.

[10] See Savannah O'Leary, "25 Years after the ADA, Navigating New York City is Still Daunting for the Disabled," *The Huffington Post* (7/27/2015), https://www.huffpost.com/entry/disabled-new-york_n_55a5084ee4b0a47ac15d5334.

[11] Anjlee Agarwal and Andre Steele, *Disability Considerations for Infrastructure Programmes* (London: Evidence on Demand, 2016).

Similar to the understanding of abuses experienced by members of ethnic, racial, gender, and sexual "others," an account of the assumptions about and experiences of people with disability follows that must be admitted if the trajectory of history's future is to be changed. With exceptions, people with disability have not been treated well. Their treatment has been identified and outlined in a system of models that distinguishes one manner of positive or negative treatment from another. Developed by people with disability, models relate closely to the ways in which the nondisabled and dominant codified their assumptions about people with disability according to the social roles to which they were assigned. The most common models of disability are (1) the religious-moral model where individuals or their parents or communities are personally responsible for the presence of disability as a punishment from God for sin or sins committed; (2) the medical model that "conceptualizes disability as deviance and lack within the individual [wherein] medical interventions are geared toward bringing the individual as close to normalcy as possible";[12] and (3) the social construction model of physical and attitudinal barriers of exclusion, such as stairs and inaccessible developmental opportunities in commerce, education, employment, recreation, and religion.[13] Parallel to these models are social roles to which people with disability have been assigned: as sick or sub-human; a menace to the "general" population; pitiable; a burden; holy innocents; inspirational; amusing; and/or a blessing.[14] Regardless of model or role, each of these assignments includes degrees of stigma: the defining mark of otherness that

---

[12] Nirmala Erevelles, *Disability and Difference in Global Contexts: Enabling a Transformative Body Politic* (New York: Palgrave Macmillan, 2011), 19.

[13] Among others, see Tom Shakespeare, "Cultural Representation of Disabled People: Dustbins for Disavowal?" *Disability & Society* 9.3 (1994), 283-299; Deborah Marks, "Models of Disability," *Disability and Rehabilitation* 19.3 (1997), 85-91; A. Llewellyn and K. Hogan, "The Use and Abuse of Models of Disability," *Disability & Society* 15.1 (2000), 157-165; Carmelo Masala and Donatella Rita Petretto, "Models of Disability," in J. H. Stone and M. Blouin, eds., *International Encyclopedia of Rehabilitation* (2010), http://cirrie.buffalo.edu/encyclopedia/en/article/135/; and Mike Oliver, "The Social Model of Disability: Thirty Years On," *Disability & Society* 28.7 (2013), 1024-1026.

[14] See Wolf Wolfensberger, *A Brief Overview of Social Role Valorization: A High-order Concept for Addressing the Plight of Societally Devalued People and for Structuring Human Services* (Plantagenet, Ontario, Canada: Valor Press, 2013 [originally published: Syracuse, NY: The Training Institute for Human Service Planning 2004, 1998]).

clears the way to marginalization and to greater or lesser degrees of direct oppression and violence.[15] The models offer a shorthand reference to understanding the presumptive figurative attitudinal and the literal excluding barriers that people with disability and their companions encounter all too frequently to this day.[16]

As disability advocates remind us:

... it's important to remember here that throughout recorded history all forms of inequality, injustice, and oppression have been sanctioned in one way or another on the basis of assumptions of biological inferiority.[17]

Contemporary efforts to decry these injustices and to reject these assumptions, such as including the perspectives and insights of people with disability, are rare. Often, they can devolve into patronizing thanks and nods. "Why, at almost the end of the second decade of the 21st century, are the [basic and fundamental] human rights of people with disability still ignored?"[18]

As suggested above, those with the power to make and shape societies have been grossly mistaken in their judgment about the inherent human value and dignity belonging to people with disability and others who do not conform to dominant norms. Those mistaken judgments are the bases of a history of maltreatment that people with disability have endured, a history that has been largely and likely intentionally ignored; in effect, people with disability themselves and their stories of success and failure and of loves and losses have been silenced over the course of time. However, that culture of silence is no longer acceptable. The truth to be told is that newborns,

[15] See Erving Goffman, *Stigma: Notes on the Management of Spoiled Identity* (New York: Simon & Schuster Inc., 1963).

[16] See Carmelo Masala and Donatella Rita Petretto, "Models of Disability," in J. H. Stone and M. Blouin, eds., *International Encyclopedia of Rehabilitation* (2010), http://cirrie.buffalo.edu/encyclopedia/en/article/135/.

[17] Colin Barnes, "Disability Studies: What's the Point?" Notes for presentation at Disability Studies: Theory, Policy, and Practice, University of Lancaster (September 4, 2003), 20.

[18] Mary Ann Jackson, "Models of Disability and Human Rights: Informing the Improvement of Build Environment Accessibility for People with Disability at Neighborhood Scale?" *Laws* 7.10 (2018), 2.

infants, children, and adults have been neglected, abused, and exterminated on account of the presence of disability in their lives.[19]

With 15% to potentially 25% of people worldwide today having one or more disability (up to 1.75 billion of 7.6 billion people), it is undeniable that people with disability have been among the members of the human economy from antiquity to the present.[20] Combining the models of disability (medical, moral, and social) to parallel social roles (menace, burden, clown), individuals were identified taxonomically as "other." This "othering" of people with disability has resulted in their oppression as a class. Given the lessons of contemporary retrievals of the historical experiences of many members of minority populations, this can no longer be tolerated; *conversion* is the order of the day.

The Stare and the Stigma Versus the Gaze

Most of us have heard a parent's command, "Don't stare!" Albeit indirectly, the imperative is an instruction that attempts avoid offense against the other deemed different from the main, at least, of our childhood formation (we may replay the voice when we become aware of the potential objectification of a contemporary subject). I suppose it is one of the ways that, as children, we come to distinguish people and things as we strive to understand who and what we are encountering in our world. Staring, looking, gazing permit us to start the catalog of categories in which we store the details of lessons learned. And yet, we still hear our parent's command, and rightly, but only to a degree. Today we must reexamine the catalog and categories into which people and things have been placed (sexual binaries, racial minorities, and abled/disabled bodies and/or minds) to recognize the potential insight in which "staring offers an occasion to rethink the status quo."[21]

---

[19] On the ramifications of a culture of silence, see Paulo Freire, "The Adult Literacy Process as Cultural Action for Freedom" and "Cultural Action and Conscientization," *Harvard Educational Review* 68.4 (1998 [originally published in *Harvard Educational Review* 40.2-3 (1970), 205-225, 452-477]), 480-498, 499-521.

[20] See World Health Organization, *World Report on Disability* (Geneva: WHO and The World Bank, 2011); https://www.who.int/disabilities/world_report/2011/en/.

[21] Rosemary Garland-Thomson, *Staring: How We Look* (New York: Oxford University Press, 2009), 6.

The categories catalogued in personal and cultural usage in reference to people with disability and other minoritized people need to be checked every now and again, particularly in light of communication technologies' speeds that unceasingly challenge reality as it has been conceived, received, and internalized—by dominant and oppressed communities alike—if not institutionalized in law and practice. On the advice of people with disability, all of us are to be encouraged to take notice of others—those with disability and the nondisabled. Why? Because:

> ... social niceties [however misguided] are less important than social justice: disabled people must be acknowledged... [consider that like] the power of Moses parting the Red Sea, when I'm pushed through a city street, people peel away from me, their faces turning aside as they do so. It's a lonely experience but it's a symptom of a bigger problem... disabled people are people, not lesser people, nor objects of fear.[22]

Unashamedly, people with disability are people first.

In order to counter the general understanding that people with disability are to be feared or avoided by the nondisabled or accosted by stares or slurs, individuals and communities of people with disability expose this narrative with transgressive resignification and self-determination. While psychologists note that eye contact and facial expressions are critical to empathy,[23] because of the shame that it inspired, the experiences of many people with disability suggest that the stare the gasp, or the distress of the nondisabled was to be avoided, even to the extent of self-sequestering. However, today's disability movements are reappropriating the terms used derogatorily against them as an honorary recognition—despite the institutionalization, sterilization, and murder over the millennia—that today, "We're here!"

---

[22] Tanya Marlow, "Don't Tell Your Children Not to Stare at Disabled People—We are Already Invisible Enough," *The Guardian* (11 October 2018), https://www.theguardian. com/society/2018/oct. Alternately, Jessica Cox, "Disability and Staring: How I Overcame this Behavior," *Humanity & Inclusion* (2017), https://www.hi-us.org/disability_and_staring_ how_i_overcome_this_rude_behavior.

[23] See Simon Ho, Tom Foulsham, and Alan Kingstone, "Speaking and Listening with the Eyes: Gaze Signaling during Dyadic Interaction," *PLoS One* 10.8 (2015), e0136905, https://www. ncbi.nlm.nih.gov/pmc/articles/PMC4550266/#!po=1.19048.

Where "spaz," "crip," "gimp," "geek," "queer" and other terms were the norms of name-calling and finger-pointing, the terms are retrieved now with deviant devotion and effect. Why?

> The embrace of denigrating terminology forces the dominant culture to face its own violence head-on... [in] recognition of its own dehumanizing precepts. What was most devalued is now righted by a self-naming that detracts from the original power of the condescending terms.[24]

In contrast to avoidance, Pope Francis extols the positive effect of the Apostles' gaze, a gaze that liberated the man at the Beautiful Gate and that, at the same time, acknowledged the potential of his self-determination. The gaze signaled restoration of this man's rightful integration among the people and access to the fullness of worship represented by the Temple. Moreover, it is "the art of accompaniment" beyond first encounters and toward a culture of encounter that tests the resolve of the community "to make the world more human by removing everything that prevents [people with disability] from full citizenship... and by promoting accessibility to places and a quality of life."[25]

More formally, Pope Francis details this trajectory in the 2017 Vatican conference on "Catechesis and Persons with Disabilities: A Necessary Engagement in the Pastoral Life of the Church." Francis refers to the liberation insights on marginalization to focus on inclusion, solidarity, and participation with:

> [the] hope that more and more people with disabilities can become catechists themselves in their communities, offering their own witness and helping to communicate the faith more effectively.[26]

[24] David T. Mitchell and Sharon L. Snyder, *Narrative Prosthesis: Disability and the Dependencies of Discourse* (Ann Arbor: The University of Michigan Press, 2011), 35-36.

[25] Pope Francis, "General Audience" (Wednesday, August 7, 2019).

[26] *Vatican News*, "Pope Meets with Participants in Vatican Disability Conference" (October 21, 2017), https://www.vaticannews.va/en/pope/news/2017-10/time-for-persons-with-disabilities-to-become-catechists.html.

Indeed, with the man at the Beautiful Gate:

> … we renew our gaze… which sees in every brother and sister the presence of Christ himself… [and] to recall that the promotion of participation rights today plays a central role in fighting against discrimination and fostering the culture of encounter and quality of life.[27]

From Troubled Assumptions to All Are Welcome

Like the social constructions of race, ethnicity, gender, and sex, the social construction of disability precludes, in many ways, an understanding of people with disability as people first. Repetitive though it may seem, the fact that many well-intentioned people do not take seriously the exercises of self-determination and potentials of participation in the common good by people with disability remains a bridge-crossing obstacle to their inclusion. More explicitly, to the extent that any of us remain unaware of the faulty bases revealed in the social constructions of disability and of race, ethnicity, gender, and sex, to that same extent the assumptions regarding people with disability will continue to impede their crossing.

Insights uncovering the social constructions of disability confront and question the inherited assumptions about and the ramifications of exclusion toward people with disability. This interrogation has yielded great benefits since its conception in the 1970s by the Union of the Physically Impaired Against Segregation (UPIAS), a United Kingdom political action group. In November 1975, the UPIAS and the UK's Disability Alliance met to discuss disability as a situation caused by social conditions that require a systemic approach to relieve the poverty, assumed dependence, and exclusion of people with disability from decision making concerning themselves in lieu of others doing so on their behalf and for their assumed benefit. Those discussions reveal tensions on the part of the Alliance regarding the principle cause of disability that rests in society's failures to meet this diverse population's needs and desires for access to education, health, and the commonweal. The UPIAS's:

[27] Pope Francis, "Message for the International Day of Persons with Disabilities" (December 3, 2019), http://www.vatican.va/content/francesco/en/messages/pont-messages/2019/documents/papa-francesco_20191203_messaggio-disabilita.html.

…own position on disability is quite clear…it is society which disables physically impaired people. Disability is something imposed on top of our impairments, by the way we are unnecessarily isolated and excluded from full participation in society. Disabled people are therefore an oppressed group in society.[28]

Indeed, many assumptions include the rather perverse notions that people with disability are either less than human or (always) sick, that they pose a (contagious or violent) threat to the nondisabled, that they are a drain on (or waste of) scarce resources, that they cannot/do not contribute to the common good, and that they have no sense of self or direction in their lives.

If our culture could expand its assumptions about "normal" to include disability, and if it were more familiar with the everyday, lived experience of real people with impairments, then those…constructed, attitudinal barriers to full participation, might become increasingly rare.[29]

Unsurprisingly, it is truth, not assumptions about what is true, that must hold sway over new and restorative bridge-building projects so as to be fully accessible to people with disability and across the spectrum of impairment. Why? Because assumptions and subsequent exclusionary barriers have long segregated—and wrongly so—people with disability in literal and figurative captivity. Thus denigrated and dehumanized, people with disability represent what many critics of comprehensive access to social services, universal healthcare, public education, employment, recreation, and religious practice might call "the surplus/disposable population."[30] The conclusions of these assumptions suggest that it would be better, in fact, that such people ought not to even to have been born or, in face of a driving force to live, to be denied post-natal

[28] The Union of the Physically Impaired Against Segregation, *Fundamental Principles of Disability* (London, Nov. 22, 1975), https://disability-studies.leeds.ac.uk/wp-content/uploads/sites/40/library/UPIAS-fundamental-principles.pdf.

[29] Patricia A. Dunn, "Challenging Stereotypes about Disability for a More Democratic Society," *The English Journal* 103.2 (2013), 94.

[30] With a nod to Ebenezer Scrooge (or Charles Dickens), *A Christmas Carol* (1843). See also Prem Kumar Rajaram, "Refugees as Surplus Population: Race, Migration, and Capitalist Value Regimes," *New Political Economy* 23.5 (2018), 627-639.

care and the subsequent whole-life support that all persons require.[31] Such services belong to the common good that builds, maintains, and improves bridges between woe and weal for the nondisabled and people with disability alike.

It is to initiatives that dismantle the unconfronted and unquestioned assumptions among the nondisabled and powerful in regard to the work of inclusion with and for people with disability to which the Body of Christ, the Church, must in earnest turn.

To continue the work of inclusion begun in the Church, everyone who holds a position of power—from the Holy See to national conferences of bishops, local dioceses, clergy, lay Church organization leaders and administrators, and other lay faithful—needs to know in concrete terms the people whom they serve so that they may serve ever more effectively and wholesale, not piecemeal, every member of the Body of Christ. A starting place requires local investments in (1) a census that will reveal the number of people with disability in our respective communities. The findings of the census ought to reveal numbers that align with the WHO's estimates of 15% or more people with disability among them. Following this hard evidence, (2) those with power and their delegates will need to reach out to and meet their community members with disability and their families so as to ascertain their level of participation in the Church (and elsewhere) and to ask how the Church may facilitate their inclusion where absent, and greater levels of participation as they desire. From this outreach (3) the Church can move forward on initiatives of bridge-building inclusion of intentional collaboration with all and especially with those who have been neglected on account of unconfronted and unquestioned dominant assumptions concerning them.

Fortunately, people with disability have been organizing in earnest for social change, just access, and welcome for more than 50 years. With their experience, genius, and activism, the literal and figurative wheels and pulleys of access do not need to be reinvented but rather engaged. Their organizing has resulted in the development of principles of inclusion for the nondisabled

---

[31] In the not-too-distant past, infants presenting a disability would have been disposed by either humane or inhumane means; denial of treatment to persons with disability remains commonplace. See Alicia Ouellette, *Bioethics and Disability: Toward a Disability-Conscious Bioethics* (Cambridge, UK: Cambridge University Press, 2011); Deborah Schurman-Kauflin, "Killing the Disabled," *Psychology Today* (June 19, 2012), https://www.psychologytoday.com/us/blog/disturbed/201206/killing-the-disabled; and Kenny Fries, "The Nazis' First Victims were the Disabled," *New York Times*, Opinion (September 13, 2017), https://www.nytimes.com/2017/09/13/opinion/nazis-holocaust-disabled.html.

and institutions of all kinds to follow that remain underutilized, perhaps particularly in faith-based institutions. But these principles have the potential to usher all persons over the physical barriers of stairs and askance attitudinal stares with a drawbridge to their pews, Church halls, schools, universities, and Church service in the name of Our Lord Jesus the Christ, the Disabled Resurrected God Incarnate.[32] Surely, the Catholic community can do better.

Conclusion

Most of this writing has pointed to raising the consciences and consciousness of the faithful in regard to people who do not have a place or who have limited access to the Good News in our Churches and evangelization efforts. The work that remains to be engaged concerns institutionalizing the changes needed so that people with disability and others who have been marginalized or oppressed are welcomed in all the places where people gather—to live, to learn, to work, to play, to pray. I leave the final word on directions forward to disability activists and educators: "implementing innovative programs... building bridges to create a new era where people with disabilities will take their rightful place in the world community."[33]

Acknowledging a human rights model of disability, Mobility International USA offers *Guiding Principles for Excellence in Development & Disability Inclusion:*[34]

[32] See Nancy Eiesland, *The Disabled God: Toward a Liberatory Theology of Disability* (Nashville, TN: Abingdon Press, 1994).

[33] "Founded in 1981, Mobility International USA (MIUSA) is a disability-led non-profit organization headquartered in Eugene, Oregon, USA, advancing disability rights and leadership globally." MIUSA, "Who We Are" (2018), https://www.miusa.org/about.

[34] MIUSA, "Guiding Principles for Excellence in Development & Disability Inclusion," Resource Library (2018), https://www.miusa.org/resource/tipsheet/principles. MIUSA offers four additional principles: Budget for Inclusion, Disability is Diversity, Twin-Track Approach, Applying a Human Rights Lens to Disability Services. Additionally, MIUSA presents "Ten Essential Strategies" that can make every community activity accessible and inclusive; see "Making Inclusive Development a Reality," Research Library (2018), https://www.miusa.org/resource/tipsheet/inclusive-development. See also Karen Heinicke-Motsch and Susan Sygall, eds., *Manual for Building an Inclusive Development Community* (Eugene, OR: Mobility International USA, 2004).

Disability Leadership
Inclusive development makes use of the strengths and potential of people with disabilities as partners and contributors to your programs—
not solely as beneficiaries.

Disability as a Cross-Cutting Issue
There is no program or topic that would not include [the interest of]
people with disabilities. To implement inclusive development effectively, you must ensure that people with disabilities can and do access
your broad range of programs alongside nondisabled people. *Whether the program focuses on food security, emergency response, education, health, livelihood, disease prevention, or workers' rights, [or
Church practices], thoughtfully include disability in your program's
design, outreach, participation, and evaluation* [emphasis added].

Infiltration is the New Inclusion
Begin a new strategy of working toward inclusion by practicing "infiltration," a more proactive and intentional approach. This means
infiltrating the disability community's events, sharing information
with disability networks, and inviting members of the disability community to your events and programs.

Although it may not seem that these secular strategies will be appropriate for
the Church, in fact, to further the work of sharing and being Good News,
those with power can come to a better appreciation of the exclusionary compound effects that assumptions about people with disability has exerted on
them, their families, and others. We are all encouraged to bend a little further backwards to accommodate all sisters and brothers who yearn to be at
the tables of Word and Worship as well as at work and play.[35] Exclusion is
contrary to the God of pathos and love, and the relationality disclosed in the
Trinity and confirmed in Jesus' self-identification as a person with disability
in the Resurrection as admitted by the Apostle Thomas with his tangible
touch of the wounds the Crucified Christ still bears (John 20:24-29).

---

[35] See Mary Jo Iozzio, "God Bends Over Backwards to Accommodate Humankind… While the
US Civil Rights Acts and the Americans with Disabilities Act Require [Only] the Minimum."
Journal of Moral Theology 6. SI 2 (2017), 10-31.

CHAPTER SEVEN

"Where There Is Hurt, There Must Be Healing":[1] Native Values, Restorative Justice, and Feminist Bridgework

KATHARINE E. LASSITER[2], PhD

Introduction: Life in a Death State[3]

SINCE THE 1970S, THE restorative justice movement in the United States has grown in response to the mass incarceration of black and brown persons. The intention in restorative justice praxis is to initiate the opportunity

[1] Robert Yazzie, *Life Comes From It: Navajo Justice Concepts.* 24 New Mexico Law Review 175 (1994). Available at: https://digitalrepository.unm.edu/nmlr/vol24/iss2/3. The Honorable Robert Yazzie serves as Emeritus Chief Justice of the Navajo Nation.

[2] Katharine E. Lassiter is Director of Theological Field Education at Chicago Theological Seminary. She is the author of *Recognizing Other Subjects: Feminist Pastoral Theology and the Challenge of Identity.*

[3] I lived in Ohio—called "a death state" given its high number of opioid fatalities—for the better part of a decade. During that time I learned the difference between physical death and psychic-spiritual death, and began to see the threads that connected the two in ways that shook me to my very bones. While the physical state of death, decay, and rot is one thing, it was all the myriad psychic and spiritual deaths that made me doubt my deepest theological convictions:

for repair of harm, particularly of criminal acts in the context of the criminal justice system. This, however, would only be a cursory understanding of restorative justice. As Roman Catholic moral theologian Amy Levad writes, most restorative justice advocates that we:

> ... view crime principally not as a violation of the law, but as a violation of relationships by offenders when they cause harm to others. The harm caused may include "material losses, physical injuries, psychological consequences, relational problems, and social dysfunctions."[4]

By attending to the violations, offenders are given the opportunity to make things right.

Importantly, restorative justice is indebted to indigenous understandings of life and justice. Chief Justice Emeritus of the Navajo Nation and proponent of restorative justice models, the Honorable Robert Yazzie, explains that "Anglo law is concerned with social control," whereas "Navajo law comes from creation."[5] He writes:

> Law, in Anglo definitions and practice, is written rules which are enforced by authority figures. It is man-made. Its essence is power and force. The legislatures, courts, or administrative agencies that make the rules are made up of strangers to the actual problems or conflicts which prompted their development. When the rules are applied to people in conflict, other strangers stand in judgment and police and prisons serve to enforce those judgments. America is a secular society,

---

[3] *(continued)* that there is inherent goodness and beauty within every creature and that systemic change is possible. I begin this essay with an acknowledgment of a world beyond this material reality as well as with this disclaimer because restorative justice must be rooted in something other than the cool functioning of a supposedly unbiased system following from a Rawlsian theory of justice. To make claims for restorative justice as bridging theological praxis is to stare down the colonizing, militaristic, dehumanizing State and all those who ensure that it functions effectively and efficiently.

[4] Amy Levad, *Redeeming a Prison Society: A Liturgical & Sacramental Response to Mass Incarceration* (Minneapolis: Fortress, 2014), 114.

[5] Yazzie, 176.

where law is characterized as rules laid down by human elites for the good of society.

> The Navajo word for "law" is *beehaz'aanii.* It means something fundamental, and something that is absolute and exists from the beginning of time. Navajos believe that the Holy People "put it there for us from the time of beginning" for better thinking, planning, and guidance. It is the source of a healthy, meaningful life, and thus "life comes from it." Navajos say that "life comes from *beehaz'aanii,*" because it is the essence of life. The precepts of *beehaz'aanii* are stated in prayers and ceremonies which tell us of *hozho*—"*the* perfect state." Through these prayers and ceremonies we are taught what ought to be and what ought not to be.[6]

It is worth reiterating what Yazzie candidly points out: Anglo law (read: white; Western; male; Christian hegemony; heteronormative; and in linear time) comes from elites who authorize and legitimate domination and subordination as social norms between vulnerable peoples, reading trauma for deviance and non-whiteness, and difference as criminality. Navajo law comes from creation, Creator, and Holy Peoples; there is no elite upon whom the machinations of legitimation and authorization rest as a stand-in for a god, a *deus ex machina,* or another invisible hand. These are two different worldviews.

Right from the start, I want to be clear about my intentions and method in writing a feminist bridge theology that argues why and to what ends a restorative justice is possible when drawn from indigenous religious practices. Although my back is not a bridge in the same sense that Cherríe Moraga or Gloria Anzaldúa wrote of, aspects of myself have allowed me to see the spiritual in the natural and made me bow in deepest respect.[7] In my bow, I stretched forth and became my own bridge. My subconscious awareness of my settlerism forces me to ensure that this bridge is a drawbridge: there must be boundaries because saviorism is brutal assistance. As such, I tell you what I can, from my on-the-ground work for healing justice with survivors of crime, returning citizens, and drug users. While teaching in Ohio,

---

[6] Ibid., 175.

[7] Cherríe Moraga and Gloria Anzaldúa, eds., *This Bridge Called My Back: Writings by Radical Women of Color,* 4th ed. (Albany: SUNY, 2015).

I came to be involved in the HELP program, a Marianist social ministry for returning citizens, through my parish. As a full-time tenure-track professor, I expected to have little to offer. It quickly became apparent that my background in psychology and theology, as well as my training in indigenous peace circle practices, had larger applications than I had ever realized and helped me to understand the deep social entrenchment in retributive systems. Additionally, my argument is informed by theory and theology. My training in psychodynamic psychology, feminist and queer theory, and pastoral and practical theology makes me attentive to difference and psychological motivations. Lastly, my argument, taking academic form for the sake of intelligibility, comes from a place of deep respect and reverence for the *Diné* (Navajo) people and all indigenous peoples whose lives and cultures have survived systematic genocide. As such, allow me to outline my assumptions.

First, human development is central to the development of a feminist bridge theology that can address mass incarceration and detention. We cannot "power" our way through to repair economic, political, legal, and criminal justice systems. Such neo-colonial systems are the world of men, masculinity, rationality, hierarchy, dominance, control, self-interest, battles to be fought and either won or lost, with resulting implications for families and individuals.

Second, the work of a feminist bridge theology in criminal justice reform must be to address harms through a restorative lens that offers healing—beginning in the earliest of childhood development, family care, and ongoing work with those most traumatized and hurt by the violence of Empire.[8] The Empire infects our organizations, cultural institutions, and social structures, rooting them in a dominating, heteropatriarchal lens even as they attempt to change the systems of the harm. Working for social justice requires working for greater care, love, nurturance, health, boundaried vulnerability, emotional intelligence, mutually beneficial growth, and inclusion. Such realms are typically deemed to be women's work and less valuable, with resulting implications for the development of all humanity, but especially those who

---

[8] Joerg Rieger, *Christ and Empire: From Paul to Postcolonial Times* (Minneapolis: Augsburg, 2007), 2-3. Empire describes the accumulation and concentration of power that seeks to control and dominate across multiple spheres: "geographically, politically, economically, intellectually, emotionally, psychologically, spiritually, culturally, and religiously." Empire ought to be a primary concern in theology as it shapes the very theology that can be thought or produced under circumstances of neo-colonialism and exploitative global capitalism.

cannot live up to a set of norms established through a hetero-patriarchal, colonial, and racist system.

Third, in the United States context, attending to carceral logics requires attention to all those whose bodies do not participate in upholding the het-ero-patriarchal, colonial, and racist systems of harm, namely, black and brown bodies, LGBTQ bodies, women's and children's bodies, and bodies of persons with neuro-difference and physical disabilities. In particular, a racial justice lens must be deployed in addition to a gender lens to account for the fact that the rapid increase in prison population came as a result of explicitly racist public policy decisions in the United States context.

Given these assumptions, my goal in this chapter is to build a bridge between restorative justice and Catholic social teaching using a gender and racial justice lens, to whet the appetite for the depths of what is needed to sit with harm reduction and healing, and to offer practical next steps for scholars, activists, institutions, and funders alike by modeling this feminist bridgework.

Pope Francis and Human Development

Structures of harm render people as Others and less than human. Since the election of Pope Francis, many more Roman Catholics have stepped up bravely to critique structural injustice and call for reforms to the criminal justice system. As an honored invitee to the Vatican to celebrate the Jubilee of Prisoners in 2016, I gathered at St. Peter's with my mentee and with other Catholics who, along with Francis, know that an eye for an eye does not bear witness to the prophetic message of Jesus of Nazareth. Francis observes:

> … the Lord has gradually taught his people that there is a necessary asymmetry between crime and punishment, that an eye or a broken tooth cannot be restored by taking or breaking another. It is a matter of bringing justice to the victim, not punishing the aggressor [and] in our societies we tend to think that crimes are solved when we capture and sentence the criminal.[9]

[9] Pope Francis, *Letter of Pope Francis to Participants in the 19th International Congress of the International Association of Penal Law and of the 3rd Congress of the Latin-American Association of Penal Law and Criminology.* 30 May 2014. Available at http://w2.vatican.va/content/francesco/en/letters/2014/documents/papa-francesco_20140530_lettera-diritto-penale-criminologia.html.

Francis' call for attention to the asymmetry at a state-level has deep roots in the Vatican II document *Populorum Progressio (PP)*. *Populorum Progressio* marks a substantial prophetic turn in Catholic social thought as the Church, under the leadership of Pope Paul VI, rejected colonizing neoliberal economic forces and argued for economic justice as the means to ensuring peace. The document offers a vision of human development that is both personal and social, aiming for spiritual maturity and growth alongside the necessities of life, cultural institutions, and the production of new knowledge. As such, what constitutes human development is a theological anthropology rooted in dignity and worth that must lead any operational procedures in every system, including the criminal justice system.

Similar to Native values, the document is explicit in stating that authentic human development must be oriented toward an ultimate purpose. "In God's plan, every person is born to seek self-fulfillment, for every human life is called to some task by God."[10] We are called toward a "full-bodied humanism," which includes the fulfillment of the whole person as well as every person.[11] However, fulfillment also necessitates personal responsibility:

> Endowed with intellect and free will, each person is responsible for their self-fulfillment even as they are for their salvation. They are helped, and sometimes hindered, by their teachers and those around them; yet whatever be the outside influences exerted on them, they are the chief architect of their own success or failure. Utilizing only their talent and willpower, each person can grow in humanity, enhance their personal worth, and perfect themselves.[12]

The document, like other Catholic social teaching documents, also makes explicit that the economy serves humanity and not the other way around. More importantly, *Populorum Progressio* lifts up technology as another mistake to avoid, stating:

> The reign of technology—technocracy, as it is called—can cause as much harm to the world of tomorrow as liberalism did to the world of

[10] PP, para. 15.

[11] PP, para. 42.

[12] PP, para. 15.

yesteryear. Economics and technology are meaningless if they do not benefit people, for it is people they are to serve. Human beings are truly human only if they are the masters of their own actions and the judge of their worth, only if they are the architect of their own progress.[13]

To be architects is a worthy goal. Yet, religious, community, and national leaders often fall back on the same tropes that punish those who already experience lack, powerlessness, and marginalization. Studies of developmental trauma suggest that poverty, lack of education, food scarcity, and other compounding factors directly impact an individual's ability to become a resilient self. Willpower is no match to the terror and anxiety fueled by these experiences, which form the psyche and devastate the soul. Failure to resist these death-dealing forces of patriarchal domination makes criminals of us all.

Return of the Repressed: Reparation and Restoration

Freud argued that society is a substitute-formation for our instincts and drives. As a society, we create structures to ensure that our instincts for survival are transformed into productive means that work toward the common good. That is, we sublimate the drive for conquest—which is first and foremost a drive for sexual domination—in order to create a more fair, just, and inclusive society in which self- and social-determination are possible. However, that which we sublimate is never gone, always living in the unconscious of both ourselves and our society. When we do not acknowledge and work with the repressed, it returns and can even overtake our conscious functioning, blinding us to that which is most abundantly evident. However, our unconscious will not leave us alone when what is repressed returns. Freudian verbal slips, dreams, and slips of the pen are clues we use to inventory the traces of that which can destroy us.

What does personal, familial, and national development require in a context where the return of the repressed takes the form of structural racism or ongoing colonization? Two developments are required: first, reparation; second, restoration. For reparation, the soul of development requires that we tear apart the fabric, thread by thread, in order to address the built-in legal and political structures within nation-states that constrict life. For restoration,

---

[13] PP, para. 34. Cf. 1 Cor 4:1-5.

the soul of development requires attention to unconscious processes that structure self, family, institutions, and society and are transmitted from generation to generation—trauma, blame, shame, fear of abandonment, fear of rejection, frozen emotions, unchecked aggression, and reactivity.

In the article "The Case for Reparations," Ta-Nehisi Coates chronicles the racialized policy of redlining in North Lawndale, Chicago, and makes the case for reparations vis-à-vis HR 40, a bill introduced by John Conyers, Jr. (D-MI) to study slavery and its effects over 25 years. The bill never made it to the House floor until January 2019 despite evidence that the wealth gap is perpetuated by a lack of inheritance and substantial gifts, impacting home ownership.[14] Although lawsuits have been brought to repair the economic damage of redlining—a system of racial caste—and also failed, the lack of a national dialogue to speak to the plunder and piracy stemming from the transatlantic slave-trade is telling. The development of nations cannot be undertaken without confronting the underlining rape and pillage that legalized the economic gap.

Coates underscores the fact that studying slavery and the possibility of reparations will require admitting that Americans, especially white Americans, lie to themselves. He writes:

> To ignore the fact that one of the oldest republics in the world was erected on a foundation of white supremacy, to pretend that the problems of a dual society are the same as the problems of unregulated capitalism, is to cover the sin of national plunder with the sin of national lying.[15]

To this end he calls for "an airing of family secrets, a settling of old ghosts. What is needed is a healing of the American psyche and the banishment of white guilt."[16]

---

[14] See the recent report *The Asset Value of Whiteness: Understanding the Racial Wealth Gap* or, for a quick overview: https://www.bloomberg.com/news/articles/2017-02-08/the-big-reason-whites-are-richer-than-blacks-in-america.

[15] Ta Nehisi-Coates, "The Case for Reparations," *The Atlantic Monthly*, June 2014, https://www.theatlantic.com/magazine/archive/2014/06/the-case-for-reparations/361631/.

[16] Ibid.

The latter task is reparative in some sense of the word, but healing the American psyche also requires diving into depths that allow for the hearing and telling of complex realities from the standpoint of survivors. Any hopes for a public policy of reconciliation will require individual, communal, and national processes that not only repair but also restore humans to their dignity and worth in ways that see beyond a rational—read male—economic actor. The wounds of not belonging are not rational, and instead the return of the repressed configures the national dialogue as making progress in America rather than a rending of the white supremacist garment. What would it take to rend the garment? How might Catholic social teaching help or hinder?

Populorum Progressio and other Catholic social teachings that advocate for human development vis-a-vis peace-building, racial justice, or criminal justice reform has its blind spots: an inability to substantially take up the psyche and the role of violence, especially sexual violence. Failure to address the colonial dyads—black/white, female/male, colonized/colonizer, Africa/United States, South/North, care/justice, and restoration/reparation—confines violence and harm to intimate interpersonal injustice rather than seeing it as central to the maintenance of hegemonic racialized and gendered economic and colonial systems that destroy the lives of the most vulnerable. Any hope for reconciliation, a necessary precursor to peace, requires enough safety so that salves of healing can be applied.

A Feminist Bridge Toward Healing and Safety

Given this context of long-perpetuated social harms, I have three suggestions for a praxis of feminist bridge theology. First, restorative justice practices are one modality of bridge theology that may advance a human development attentive to the internalized trauma that is a direct result of built colonial projects, including the criminal justice system. They do so by authorizing a double decolonization which attends to the harm on all sides and offers redress through empowerment "in the construction of a new world order."[17] A new world order, the development of people for the sake of peace, must be oriented toward restoration and healing. The soul of development is the development of selves, and it, supported through structural change that can

[17] PP, para. 83.

attend to the gynocentric-affective dimensions, is what will make possible the transformation of nations into places of belonging. In the context of circles processes, which are one aspect of restorative justice, defining what is at stake can create the conditions to develop critical and strategic questions for public or private dialogue.[18]

Second, a feminist bridge theology endeavors to build mechanisms of healing and safety as a response to the endless recitation of social injustices. The building of mechanisms requires the political, social, and theological engagement of underrepresented actors dedicated to the common good, a realm certainly familiar to all those who claim the authority of Catholic social teaching for praxis. Problematically, the crux of the matter is that organizing the hard to organize—prisoners, returning citizens, detainees, drug users, survivors of crime—requires attention to healing and safety, particularly in faith-rooted organizing that in practice mirrors the very systems it seeks to transform. Given my psychological analysis in previous sections, this ought not to come as a surprise.

Faith-rooted organizing for social justice and social activism relies on individuals who already serve and participate in social voluntary organizations—churches, political associations, parent-teacher organizations, nonprofits—which is to say, people whose lives reflect middle-class values, social capital, and economic opportunities. This, however, leaves out a wide range of communities and people throughout the country whose lives have been destroyed by the structural violence of American society—crime survivors, returning citizens, and people in poverty—who are also, too often, people of color, women, and children. They do not flourish and cannot thrive. They continue to experience trauma and to pass trauma intergenerationally, shifting their economic, socio-political, and psychic burdens to their children. They have little chance of achieving a middle-class lifestyle. They struggle to survive in the world. They lack social and emotional supports while at the same time facing greater health disparities and social injustices. Let's face it:

[18] Fran Peavey, "Strategic Questioning: An Approach to Creating Personal and Social Change," ed. Vivian Hutchinson, n.d. Available at https://gustavus.edu/provost/faculty-l/attachments/strategic-questioning.-short.pdf. Strategic questioning is both political and personal. The objective is not to merely gather data but to encourage individuals and groups to cope and proactively respond to change, a feature of leadership according to Harvard Business School professor John P. Kotter (see his oft-cited article "What Leaders Really Do" in *Harvard Business Review* from December 2001).

it is difficult to be an activist, and to lead and organize in your community, if you experience crippling anxiety and depression when thinking about your future and your children's future.

If organizing intends to change public policy to effect material changes for those who are most marginalized, then it is necessary to reform practices and leadership structures so that the "hard to organize" are not further marginalized. Instead, they must be brought into the center of powerful and prophetic movements for justice and healing. To do this, we must address trauma, especially the trauma experienced as a result of the new racial caste system that is mass incarceration, which decimates families and communities materially and emotionally. Trauma is insidious and pervasive. Bessel Van der Kolk has described developmental trauma as "the hidden epidemic" in which "hundreds of thousands... absorb enormous resources, often without appreciable benefit."[19] Resolving trauma requires the restoration of the proper balance between the rational and emotional brains. Executive functioning and critical thinking—two necessary prerequisites for building powerful movements that pull people together to act in their self- and communal interest—cannot occur without owning one's voice. That is, movements such as the Poor People's Movement, or movements to organize returning citizens or survivors of crime to impact the criminal justice system in substantial ways, cannot gain traction when survival is the primary goal.

As such, strategies are needed to embed healing justice practices and to create structures of leadership within organizing. Leadership development from the grassroots to the elite requires an ability to speak without the hyper- or hypo-arousal—feeling "triggered"—that trauma induces. We cannot win substantial public policy changes that promote dignity and respect for all people because harm and trauma literally rewire the brain to shame, panic, terror, and fear—fight, flight, freeze, and appease. This is true across color lines. Joblessness, insecurity, and lack of safety make people hand over their power or collude with those who do not serve their interests in the hopes of being recognized as people of dignity and worth. Thus, developing new rhythms of leadership training with the hard to organize is one critical intervention to interrupt internalized self- and other-defeating narratives that collude with power.

[19] Bessel Van der Kolk, *The Body Keeps the Score: Brain, Mind, and Body in the Healing of Trauma* (New York: Penguin, 2014), 151.

Feminist bridge theology is, third, dialogical and political. It shapes meaning and worldviews for hope and emancipation and leads and supports the mechanisms and institutions that enable this shaping. One such example was the evidence-based, trauma-informed "Safe and Healthy Ohio" legislative ballot issue in November 2018. Ohio voters did not pass it. Modeled after legislation that passed in California, the ballot initiative sought to increase public safety while decreasing incarceration through four proposals. These proposals were shaped by evidence-based outcomes from public health experts about the impact of trauma as well as a worldview that favors healing, creating safety, and rewarding rehabilitation over domination, punishment, and social control:

- Drug addiction does not belong in prison. The amendment proposed turning fourth- and fifth-degree drug-possession felonies into misdemeanors. The first two convictions would necessitate a form of community control, including mandatory residential drug treatment. This does not apply to drug trafficking.

- Probation violation does not belong in prison. The amendment required local probation departments to hold supervised people accountable with smaller, swifter sanctions (electronic monitoring, one night in jail, more intensive programming, more meetings with an officer) when rules are broken. At the time of the amendment, judges sent nearly 5,000 Ohioans to prison per year for breaking a rule of probation, not for committing a new felony.

- Personal rehabilitation is rewarded. The amendment proposed an expansion of Ohio's system for awarding modest sentence reductions to prisoners who genuinely work hard to rehabilitate themselves.

- Investments in healing would ensure safety. Each of these evidence-based public health proposals would have resulted in nearly $100 million in savings per year from the state prison budget. The amendment proposed redirecting these savings into drug treatment for suffering Ohio communities and trauma recovery services for crime victims.

While colleagues in Ohio shared with me some of their thoughts about why this legislation did not pass, I cannot help but think that internalized shame and fear-based submission to all forms of "father" had a part to play. As such, feminist bridge theology that can meet the demands outlined in this chapter requires investment in infrastructure that supports liberation, not institutions of patriarchy, fear, and domination. Significant institutes and networks led by women and people of color—beyond higher education and graduate level theological education—are needed to support our most deeply held values, including democracy, solidarity, and equality. In particular, I call for investment in institutes and networks to effect this work. How they function and what they do will, by necessity, be different from what has existed to date, and yet they will work with all of creation to effect social change through structural reforms. Perhaps they could even function as places where the sacredness of all creation is honored and attended to through boundaried lovingkindness. Perhaps, one day, we might even say to each other, wholeheartedly, that life comes from it.

CHAPTER EIGHT

Economy of Communion as Lived Bridge Theology: Redemptive Transformational Entrepreneurship for Persons

ANDREW GUSTAFSON, PHD

THE ECONOMY OF COMMUNION (EOC) is a form of business that can build bridges to the poor and marginalized in many ways, seeking to bring about communion through practice animated by gratuity and reciprocity. The following chapter shares this unique EOC business vision by first considering the thought of Stephano Zagmani, an Italian economist heavily involved in the EOC who characterizes the EOC in terms of generativity, reciprocity, and gratuity. Second, it will consider the recent exhortations of Pope Francis himself to the EOC as a bridge the contemporary world desperately needs. Third, it will consider Luigino Bruni's description of the EOC as a stance that accepts both the wounds and blessings of a person-centered approach. Finally, Luca Crivelli, a Swiss economist also involved in the EOC, discusses the love-centered approach of the EOC, which embraces poverty by participating in it.

Economy of Communion: An Introduction

Pope Francis recently called on ethicists to develop "a praxis that is compassionate and attentive to tragic human situations and concerned with accompanying them with merciful care."[1] The EOC is one practical movement that has arisen in recent years, acknowledged and supported by the Vatican in its efforts to foster communion and help alleviate poverty through private entrepreneurship and promote sustainable development and communion between all people. The Focolare, a Catholic-based interreligious movement of almost 5 million people, works for greater dialogue and social integration at all levels of society. Chiara Lubich, leader of the Focolare, helped initiate the EOC during a 1991 visit to the slums of Rio to the Focolare community there. The EOC saw that many of the Focolare members were living in poverty and the community had more needs than it could address through simple charitable giving. A plan was made to create profitable businesses that could employ many of the poor.[2] These entrepreneurial for-profit enterprises began with the goal of providing employment and helping the poor gain financial stability. They also helped them more fully integrate into society and experience the dignity of productive work in community with others. Not only would financial poverty be overcome, but the lack of dignity and community would be overcome by building relationships based on communion and radical sharing.[3] Today there are over 750 EOC businesses worldwide, the majority in Europe (especially Italy), a large number in Latin America, and over 40 in the United States.

EOC companies operate with a vision quite distinct from traditional ways of doing business as well as how for-profit businesses think of people. As Lorna Gold states, "Market enterprises... have been perceived as the realm of an instrumentalist logic in human relationships, with the profit

---

[1] Pope Francis, *A Critical Time for Bridge-Building: Catholic Theological Ethics Today* (A Message of the Holy Father Francis to Participants in the 3rd International Conference of "Catholic Theological Ethics in the World Church"). [Sarajevo, 26-29 July 2018] http://w2.vatican.va/content/francesco/en/messages/pont-messages/2018/documents/papa-francesco_20180711_messaggio-etica-teologica.html.

[2] Lorna Gold, "The 'Economy of Communion': A Case Study of Business and Civil Society in Partnership for Change," *Development in Practice* 14.5 (2004), 636.

[3] For more on the Focolare movement, see Luigino Bruni and Lorna Gold, eds. *Toward a Multidimensional Economic Culture: The Economy of Communion* (New York, NY: New City Press, 2002); Focolare (2001) "Economia di Comunione," available at https://www.focolare.org/in-dialogo/cultura/economia/ (accessed March 21, 2020).

motive dominating other concerns such as human rights and the environment."[4] Stefano Zamagni, an Italian economist who has written extensively on the EOC, says it "represents a real challenge to the still dominant mode of doing economic theory."[5] Rather than assuming *homo economicus* (economic man), the EOC assumes *homo reciprocans* (reciprocal man) as its starting point.[6] This radically alters one's notion of what the economy is for and about. The EOC views economic phenomena with an interpersonal dimension frequently ignored by the individualism and self-interest characteristic of most economic thought.[7] Insofar as it thinks of "economics as if people mattered,"[8] the EOC is in a very real sense an attempt to "civilize the economy" that Pope Benedict XVI argues for in *Caritas in Veritate*:

> ... there must be room for commercial entities based on mutual principles and pursuing social ends to take root and express themselves. It is from this reciprocal encounter in the marketplace that one may expect hybrid forms of commercial behavior to emerge, and hence an attentiveness to ways of *civilizing the economy*.[9]

The EOC "demonstrates empirically that it is possible to use the market as a means to reach goals which are by their nature public," including alleviating poverty.[10] In this sense, EOC demonstrates bridge economics.

Zamagni helpfully characterizes EOC in three words: generativity, reciprocity, and gratuity. He explains, "Generativity in the present context means the capacity to generate new forms of doing business, new modes of organizing the productive process, new ways of realizing the specific role of entrepreneurship."[11] EOC does not see entrepreneurship primarily as a

---

[4] Gold, 633.

[5] Stefano Zamagni, "The Economy of Communion Project as a Challenge to Standard Economic Theory," *Revista Portuguesa de Filosofia*, T 70 Fasc. 1 (2014), 52.

[6] Ibid., 52.

[7] Ibid., 44, 60

[8] Ibid., 48.

[9] Pope Benedict, *Caritas in Vertitate*, n. 38

[10] Zagmani, 50.

[11] Zagmani, 46.

pursuit of personal profit, but rather as a bridge connecting the practice of business to the construction of the common good. This occurs by providing employment and community to the poor, which in turn recognizes their dignity, freedom, and sociality in relationship to others as they take their place in society through productive and contributive work.

Reciprocity is not merely an exchange of equivalents, but rather;

> According to the EOC perspective, the firm is visualized as a community, not as a commodity that can be bought and sold in the market according to the conveniences of the moment. A community to function on presupposes that its members practice the principle of reciprocity.[12]

Far from a transactional this-for-that approach, this view of reciprocity sees business as a communal bridge where everyone is committed to the good of the whole, and each is willing to sacrifice and give to the other. This is not a guarded relationship, but a free relationship of real trust that risks my wellbeing in the hands of others without caveat. When relational reciprocity is the principle of economic behavior, "transfers cannot be dissociated from personal relationships" because "the objects of exchange, are not detached from the subjects who create them, with the result that the exchange that takes place within the market ceases to be anonymous and impersonal."[13]

Finally, in terms of gratuitousness, Zamagni says, "The ultimate challenge that EOC invites us to take up is to strive to bring the principle of gratuitousness back into the *public* sphere." Gratuitousness is not merely giving or getting something for free, but "the content of gift as gratuitousness is the specific interpersonal relation that is established between the donor and the donee."[14] There are goods of justice, and then goods of gratuitousness. Goods of justice are required by duty rooted in justice—they are rooted in the requirements of a contract, for example. "Gratuitous goods on the other hand—such as relational goods—create an *obligation* that is based on the special ties that bind us to one another."[15] Ethics is in the realm of justice.

---

[12] Ibid.

[13] Ibid., 50.

[14] Ibid., 46.

[15] Ibid., 53.

Gratuitousness is beyond justice—"It has more to do with the supra-ethical sphere of human action; its logic is that of superabundance" rather than mere equivalence (this for that) which is the domain of justice and ethics.[16] Gratuitousness, fraternity, and the innovative countercultural ethos of EOC will be explored in the rest of this chapter.

The EOC as "Agents of Communion"

Pope Francis invited members of the EOC from around the world to come to the Vatican, where he spoke to them in February 2017. He spoke directly to the members of the EOC to challenge them to be agents of communion in the world. He began by pointing out that economy and communion are often considered apart from each other, but the EOC bridges these two apparent opposites:

> By introducing into the economy, the good seed of communion, you have begun a profound change in the way of seeing and living business. Business is not only incapable of destroying communion among people but can edify it; it can promote it.[17]

This is a very interesting idea—we frequently think about how faith can inform and direct business practices (business informed by faith), but we do not so often think about how business might actually promote and even edify communion among people. This is the new bridge-building perspective of the EOC:

> With your life you demonstrate that economy and communion become more beautiful when they are beside each other. Certainly, the economy is more beautiful, but communion is also more beautiful, because the spiritual communion of hearts is even fuller when it becomes the communion of goods, of talents, of profits.[18]

---

[16] Ibid.

[17] Pope Francis, Address of His Holiness Pope Francis to participants in the Meeting "Economy of Communion," sponsored by the Focolare Movement. Paul VI Audience Hall Saturday, 4 February 2017. https://w2.vatican.va/content/francesco/en/speeches/2017/february/documents/papa-francesco_20170204_focolari.html.

[18] Pope Francis, 2017.

EOC envisions business practice itself as a bridge—a spiritual enterprise—which can bring about unity, not as an individual pursuit of
self-benefit that inadvertently helps the common good due to impersonal
market forces (the invisible hand). Pope Francis had three things to say to
the EOC members gathered at the Vatican, all of which are related to the
concept of bridge building.

The first thing Pope Francis brought up was *money*: "It is very important that at the center of the economy of communion there be the communion of your profits. The economy of communion is also the communion
of profits, an expression of the communion of life." It has always been a
principle of the EOC to divide profits three ways:

- **Support** the development of persons and communities that find themselves in need, through shared projects based on reciprocity, subsidiarity,
and communion.

- **Spread** the culture of giving and of reciprocity, a precondition to integral
development and of an economy and society characterized by fraternity
and solidarity.

- **Develop** business, create jobs and wealth, orient all internal and external
business life towards the common good.[19]

Thus, profit becomes a bridge to development of the common good rather
than simple individual reward. Pooling and giving away some of the profit
is essential, as Pope Francis says:

> The best and most practical way to avoid making an idol of money is
> to share it, share it with others, above all with the poor, or to enable
> young people to study and work, overcoming the idolatrous temptation
> with communion.

Pooling our money with others for the common good is a very practical spiritual exercise enacted through our business practices. Project Lia in
Indianapolis is an example of a nonprofit social enterprise project started with

[19] EOC website: https://web.archive.org/web/20110726014843/http://www.edc-online.org/index.
php/en/component/content/article/18-idee-forza/1-benvenuto.html.

pooled money from EOC business owners. Project Lia helps previously incarcerated females learn job skills through work repurposing discarded materials into home furnishings (projectlia.org). In other cases, EOC businesses simply make financial decisions that favor environmental sustainability, employee support, or customer wellbeing over making greater profits. Francis says, "When you share and donate your profits, you are performing an act of lofty spirituality, saying to money through deeds: 'you are not God, you are not lord, you are not master!'"[20]

A second issue Francis addressed with EOC members was poverty. Essentially, he argued that we should bridge the chasm between rich and poor not through charity but by helping eliminate the needs of the poor through EOC enterprise. He said, "Capitalism knows philanthropy, not communion. It is simple to give a part of the profits, without embracing and touching the people who receive those 'crumbs.'"[21] The EOC does aid the poor at times with its excess profits, but more importantly it seeks to employ the poor and use private enterprise to lift up those in need, not only financially but socially. Those who are financially poor are typically poor in terms of social capital, that is, community, and this is the ultimate goal of the EOC—to create a bridge to the poor through communion with others.

Pope Francis, in speaking of philanthropy and charity, pointed to the sad fact that "capitalism continues to produce discarded people whom it would then like to care for."[22] He provided examples such as airlines polluting the atmosphere but donating a part of the cost of the ticket to plant trees, or gambling casinos financing campaigns to care for addicted gamblers (one could also suggest tobacco companies donating to fight lung cancer). Pope Francis points out the absurdity of this charity when he says, "And the day that the weapons industry finances hospitals to care for the children mutilated by their bombs, the system will have reached its pinnacle. This is hypocrisy!"[23] The poor whose wellbeing is at times undermined by the companies that provide charity to them are the discarded people. Pope Francis said that "the creation of discarded people, then trying to hide them or make sure they are no longer seen" is the principal ethical dilemma of capitalism. We might think here of

[20] Pope Francis, 2017.

[21] Ibid.

[22] Ibid.

[23] Ibid.

Zygmunt Bauman's notion of "wasted lives." The poor are unable to participate in the economy, and so are "wasted lives" in terms of being able to be
active consumers in a consumer society.[24] Pope Francis' point is that charity
is not enough, when we continue to produce and then hide discarded people.

Instead of charity, Pope Francis calls the EOC to live out its purpose
to become a bridge to the marginalized and bring about communion: "The
economy of communion, if it wants to be faithful to its charism, must not
only care for the victims, but build a system where there are ever fewer
victims, where possibly, there may no longer be any."[25] This represents a
change in how business and economics are envisioned—a vision in line with
the EOC. According to Francis:

> Therefore, we must work toward changing the rules of the game of
> the socio-economic system. Imitating the Good Samaritan of the Gos-
> pel is not enough. Of course, when an entrepreneur or any person
> happens upon a victim, he or she is called to take care of the vic-
> tim and, perhaps like the good Samaritan, also to enlist the fraternal
> action of the market (the innkeeper).... But it is important to act
> above all before the man comes across the robbers, by battling the
> frameworks of sin that produce robbers and victims. An entrepreneur
> who is only a Good Samaritan does half of his duty: he takes care of
> today's victims but does not curtail those of tomorrow.[26]

Charity often meets the immediate needs of people, but it is rarely a means of
building bridges, or sustainable change for those being helped. Pope Francis
is calling the EOC to create sustainable enterprises that can consistently help
prevent people from falling into poverty and calls us to bring people into
communion—to help to change the system that creates victims. Bruni and
Crivelli provide more explanation of this below. But this approach requires
gratuitousness, foregoing typical business concerns about merit:

> For communion one must imitate the merciful Father of the parable
> of the Prodigal Son and wait at home for the children, workers and

[24] Zygmunt Bauman, *Wasted Lives* (Cambridge, UK: Polity Press, 2004).

[25] Pope Francis, 2017.

[26] Ibid.

coworkers who have done wrong, and there embrace them and celebrate with them and for them—and not be impeded by the meritoc-
racy invoked by the older son and by many who deny mercy in the
name of merit.[27]

Gratuitousness is at the heart of the EOC approach—a gratuitousness that
imitates the mercy of God and reaches out to bring the outcast back into
the fold. The graciousness Pope Francis calls us to—to ignore merit and
embrace those who have failed us—is an act of gift and mercy.

The last thing Pope Francis spoke of was the future. The EOC needs to
build bridges to those who are unaware of it and plant seeds to establish and
support more EOC entrepreneurs. Francis says:

> The economy of communion will have a future if you give it to ev-
> eryone and it does not remain only inside your "house." Give it to
> everyone, firstly to the poor and the young, who are those who need it
> most and know how to make the gift received bear fruit! To have life
> in abundance one must learn to give: not only the profits of business,
> but of yourself…. Today's economy, the poor, the young, need first of
> all your spirit, your respectful and humble fraternity, your will to live
> and, only then, your money.[28]

We see Pope Francis taking this call very seriously by creating the EOC
Francesco event in Assisi in November of 2020, which was attended by
youth from over 120 countries (https://francescoeconomy.org/). The EOC
provided a constructive bridge-building and socially unifying alternative to
the profit-maximizing approach of the traditional contemporary market
and business structure.

This very powerful message from Pope Francis to the EOC members
who travelled to the Vatican from around the world to hear his address was
full of challenges to the status-quo economy. In his closing remarks, he challenged us with the following: "May the 'no' to an economy that kills become
a 'yes' to an economy that lets live, because it shares, includes the poor, and

---

[27] Ibid., 2017.
[28] Ibid.

uses profits to create communion." This is the radical challenge the EOC presents to the standard economic business models around us—a challenge to build bridges to the poor not through charity handouts but by providing a sustainable means of financial support through meaningful work, and a communion that is possible only by fully engaging them as human beings.

Human Nature (Anthropology) and the Place of the Other

Every theory reveals an understanding of human beings. This applies especially to business and economic theory. As mentioned above, the EOC replaces the standard *homo economicus* with *homo reciprocan* as the model of economic persons.[29] The EOC assumes we are not merely self-interested beings who only seek our own fulfillment, but rather we are social beings who desire relations of reciprocity, found in communion with others. A theory's fundamental view of human beings has profound effects on its view of others, as well as its fundamental conception of the purposes and ends of business. The radical individualism frequently assumed in economics inevitably nurtures a suspicion of others who compete with me for what is mine. Karol Wojtyła (Pope John Paul II) speaks of the isolated self:

> Individualism accomplishes this isolating of the self—to itself and to its own good, that is, a good that exists in isolation from the good of the others and from the common good. In this system, the good of the individual has the quality of being opposed to every other individual and their good. This kind of individualism is based on self-preservation and is always on the defensive and is also defective. Acting and existing jointly with others is, according to this individualism, an imposed necessity to which an individual has to submit. But there is no positive aspect in this necessity. It does not serve the development of

[29] *Homo economicus*, or "economic man," traditionally refers to the concept that humans attempt to maximize utility as consumers and economic profit as producers—with economic efficiency as the basis of all decisions. In contrast to this, *homo reciprocan*, or reciprocating man is the concept that humans are cooperative actors who are motivated by positive reciprocity with other human beings.

their individuality. "The others" are for the individual only a source of limitations and may even be opponents and create polarizations.[30]

Our stance towards the other directs our actions. Jean Paul Sartre famously characterized the other as a threat to my self-project and was known for his phrase "Hell is other people,"[31] in part because people can look at you as an object, undermining your subjectivity and freedom. The Catholic philosopher Gabriel Marcel, in contrast, said we should take the stance towards others that they are a gift, not a threat. Through being humbly present and open to others with one's whole being, this very vulnerable stance of availability enables a dynamic and creative encounter between people allowing us to "make contact."

Luigino Bruni, an Italian economist deeply involved in the EOC, has an economics that gets the anthropology correct. He frames what it means to be human and how we become truly happy, as well as what kind of economic practice promotes this happiness. As Charles Clark says of Bruni,

> This understanding of what it means to be human emphasizes the social nature of being human, and that economic relations are built up from 'gift' and not 'gain.' Such an understanding of 'persons' stands in contrast to 'autonomous rational economic man.'[32]

The EOC is an economic outlook that does not see me in opposition to others—in fact a stated goal of the EOC is to unite all people.[33]

In his book *The Wound and the Blessing*, Bruni characterizes modern economics as providing an illusory promise of "a life together without sacrifice" where the market or corporation can "offer a painless and peaceful society, mediating encounters with others with whom we interact harm-

---

[30] Karol Wojtyła, *Towards a Philosophy of Praxis*, edited by Alfred Bloch and George T. Czucka (New York: Crossroads Publishing Co., 1981), 40-41.

[31] Jean Paul Sartre, "Hell Is Other People," 1944.

[32] Charles Clark, Foreword, *The Wound and the Blessing: Economics, Relationships and Happiness* by Luigino Bruni. (Hyde Park, NY: New City Press, 2012), xi.

[33] The spirituality of unity in the management process has been discussed extensively. See Stanisla Grochmal, "Spirituality of Unity in Management—Economy of Communion," *Cogent Business & Management Journal 3.1* (2016).

lessly, without contention or wound."[34] In this view, interpersonal relationships are a problem to be overcome, and the "other" is a source of wound,
to be avoided. "Modern humanity has seen primarily the wound, rather
than the blessing, of the other."[35] The blessings that also come with these
wounds are ignored.[36] The effect of this economic viewpoint "represents
an important stage toward an individualistic, non-communitarian and immunizing humanism in western modernity."[37] Friendship and fraternity
cannot be characteristic of "normal market relations" under such a system.[38] Multiple aspects of business theory contribute to this immunization
to human interaction. Through policies and procedures that contemporary
business create to help avoid personal judgments and relational decisions
(as in, "it's just our company policy; it's nothing personal"), the market is
constantly "searching for ways to avoid eye contact with the other." And
even "economic personnel theory and agency theory are worthy attempts
to foresee, mitigate and minimize the 'wounds' that face-to-face encounters
cause, exactly as in market theory."[39] The owners don't have to deal with
labor directly—they pay the manager agents to deal with the humans in their
organization, etc., etc. Most business transactions happen without human
interaction—shareholders need never meet an employee, owners need never
interact directly with customers, and frequently customers need never meet
an employee, particularly in contemporary online sales. When transactions
do occur, they are governed by contracts, agreements, customer service policies, small print, etc.

Bruni points to the pessimistic view of humanity in Machiavelli and
Hobbes, as well as a desire to eliminate beneficence from market interactions
in the work of Adam Smith as the foundation of these stringent attempts to
avoid relationality in business. In *The Prince*, Machiavelli describes humans as:

---

[34] Luigino Bruni, *The Wound and the Blessing: Economics, Relationships and Happiness* (Hyde
Park, NY: New City Press, 2012), xxi.

[35] Ibid., 10.

[36] Ibid., 1.

[37] Ibid., 5.

[38] Ibid., 29.

[39] Ibid., 34.

... ungrateful, fickle, deceitful and dissembling, cowardly, and covet-
ous for gain; as long as you do well for them they are wholly yours,
offering you their blood, property life, and children... when need is
distant; but when it approaches, they turn against you.[40]

Hobbes, who considered life "nasty, brutish, and short," saw contracts as
the basis of civil society, and Smith saw them as the basis of market relations.

We must gratefully remember that it was Adam Smith who pointed out
the beneficial civilizing influences of commerce on society when he wrote
"Whenever commerce is introduced into any country, probity and punctual-
ity always accompany it. These virtues in a rude and barbarous country are
almost unknown."[41] In addition, there is an equalizing effect in an economy
based not on class but on capital: a worker who has money to participate
in the market has equal footing with a nobleman in a market that treats all
with money equally. As Bruni puts it:

... in the interaction of the market we meet on equal footing, where,
thanks to the contract, we are freed from dependence on the benevolence of others. The market is a high expression of a civil society... the
market frees one from vertical and asymmetrical relations and from
those that are not chosen, and it creates conditions for a horizontal
sociality between subjects that tends to be free and equal.[42]

This equity is an advantage of Adam Smith's market economy, no doubt,
and a type of bridge between the middle class and upper class. But while
Bruni acknowledges the civilizing effects of the market, he also sees negative
effects of letting the market direct our society too much:

[40] Nicolo Machiavelli, *The Prince*, trans. by W.K. Marriott, ch. XVII. https://www.gutenberg.
org/files/1232/1232-h/1232-h.htm.

[41] Adam Smith (1763, 1896), "Of Police," in *Lectures on Justice, Police, Revenue and Arms*,
ed. by Edwin Cannan (Oxford: Clarendon Press), 253. https://oll.libertyfund.org/titles/smith-
lectures-on-justice-police-revenue-and-arms-1763.

[42] Bruni, 29.

> There is, however, a tipping point, a threshold beyond which the anonymous relationships of markets produce lawlessness, loneliness, and the loss of bonds of identity with others. My impression is that wealthy Western societies have already passed beyond this threshold, which delimits what it means to be human.[43]

Bruni argues that Adam Smith's market is one without benevolence or gratuity. We all know the famous quote from Smith that "it is not from the benevolence of the butcher, the brewer, or the baker, that we expect our dinner, but from their regard for their own interest."[44] This quote is the basis of modern economics insofar as the market is one of self-interest that happens to bring about good for others. Again, according to Smith, "Society may subsist among different men, as among different merchants, from a sense of its utility, without any mutual love or affection."[45]

In this modern market envisioned by Smith, it is not love or affection, but the impersonal motives of the market itself that bind us together, and those are typically written out in contracts. Connecting Hobbes' social contract and Smith's economics, Bruni says:

> In Hobbes's politics and Smith's economics there is no direct intersubjectivity, but rather a mediated and anonymous relationality, for fear of the negative and the suffering that a personal "you" carries in him or herself. The contract—private for Smith, social for Hobbes—thus became the main instrument of this interaction, where the "contract is above all that which is not a gift, but the absence of *munus*" [that is, a gift].[46]

Modern society pursues a justice that is faceless and without personal bias. Bruni points to "mutual disinterest" for one another as being a fundamental

[43] Ibid., xxiii.

[44] Adam Smith, *Wealth of Nations* (London: Methuen & Co. Ltd, 1776, 1904), I.ii.2. https://www.econlib.org/library/Smith/smWN.html.

[45] Adam Smith, *Theory of Moral Sentiments* (Boston: Well and Lilly, 1817), I.ii.3.4. https://www.google.com/books/edition/The_Theory_of_Moral_Sentiments_Or_An_Ess/ifIoAAAAYAAJ?hl=en&gbpv=1&printsec=frontcover.

[46] Bruni, 11.

condition of the social contract, according to contemporary ethicist John Rawls.[47] For the contract to be fair:

> ...since feelings, a sense of belonging, friendship and strong bonds are all dangerous, ever tending toward partiality and exclusivity. To be "just," a broad pluralistic and liberal society needs individuals without ties and passions...each protects him- or herself from these differences by increasingly sophisticated social and private contracts that do not require a dialogue, much less an interpersonal encounter, but precisely a mutual indifference.[48]

This has led to a "famine of gratuitousness" in contemporary markets.[49] The efforts put forth to eliminate the possibility of wounds have simultaneously eliminated the possibility of blessings from human encounter (xxi-xxii). As Bruni says, "we can live a long time without markets and income, but much less without giving and receiving gratuitousness."[50] The current situation as seen in market economies where the wound and blessing have been eliminated show us that such a world "is not a habitable place, much less a place of joy."[51]

There is an alternate to the modern contract-oriented market model that normalizes the contractual, anonymous, and impersonal relationality of the market, and that, as it immunizes us to others, eliminates *community*. In contrast, the social-cooperative economy tradition, as exemplified in the EOC, does exactly the opposite. It starts from the cooperative principle of reciprocity, where equal persons live in solidarity with one another. As Bruni says, its goal is "to 'commonize' the market and the civil society. Its goal is *community* instead of *immunity* (the latter as typical of the contract)."[52] The EOC enables the possibility of blessing:

---

[47] John Rawls, *Theory of Justice* (Boston: Harvard University Press, 1971), 128-29.

[48] Bruni, 13.

[49] Ibid., 45.

[50] Ibid., 46.

[51] Ibid., 17.

[52] Ibid., 40.

The EOC demonstrates precisely this: the market can be a place where the other can truly be encountered, a place of blessing as long as we open ourselves to gratuitousness and do not flee from being wounded by the other.[53]

Markets need to become a bridge for relationality, where people truly engage as humans with one another. But to accomplish this, "economic theory must surpass Smith and envision an economic science capable of gratuitousness, beyond a merely contractual and immunizing relationality."[54]

On the Reciprocity and Communion of the EOC

It could be said that the very point of the EOC enterprise is to build bridges to everyone it engages to the point of communion. Luca Crivelli points out that the EOC is distinctive because it has a primary goal of promoting communion—"the highest degree of mutual openness and brotherhood among people, within the economic sphere."[55] This truth was clear when Chiara Lubich, leader of the Focolare Movement at the time of the founding of the EOC, said that giving and loving were fundamental to EOC practice: "Love your employees, even your competitors, your clients and suppliers too, love everyone. The life-style of the company has to change, everything has to be evangelical, otherwise it isn't Economy of Communion."[56]

This evangelical mission is seen in Pope Francis' call for EOC entrepreneurs to be "agents of communion" through their business activities.[57] EOC has a culture and ethos that serves as a bridge between one's life and the common good. It sees one's commercial life as a way to make life better for others, particularly the poor. Living out the EOC ethos is more than a matter

---

[53] Ibid., xxiii.

[54] Ibid., 19.

[55] Luca Crivelli and Benedetto Gui, "Do 'Economy of Communion' Entrerprises Deserve the 'Social' Label? A Comparative Discussion of their Aims and Logic of Action," in *Revista Portuguesa de Filosofia* (2014), T. 70, Fasc.1, 37.

[56] Luca Crivelli, "Economy of Communion, Poverty, and the Humanised Economy" Journal of Religion and Society, Supplement 22 (2020)

[57] Ibid.

of acting generously, giving charitably, philanthropy, or providing assistance, but rather, "it has to do with acknowledging and living the dimension of giving and giving of oneself as essential to one's own existence."[58]

Making a profit for owners is not the primary goal of EOC companies and, similarly, the commitment to create value for stakeholders "is not just a simple restriction they have to fulfil in order to maintain social legitimacy over time, but is an essential objective of EOC firms' activity."[59] Bruni and Sugden have argued that the market economy itself requires a specific form of sociality or fraternity that is not charity or altruism but an intention for mutual benefit, which entails avoiding opportunities to behave opportunistically towards customers, suppliers, or even competitors.[60] The EOC expects a demanding fraternity that goes against typical business behavior in that it is much more generous and forgiving and frequently acts "in an other-regarding or superogatory way...."[61]

Crivelli points out why the "love" that animates EOC is so scandalous to economics. First, economics "considers that the more the market is able to cut down on 'love,' the more efficient it will be." In addition, love requires the gift to be free and unconditional "which is a scandal for economics which believes a price must be attributed to everything."[62]

But the love of EOC is practical. Loving one's neighbor means:

> ... to put itself in its neighbor's place without being intrusive. When a solution to the problems does not emerge in the short run, love requires to be concerned by sharing the difficulties of the employees, providing support in seeking an alternative solution and in certain cases offering help which goes beyond the company's expected role. This "something more" of unconditional giving in relationships is the secret behind the companies of the EOC.[63]

[58] Ibid.

[59] Crivelli and Gui, 30.

[60] Crivelli.

[61] Crivelli and Gui, 2014, 39.

[62] Crivelli, 6.

[63] Ibid., 6-7.

The original point of the founding of the EOC in Sao Paulo, Brazil in 1991 was to help the poor by creating businesses to gainfully employ the poor. This was to help alleviate financial poverty. But Crivelli highlights another type of poverty:

> On the other hand, there is a second type of poverty, one that is freely chosen and which truly renders a person blessed. This is the poverty which is born from the awareness that all that I am has been given to me; likewise, all that I have must, in turn, be given. This is the foundation of the dynamics of reciprocity.[64]

One is reminded here of the *Vocation of the Business Leader* (derived from *Caritas en Veritate*), which argues that "the first act of the Christian business leader, as of all Christians, is to receive; more specifically, to receive what God has done for him or her."[65] Receiving and accepting the gifts of life as gifts enables us to reciprocally act with gratuitousness. In conclusion, Crivelli provides an excellent summary quote describing the EOC:

> In seeking a new relationship between market and society, the Economy of Communion sees companies as a social good and as a collective resource and it transcends the idea of the market as a place where relationships are only self-serving. In envisioning and living business in this way while remaining fully inserted in the market, the experience of the EOC joins together the market and civil society, efficiency and solidarity, economy and communion. And this is not trivial. If market economy wants to function and to have a future which is sustainable and human, it must allow for the development of behavior founded on these other principles.[66]

---

[64] Ibid., 7.

[65] Pope Benedict XVI, *Caritas in Veritate* (no. 70). http://www.vatican.va/content/benedict-xvi/en/encyclicals/documents/hf_ben-xvi_enc_20090629_caritas-in-veritate.html.

[66] Crivelli, 10.

We may remember that Adam Smith said derisively that "I have never known much good done by those who affected to trade for the public good."[67] Adam Smith never knew the EOC. The EOC demonstrates that it is possible to successfully practice entrepreneurship as a bridge to the common good, and especially communion with the poor.

---

[67] Adam Smith, *An Inquiry into the Nature and Causes of the Wealth of Nations* (London: Methuen & Co. Ltd, 1776, 1904), Book IV, Chap 2, para. IV, 2.9.

PART III

Bridge Theology: Latin American Models of Theological Praxis

Rutilio Grande, SJ: Ignatian Spirituality, and Human Agency: The Bridge to Integral Human Development

THOMAS M. KELLY, PhD

A T THE END OF 16 months of deliberation, after engaging various levels of the Society of Jesus, the following universal apostolic preferences for the years 2019-2029 were offered to Pope Francis by Father Arturo Sosa, SJ:

    A. To show the way to God through the *Spiritual Exercises*
       and discernment
    B. To walk with the poor, the outcasts of the world, those whose
       dignity has been violated, in a mission of reconciliation and justice
    C. To accompany young people in the creation of a hope-filled future
    D. To collaborate in the care of our Common Home.[1]

---

[1] General Curia of the Society of Jesus, *Universal Apostolic Preferences of the Society of Jesus, 2019-2029* (June 2019), accessed at http://image.jesuits.org/UCSPROV/media/Fr_Sosa_Letter_UAP.pdf.

This essay argues for the intrinsic connection of priority A to priority B. It does so by arguing that the *Spiritual Exercises* of Ignatius can be used as a bridge to integral human development framed by Catholic social thought. It begins with the importance of spirituality in general and Ignatian spirituality in particular. Spirituality is then integrated into an understanding of human agency. Next, integral human development is understood using Ignatian spirituality through the pastoral action of Father Rutilio Grande, SJ, a Salvador Jesuit martyred in 1977.[2] Finally, this essay concludes with personal and communal meditations related to integral human development through each week of the *Spiritual Exercises*.

Introduction

Ignatius of Loyola was many things *before* his conversion. In these he was certainly a man of his times. As the youngest son of a family of minor nobility he had much to prove, both to his family and to wider society. The following description gives a sense of the state of his mind as a young adult:

> His fantasies became those of intrigue and gallantry and knightly romance. Of him in his twenties it was written: "He is in the habit of going [a]round in cuirass and coat of mail, wears his hair long to the shoulder, and walks about in a two-colored, slashed doublet with a bright cap." We have evidence he was cited in court for brawling, and he himself confessed that "he was a man given over to the vanities of the world; with a great and vain desire to win fame, he delighted especially in the exercise of arms."[3]

Ignatius lived in the world of the late medieval Spanish court without much reflection or self-awareness prior to his conversion. After a career-ending

[2] For more on Rutilio Grande, SJ, and his life, ministry, and death see: Thomas M. Kelly, *When the Gospel Grows Feet: Rutilio Grande, SJ, and the Church of El Salvador* (Collegeville, MN: Liturgical Press, 2013); *Rutilio Grande, SJ, Homilies and Writings*, edited, translated, and annotated by Thomas M. Kelly (Collegeville, MN: Liturgical Press, 2015).

[3] Ron Hansen, "The Pilgrim: Saint Ignatius of Loyola," in *An Ignatian Spirituality Reader: Contemporary Writings on St. Ignatius of Loyola, the Spiritual Exercises, Discernment and More*, ed. by George Traub, SJ (Chicago, IL: Loyola Press, 2008), 25.

injury at the Battle of Pamplona, however, everything changed. Ignatius became a different person after reflecting upon his life, his God, and the world in which he lived while convalescing from this serious battle injury. In this essay, "spirituality" refers to these three interconnected relationships—self, God, world. Reframing these relationships was the key to Ignatius' transformation—it is also the key to understanding human agency.

Human agency is the capacity for a person or community to understand, act upon and realize one's vision and goals. Human agency requires self-awareness, self-reflection, knowledge, commitment, and action. The people we serve must become protagonists of their own integral human development or else no outside funding, action or program will succeed. When this agency is shared with others, it is called *community agency*. Without this agency, a person cannot develop as an individual, nor can a group of people develop as a community; that is, they cannot become the creators of their own history. Many attempts to aid those in poverty use strategies that undermine the personal and communal agency of the poor. For this reason, they fail. For those who wish to work for integral human development, how does one facilitate both individual and community agency? To better understand this, a primer on "spirituality" is necessary. Spirituality should play a vital role in integral human development. Unfortunately, it is often viewed as an "add-on" or an "extra"—even something to avoid in the *real* work of development. The spirituality of St. Ignatius is essential to encouraging agency through the formation of leaders and communities.

When a human development paradigm begins from a spirituality—and for us this is Ignatian spirituality—it configures and reconfigures these fundamental relationships to "self," "ultimate," and "world"—both individually and communally. It does so according to the criteria of the *Spiritual Exercises*. This is what is at stake in a development paradigm based on Ignatian spirituality. It is much more than embracing a set of "values" or "methods" or "desired outcomes," which are typical of secular approaches to development. It means understanding our communities, our God, and our wider world as Ignatius would.

The question of where to begin with integral human development is important. "Integral" signifies what is necessary for the completeness of the whole. Thus, it is the unifying factor that gives meaning to everything else and holds it in unity. This unifying factor is spirituality. Different understandings of self, God, and world (spirituality) will lead to different understandings of "integral." For our purpose here, we begin with Ignatian spirituality (in the larger context of a Catholic worldview) for the framing of our fundamental orientation.

Ignatian Practice for Development

When we aspire to integral human development as the way to orient ourselves and our organizations, where do we begin? Do we begin with the community? Do we begin with leaders? How do we decide? Who decides leadership in a community? These are important questions because the very identity of the "leader" and a "community," as well as the purpose of development, is at stake.

Shortly after Vatican II, the Catholic bishops of Latin America met in Medellín, Colombia (1968), where they applied the conclusions of Vatican II to their own context. The intuition that grounded their pastoral approach to questions of poverty, suffering, and integral human development was based on the importance of human agency. "Our pastoral mission is essentially a service of encouraging and educating the conscience of believers, to help them to perceive the responsibilities of their faith in their personal life and in their social life."[4] That intuition was to encourage agency by lay leaders in the community to deepen the faith life of all, in collaboration with priests and bishops who support them. The missing element was a way of informing and forming people to respond to their own situation, motivated and sustained by their faith commitments. This forming and informing would then bridge their response to social, political, and economic issues in their context.

A Jesuit who made great strides toward this in his own pastoral work was a Salvadoran priest named Rutilio Grande, SJ. He was a friend of St. Oscar Romero, and his pastoral work was important for demonstrating to Romero that one could work for the Kingdom of God in this world, in a highly politicized environment, without resorting to secular philosophies contradictory to Christianity. As a Jesuit who was spiritually integrated himself, he introduced Ignatian spirituality to the communities he worked within—not as an "extra" or an "add-on," but as intrinsic to the transformation of leaders and the communities they served.

---

[4] Medellín, *Document on Justice*, no. 6.

Grande began his ministry with a social analysis of El Salvador. This was consistent with the Latin American bishops' method for approaching social issues: See-Judge-Act. While this was essential for understanding the problems in that context, Grande believed it would take more than knowledge of the problems or changing "structures" to reverse the injustices in that society.[5] Marxists in his context thought structural change alone would create justice. Grande's vision was much broader:

> We need people convinced of the necessity of modifying the existing structures and who will do so despite the greatest enemy—human selfishness. To change the structures, alone, would only promote a harmful revolution. People with preparation and disinterest have the capacity to change the necessary structures, but this must be a struggle for justice and development as well.[6]

Grande advocated a vision of justice and development that involved spiritual conversion and personal growth.

For Grande (and consistent with Vatican II) the primary work of Jesus of Nazareth was "to restore the Kingdom of God, or better, to re-establish the proper relationship between humanity and God, to re-establish relationships between people, to re-establish God as the final end for the world, to re-establish a sense of History."[7] At Vatican II, the Church put itself in service to the Kingdom of God.[8] The Kingdom of God was opposed to the arrogance and power of the Kingdom of wickedness.[9] Not only did this embrace of the Kingdom of God fight personal sin, it also denounced social sins and the structures that embodied them:

---

[5] "Structures" are systems and institutions in whose name society is managed. They include the structures of education, health care, tax systems, religion, government institutions, etc.

[6] Grande, *Violence and the Social Situation*, ECA, Vol. 262 (1970), 262, 370. Translation mine.

[7] Ibid.

[8] Second Vatican Council, *Lumen Gentium*, 9.

[9] This is a very Ignatian formulation reminiscent of the two standards of Ignatius. See also Jon Sobrino on the "kingdom" vs. the "anti-kingdom" in *Jesus the Liberator: A Historical-Theological View* (Maryknoll, NY: Orbis Press, 1993), ch. 4.

Jesus fought in a practical and devastating way the social structures
of sin, works of legalism and appearances, oppressive structures and
slavery. He said for example that the Sabbath is made for human beings; human beings are not made for the Sabbath.[10]

This effort to confront not only personal sin but social and structural sin as
well was the intention of the term "Christian liberation."[11]

Rutilio Grande's Pastoral Practice

The overarching pastoral goal for Grande was "evangelization," which he
defined as "recreating a Church of living communities of new people with
pastoral agents conscious of their human vocation who become promoters
of their own destiny and who bring change to their reality along the lines of
Vatican II and Medellín."[12]

The method for doing this was the following: it was to be:

Personalizing, dialogical, creative, and critical, based on the pattern of
action-reflection-action, which would theologize their reality starting
from the solidarity of love, faith, and hope in this person, here and
now. To make a person say their "word," be responsible and engage in
the historical process of re-creating new individuals and communities.[13]

Note that the beginning of transformation is a spirituality lived out in community that rereads its own reality with a God who is present and active in
their integral human development.

---

[10] Proaño, 16.

[11] *Personal sin* is the breaking of a good relationship with self, others, and God through
personal actions or attitudes. *Social sins* are sinful realities that everyone participates in but no
one individual is responsible for (e.g., racism). *Structural sin* is when institutions embody and
promote social sin (racist governments that exclude indigenous people from voting, for example).

[12] Thomas M. Kelly, ed., *Rutilio Grande, SJ, Homilies and Writings*, a translation of Rutilio
Grande, "Aguilares: Una Experiencia de Evangelización Rural Parroquial," *Búsqueda, Organ
of the Pastoral Commission of El Salvador* 3, no. 8 (March 1975), (Collegeville, MN: Liturgical
Press, 2015), 42.

[13] Rutilio Grande, SJ, *Homilies and Writings*, 42.

Grande's goals included the "removal of their own mindset and life (fatalistic surrender to poverty and their situation) to welcome and accept outsiders."[14] *Awareness*: to realize the surrounding problem through reflection and structural analysis. *Conscientization*: a constant critical attitude in a dialectical unity of "action-reflection" in service to continuous historical commitment."[15]

Initially, Grande followed the method established by Paulo Freire on conscientization, but then he proceeded quite differently. Freire's method began his entry into the community, but it was Ignatian spirituality that complemented it. The following is how Grande framed both the challenge and the goal of a transformed people:

> Our people live in the center of the coordinates between God and world, time, and history. We can affirm with the language conscious of Paulo Freire that the great majority have an immersed or quasi-immersed consciousness, magical and intransitive of their reality. They cannot distance themselves from it in order to objectify and criticize that reality. This reality dominates and crushes the human being who becomes an object rather than a subject and ruler. This person does not make history, and without being this maker of history, they cannot be liberated. A small number of people have an emerging consciousness or are in transition to one, even if it is naïve. They are leaving their oppressors—king, priest, God—there is a widening of the horizon of perception and awareness that the problems of the world raise, but their consciousness is not easily manipulated, nor does it have the capacity to respond. They will be the subject of their own liberation and begin to make history. It is the man in exodus who is very appropriate to receive the Easter message from the New Man, brother of human beings and Lord of history and the universe. These will be able to build a new, open society in which there is room

---

[14] Parentheses mine. I believe Rutilio is referring to "fatalism" when a person is resigned to reality as it exists with no possibility of changing it.

[15] Ibid., 43. "Concientización," translated as *conscientization*, is a phrase used by Paulo Freire in his seminal work *Pedagogy of the Oppressed* (New York: Continuum, 2006). The significance is captured in the following: "A deepened consciousness of their situation leads people to apprehend that situation as an historical reality susceptible of transformation" (85).

for the Word and for criticism, for dialogue and responsibility, to be
the managers of their own destiny and creators of history.[16]

One can see in this text a move well beyond the secular conscientization
offered by Freire. What is required for community transformation is more
than a new theory of understanding and praxis—though that is very important. What is necessary is a new spirituality. If one analyzes the article
written by Grande describing his two-year mission to the area around Aguilares, El Salvador, the stages of that mission reflect the movement of the four
weeks of the *Spiritual Exercises*. What follows is an effort to understand
those weeks through both individual and communal meditations on integral
human development.

Ignatian Spirituality: Week 1

Week 1 of the exercises has two foci. The first is concerned with who God is;
the second is a recognition of human brokenness in light of our understanding of God. Grande was clear about his own perspectives on the Church and
how God was understood in the Salvadoran context:

> The priest has some knowledge and magical powers with which he
> can manipulate everyone. God is an unpredictable and undependable
> king with whom we must be content. His will is blamed for all that
> exists and happens and is something with which 'we must still comply
> in all things.' To Him they go for certain needs and at certain times,
> like a pharmacy or a benefactor.

Many organizations work for development with a focus on social, economic, and political education and practice. Grande knew it was essential to
change how people understood themselves and their agency *first*. This required self-reflection, self-awareness, and self-knowledge *first*. He did this
by challenging traditional perceptions of who God is and what the Gospel

[16] Rutilio Grande, SJ, *Homilies and Writings*, 65, translated from Rutilio Grande, "Aguilares:
Una Experiencia de Evangelización Rural Parroquial," *Búsqueda, Organ of the Pastoral
Commission of El Salvador* 3, 8 (March 1975), 21-45.

demands. For this reason, he began all development work with what he called the "religious" option:

> Jesus openly rejected political and temporal power as well as any kind of direct leadership. His primary power is of the Word on the conscience and secondarily on what is done; the movements of conscience trigger those options. More than finished doctrines, Jesus brought values that serve for all times and which will be corrosive on all negative values, idols, and absolutizations. Jesus cannot be pigeonholed into specific models or programs or we run the risk of privatizing or ossifying him. He is found in the most notable ideals of all authentic revolutions. He was accused of "being political" and his followers will not be free from this accusation. Jesus was tempted to leave this ambiguity as all true Christians will be tempted. To fall into the temptation to reduce Christianity to a political program would negate the most dangerous and profound message against oppressive powers. The Christian message is more thorough than any political proclamation.

Grande began the initiation of community agency by reading the Bible with the community and emphasizing the historical Jesus in his practice with the poor and vulnerable.[17] He and his pastoral team did not teach this to them; he accompanied them as they read the texts together and interpreted it in light of their own lives. People often exclaimed, "I can't believe the Bible says this!" They had always been taught that their poverty was God's will. When Jesus was better understood in his context, Grande then asked the community whether the lives of those he was evangelizing reflected "God's will" as they read about it in scripture. Because he had researched the realities of the communities he was serving he could say, with conviction, that No, it is not God's will that half their children die before the age of five. It is not God's will that so many people live without food security, adequate housing, or living wages. It is not God's will that poor communities are oppressed by the powerful and suffer from a lack of the rights guaranteed by their own constitution. These things happen, not because of God's will,

---

[17] This specifically refers to Jon Sobrino on the "way of practice" in *Jesus the Liberator: A Historical-Theological View* (Maryknoll, NY: Orbis Press, 1993), ch. 4.

but because broken human beings organize human affairs in selfish ways. We see here in this initial encounter the content of week 1 of the exercises. God wills the good of all. Human beings suffer from sinfulness that is both personal and structural.

Once the people in these communities understood God as loving and committed to their earthly flourishing, the road to community agency began. They were not alone; God accompanied them. Through the process of reading scripture together, leaders emerged naturally from within the community. These leaders were participants who had fully engaged the conversations, were committed to listening to others, and provided some concrete service while they did so. This stage of the community transformation corresponded with the first week of the *Spiritual Exercises* both personally and communally—God is love and we are broken.

Personal Meditation

To begin this journey, I surrender. I am convinced that "God will direct a person's life" and so I freely enter into the first week of the exercises.[18] I recognize that God is absolute and unconditional self-giving love. I then begin a reflection on my sins. I reflect on my disordered desires that move me away from God. They cause me to harm myself and others. This reflection acknowledges both the individual and social dimensions because our identity comprises both. Why does a deep fear of insecurity or a fear of lack of status drive many of my personal decisions? There is a tension within me from living in a consumer society. Such a society defines the ideal person in ways the Gospel never would. Careful not to believe that I can overcome my sinfulness by myself, I ask God for help.

By praying honestly about my forms of sinfulness and disordered desires, I ask for God's graces to remove my defects and give me insight into God's will for me. I contemplate seriously what it would be like to live outside of God's love, and I affirm a desire to proceed more deeply toward God. While the first rules of discernment allow me to discern between good and evil, the second rules allow me to identify "deceptive consolation"

---

[18] Michael J. Buckley, SJ, "The Structure for the Rules of Discernment," in *The Way of Ignatius of Loyola: Contemporary Approaches to the Spiritual Exercises*, ed. by Philip Sheldrake, SJ (St. Louis, MO: The Institute of Jesuit Sources, 1991), 220.

when choosing among "goods."[19] This form of discernment is more nuanced. Temptations that are tailor-made for me are finally understood for what they are. During this first week I see "consolation" and "desolation" as either a movement toward God (through faith, hope, love, joy, etc.) or away from God (through despair, mistrust, apathy, aridity, etc.). How do I experience the people in my life, my relationships, my work? What is God inviting me to do through these experiences?

Communal Meditation

As a community, we recognize the Kingdom of God as a gift. It is our goal and hope—and yet we often fail to care for one another justly. Jesus mentioned the Kingdom many times in the Gospels, and the Church commits itself to the service of the same. We reflect first on the gifts God has given our community. What are we grateful for, and how can we put the gifts we have received at the service of all?

We then reflect on our deficiencies *as a community* considering who God calls us to be. Why is there suffering here, and what suffering is preventable? How is power exercised in our community, especially by its leaders? How do we relate (horizontally) with each other, and how is this inconsistent with our faith? Why do some lack food? Why do some lack health care? We live within systems and structures we are not responsible for, but they affect us every day. We know that God wants us to be members and citizens of the Kingdom of God, a collective reality where God's will and human will come together to humanize everyone. What disordered desires do we have as a community? How can we better use our collective resources as well as the gifts and talents of our leaders? How can we better advocate for ourselves as a community? Having received (we hope) the grace of understanding ourselves as "sinners loved by God," we are invited to the second week.

Spiritual Exercises: Week 2

Reflecting on the Word of God is central to all Christians. Ignatius encouraged a unique form of entering scripture through one's imagination. The person or community engaging in the *Exercises* is encouraged to put themselves

---

[19] Buckley, "The Structure for the Rules of Discernment," 226-227.

into a scene, parable, or section of the Bible where Jesus is present and to pray with it. For example, Ignatius encourages reflection upon the nativity scene and the extreme poverty into which Jesus was born. We are to place ourselves there in that cold barn with the animals and watch this poor woman give birth. "I will make myself a poor little unworthy slave, and as though present, look upon them, contemplate them, and serve them in their needs with all possible homage and reverence."[20] In this prayer we imagine ourselves with Jesus and we allow our imagination to ruminate over the scene, where we are in it, and what we feel, noting what brings consolation and desolation. Ignatius also encouraged imaginative reflections on the presentation in the Temple, the flight into exile in Egypt, and many more meditations on the life of Jesus up to his passion and death.

As we imagine these biblical scenes from the life and ministry of Jesus, we do so with an eye to the social/communal aspect of our lives as the context that both forms and informs our perspectives on reality. This comes naturally to many Latin American communities. When we focus on the Jesus of the Gospels we leave behind the abstract Christ of doctrine and emphasize the "practice of Jesus" as we read and indicate what is most important and why. All good doctrine will be consistent with the actions of Jesus. The people themselves build their interpretation, with only occasional guidance from those "evangelizing." This allows their "voice," their "word" to emerge.

Personal Meditation

In the second week I follow Jesus through his ministry in imaginative prayer. I "watch what he is doing," "listen to what he is proclaiming," and consider what this means for me.[21] Once I see and understand the "standard" to which I am drawn, I desire to commit myself to Christ and his Way through "spiritual poverty certainly—but even actual poverty," if that is where I am called. I begin to see the ministry of Jesus and the humiliations he experienced in his temptations, his rejection, the misunderstandings about him, as well as his embodied message of compassion, love, and service. I try to deepen my own humility, through honest and continual self-appraisal, to better

[20] Ignatius of Loyola, *The Spiritual Exercises of St. Ignatius Loyola Based on Studies in the Language of the Autograph*, ed. by Luis Puhl, SJ (Chicago: Loyola University Press, 1951), 52.
[21] "Meditation on the Call of the King," 134.

serve Him. I understand this humility fundamentally as self-honesty—I am not God and I need God. How committed am I to being a disciple and what am I willing to do? I reflect on discipleship and what it means. What had been a personal disposition now has a social dimension as I am required to move toward others as Jesus did, suffer what Jesus did, spread the hope and love that Jesus did. In doing so, my view of the world and all the people in it takes on the perspective of God's view. As a loved sinner trying to imitate the Jesus I serve, I commit myself to this standard.

Communal Meditation

As a community we read scripture together and ask what some of the parables would look like if we imagined them in our context. What would Jesus say to us if he walked through our community right now? We ask what it means to be a leader in the eyes of Jesus. Perhaps we focus on the story about James and John when they compete to see who is greatest?[22] Jesus teaches them that servant leadership is a different way of understanding power and always comes "from below." We think about what that means in our context. How do we want power to be exercised in our community? This will inspire and frame how leaders in our community understand power.

Perhaps we read the parable of the Good Samaritan together. Who is the priest and who is the Levite in our context? Who leaves people on the side of the road but is perceived as the "most religious"? Who is the Good Samaritan who stops and helps but who doesn't always think about God correctly? Who is the injured person on the side of the road? Who is the innkeeper who receives and cares for the injured person rescued from the side of the road? We read and reflect on the story of the Rich Man and Lazarus. In our society, who is the Rich Man? Who is Lazarus? Why should we share goods with the poor at our gates? When we "read" our community through the eyes of Scripture and learn about the Kingdom as taught by the Church, we have entered the second week. We focus on many passages in the Christian scriptures that remind us of Jesus' practice as well as our social obligations to each other, especially the poor.

[22] Mk. 10: 35-45; Mt. 20: 24-28.

Spiritual Exercises: Week 3

Week 3 of the exercises focuses on the consequences of Jesus' love and the persecution he suffered for that love. We imagine ourselves in the scenes from Jesus' travels to Jerusalem, from the Last Supper to the Garden of Gethsemane and on through His passion and death. We use this week as a reminder that there will be resistance to integral human development both inside and outside our community—that this is to be expected and it is normal. When the poor and marginalized exercise agency, other parts of society can feel threatened, even if that agency is nonviolent. We prepare ourselves for that resistance, understand that it comes from fear, and commit to supporting each other through that suffering. All of our vocations pass through our own "Jerusalem." What consequences do my choices have? How do I enter into and experience suffering in my own context?

Personal Meditation

In the third week, I witness Jesus paying the price for the love he demonstrated. He does not desire to suffer, but he is willing to suffer so that we might know absolute and unconditional love. Like a person willing to take on a burden for another whom they love deeply, Jesus entered freely into the misunderstanding, fear, and greed that ultimately led to his death. His message was peaceful and inclusive; the response to this message was not. As fully human, he experienced fear, suffering, and death—but he did so with hope. He held to the conviction that death would not be his final reality.

His divinity, understood as his capacity to love absolutely and unconditionally (perfectly), became evident in and through his humanity—especially in his actions of compassion toward others.[23] I am called to imitate these actions. I consider what this means to me. Jesus does not need me to suffer for him. By following Jesus, I choose to suffer for others the way he suffered for me. I do this out of gratitude, not from guilt or from a desire to suffer—both of which are selfish. Can I freely enter relationships where I

---

[23] This is important. Christology requires categories that do not frame the humanity and divinity of Jesus as a dualistic contradiction. This theological anthropology must be relatable; understandable; and, more importantly, possible to imitate (always imperfectly).

am misunderstood, persecuted, hated, and even rejected? How can I deepen
my discipleship to Jesus? I pray for the grace to do this. When I embrace
the vulnerability and weakness of what it means to love unconditionally, I
experience a glimpse of who Jesus is and what he did and it gives me joy
that someone loves me so perfectly.[24] At the same time, I see and experience
his death, not only his death on the Cross, but his death in all the crucified
peoples who, throughout history, have been oppressed and killed at the
hands of the powerful:

> We do not desire any more pain in the world. We simply want, and
> need, to share the pain that is there, in order to lighten the load for all
> of us. We want to be more and more a part of humanity's march, with
> its suffering, its hope, and its joy. For unless we share the suffering of
> the world, its beauty and grace cannot heal us, and solidarity cannot
> fill our void.[25]

In contemplating the passion and death of Jesus, I also contemplate the love
he had for those who betrayed him. That utter vulnerability bespeaks an
absolute love that suffers with humanity, first in Jesus, and later through
His continual presence with us in the Holy Spirit. God does not will our
suffering. God accompanies the world in the suffering it experiences. Jesus
embodies that presence of God absolutely. We are never alone.

Communal Meditation

Who is crucified in our community, and what role does our community
have in that crucifixion? Why are they crucified? How do uses and abuses of
power contribute to suffering in our community? What is our role in allowing, accepting, or even assisting in that suffering? What can we do as a community to take our crucified neighbors down from their crosses? What can
the community itself do for the community? Injustice permeates all human
societies; the question is, Do we see Jesus crucified today in our context?

[24] Joseph Tetlow, SJ, *Choosing Christ in the World*, "Going Through Jesus' Passion and Death."

[25] Brackley, p. 178.

In contemplating these realities of suffering in our context, how can we be moved, *as a living community*, to respond? Are we willing as a community to embrace suffering to love others? If so, what form might that take?

Spiritual Exercises: Week 4

The fourth week of the *Spiritual Exercises* asks us to contemplate and celebrate the victory of Jesus' resurrection over his death. Love triumphs over death. In the context of Grande's ministry in El Salvador, this took the concrete form of responses to suffering and oppression in the communities he served. These responses were transforming the oppression of the poor through actions of faith, hope, and love lived out in solidarity. This included the establishment of agricultural cooperatives, the continuing education of leaders in the community through the University of Central America (UCA), teaching leaders social analysis and how to be critical of their own context, the emergence of pastoral workers in communities that were dedicated to serving others, and teaching people literacy. All of these actions improved the quality of life and celebrated the hope of community agency through transforming a situation from suffering and death toward solidarity and life. These are values we associate with the Kingdom of God.

Personal Meditation

There is a great difference between optimism and hope. Optimism looks at external indicators and says, "that looks good," "that is strong," "that is positive," and because of these one is certain things will continue in a favorable manner. Conversely, hope is a gift of the Spirit. It springs from within when no external indicators suggest anything good is even remotely possible. What is confirmed in the fourth week of the exercises is hope. It is a hope that good will triumph over evil—even in the face of nuclear arsenals, global climate change, and the forced migration of millions of people.

Something interesting happens repeatedly throughout the Gospels. Jesus affirms that people who were considered outside of God's favor in his time were loved by God absolutely. Usually these people and their conditions were perceived as symbols of "evil" (in that historical context). Jesus transforms them. Perhaps it was a woman who had bled for a long time, a blind person, or a leper—all conditions thought to be a punishment from God, and thus representative of the power of evil. When something "miraculous" occurred to transform these people, Jesus often said "your faith has healed you." I have often wondered what this means. What could "faith" mean when no doctrines had been written, no dogmas established, and no creeds articulated? I believe it meant that the *hope* within those people that God loves them was stronger than what their religious tradition taught them. They did not believe God was punishing them; they believed God loved them. They consented to being loved. They surrendered to this love. This was the key to their healing. Jesus confirms this when they respond in hope to his actions.

Personal Meditation

During this fourth week, I contemplate the resurrection scenes of the Gospels. I imagine a group of close friends shattered by betrayal and denial. How must they have felt when they heard (after the fact) that Jesus had forgiven them from the Cross? How could anyone forgive those who had abandoned him during his own misery and suffering? Suddenly, something extraordinary happens and the lives of these people are changed forever. They move from being those guilty of betraying and denying to those who proclaim and praise! Whatever happened (they called it "resurrection") completely transformed the dejected group hiding in the upper room immediately after the crucifixion.[26] Was Jesus the *literal* sacrificial lamb for the Apostles? Did they live because he died? Only when they realized his continued love for them could they proclaim this as universally true—not just for them—but for the entire world.

While contemplating this love and the victory of Jesus over death, I come to two realizations with Ignatius. First, "love ought to be expressed more by deeds than words." Words are easy and often treated as if they matter more than actions. How do we express love? How do we experience

---

[26] "Hiding," by the way, is doubtful. The Old City of Jerusalem is small enough to throw a rock across—everyone would have known where the "Jesus group" had held their Passover meal. This is the argument of Shusaku Endo in Chapter 13 of *A Life of Jesus*. Admittedly, this is an explanation based on biblical scholarship that makes sense to me, even though it is not the traditional narrative.

love? Reflection on this gives us insight into how Ignatius understands love. Second, "love consists in a mutual sharing of goods; that is, the lover gives and shares with the beloved what he or she has, or out of what she or he has or can do, and vice versa. . ."[27] Because of my gratitude for the love given in Jesus' life, ministry, and death I can now say with Ignatius that I must live out my love for others through concrete actions.

Communal Meditation

Where do we experience hope and resurrection in our communities? Where are the victories that improve life, uphold justice, and care for the vulnerable? How can power exercised as service to others, as servant-leadership, take care of each of us in our community? How do we sacrifice for each other? How do we hope as a community? What do we aspire to? Sometimes asking these evocative questions is enough to encourage community agency toward our shared goals. Love is not an idea; it is an action, a way of embodying our ideals in the real. We do not "fall in love" or "out of love"; we either freely choose it or we do not. How does our community do this well? How should we celebrate and encourage this more?

Conclusion

> In the years following GC 32, justice was understood mainly in terms of working for the transformation of economic, political, and social structures. Such work was certainly encouraged by Decree 4 (no. 31), but that was not the only recommendation of the decree. *The document also pointed out that injustice was embedded in the human heart so that it was necessary to work as well for the transformation of attitudes and social tendencies* (no. 31).[28]

Spirituality must be intrinsic to integral human development if challenging "attitudes and social tendencies" is necessary for a better world. A healthy Ignatian spirituality lived out authentically can transform power into ser-

[27] Brackley, 212.

[28] Society of Jesus, Social Justice and Ecology Secretariat, "Special Issue: The Promotion of Justice in the Universities of the Society," in *Promotio Iustitiae*, 116 2014/3, 10. Emphasis mine.

vant leadership. Working for justice through integral human development requires a program of spiritual formation both for those accompanying the poor and for the poor themselves. Supported by a spirituality convinced that God wills both their agency and their human flourishing and accompanied by organizations committed to the global common good, the poor and marginalized can activate their own agency and transform their world both individually and communally. Those working for integral human development must trust the human agency intrinsic to the human condition, allow it to blossom, and help guide its actualization through a spirituality that liberates. Only then can we say with Rutilio Grande, SJ, that we don't walk in front of or behind those we serve, but next to them. We accompany.

CHAPTER TEN

Each Saint Is a Mission— and a Bridge[1]

Damian Zynda, ThD

In *Gaudete et Exultate* Pope Francis encourages us, given the current world and church order, to take seriously the vocation to holiness. In writing this exhortation, Francis cites Vatican II's *Lumen Gentium*, "The Universal Call to Holiness"[2]— a holiness for all people. The holiness Francis advocates is personal and transformational, mutual and communal. It is rooted in an enduring mutual relationship with Christ, one's neighbor, and self. And because relationships make claims upon us Francis urges the practice of the ancient discipline of discernment to guide growth in holiness. Lacking the superficial trappings of exaggerated religiosity, piety, and sentimentality, this holiness is real and exacting; the Gospel demands it be lived out in a world deeply scarred by the evils of isolation, narcissism, greed, consumption, and entitlement. In essence it is a holiness that bridges God with humanity and humanity with God.

Formed by and equipped with the wisdom of the *Spiritual Exercises of St. Ignatius*, Pope Francis is both a mission and a man on a mission to build bridges; one who mediates to bridge humanity with God and God with humanity, humanity with humanity, and humanity with creation.[3] More specifically, his mission is to expose deceits and sin (personal and social),

---

[2] http://www.vatican.va/archive/hist_councils/ii_vatican_council/documents/vatii_const_19641121_lumen-gentium_en.html.

[3] The word **pontifex** has its origins in Latin *pont, pons*, bridge, and *facrer*, to make.

to call to conversion, to work toward humanizing the world, to be with others in their suffering, and to rejoice in the creation of a new world order based on mutual respect, economic and social justice, and reconciliation. Bridge theology lays a foundation for a Bridge spirituality—a way of life that is dependent on the complex web of interrelationships between God, humans, and the rest of the world; a way of life that bridges reason and affect, psychology, and spirituality, church and society; a way of life that bridges pastor and people, between the poor and the authorities that should protect them; a way of life that bridges the Catholic intellectual tradition with praxis that is interiorly transformative and leads to social change; a way of life that features at its core vulnerability and humility.

How, then, does one become holy—a saint—as Pope Francis invites us to become? In this context, what is the saint's mission in the world today? Keeping in mind that the making of saints in the Catholic Church is always political, Pope Francis clearly communicated to the world a new paradigm when he raised Oscar Arnulfo Romero, whose canonization was long stalled under the pontificates of John Paul II and Benedict XVI, to the high altars on October 14, 2018. Since becoming a saint is best understood through biography, this chapter demonstrates bridge theology and spirituality in the life and conversion of Oscar Romero, who, in saying "yes" to whatever God asked of him, became a saint who was a mission.

Oscar Romero: A Man Toward Himself

Saint Oscar Romero was transformed from a theologically traditional, autocratic, rigid, domineering, fearful man to a theologically moderate, collegial, empowered prophet who by the time of his assassination in 1980 was a controversial figure, regarded by the international community as a prominent advocate for human rights. His courageous defense of the rights of indigenous Salvadorans won him a nomination for the Nobel Peace Prize from members of the British Parliament and the United States Congress. Following his death, Romero's vicar general, Ricardo Urioste, captured Romero best: "You must understand, Archbishop Romero was the most loved person in the country. And the most hated."[4]

---

[4] Kenneth Woodward, *Making Saints: How the Catholic Church Determines Who Becomes a*

Born in poverty on August 15, 1917, in the small village of Cuidad Barrios, Oscar, a shy, anxious, bright introvert, left home and entered priestly formation in 1933 at the age of 13 (a norm for the time). As a minor seminarian (high school seminary) he established a reputation as an above-average student who was prayerful, responsible, and virtuous, and who had a penchant for serving the poor.

Graduating in 1937, he was sent to study in the major seminary in El Salvador staffed by the Jesuits. His academic performance, distinction as a model seminarian, and loyalty to the magisterium led Bishop Dueñas of the Diocese of San Miguel to send Romero to study at the Jesuit Seminary at Gregorian University in Rome. Sending a man to study in Rome meant he was being prepared to teach in seminary or he was being prepared for a career of ecclesial administration. While Romero demonstrated aptitude and potential in both arenas, it sent a message that he was being groomed for a mission beyond pastoring a parish in the Archdiocese of San Salvador.

In 1941 Romero graduated *cum laude* with a licentiate in theology; he was ordained and began doctoral studies in ascetical theology. His dissertation research focused on the 16th-century Jesuit Luis de la Puente,[5] a priest whom it seems Romero may have patterned his priesthood after. Unfortunately, due to the privations, threats, and risks of the Second World War, Romero was called back home; his academic dream, dissertation, and degree were never realized.

In El Salvador, Romero was assigned as secretary to the bishop of San Miguel, Monseñor Miguel Angel Machalo, who was narcissistic, irresponsible, and frequently absent. Over time he delegated the direction, organization, and governance of the diocese to Romero. It was the perfect storm for the newly ordained Romero, who administratively capitalized his organizational strengths to turn a diocese around that had become lax, corrupt, and pastorally negligent. He governed with firm authority fueled by ambition and fear of failure. Even as the bishop's secretary, Romero was pastor of the cathedral parish (and completed construction on the church), and chap-

---

Saint, Who Doesn't and Why (New York: Simon & Schuster, 1996), 40.

[5] Luis de la Puente, SJ (1554-1624) was a Spanish nobleman admitted to the Jesuit Novitiate in 1574. Throughout his Jesuit life he served in key positions within the Society as rector of Jesuit Colleges, as novice master and prefect of studies, and as spiritual director to countless Jesuits. He is known for possessing an extraordinary love of God, hard work, and performing extraordinary penances.

lain of the Church of San Francisco (a small colonial parish). At both sites he organized and facilitated catechetical classes, the Legion of Mary and Knights of Columbus, Alcoholics Anonymous, Cursillos de Christianidad, the Apostleship of Prayer, the Guardians of the Blessed Sacrament, the Rosary Association, the Third Order of Franciscans, and the diocesan branch of Caritas (an association that provides food for the poor). He was the editor of *Chaparrastique*, the diocesan newspaper, rector of the seminary, and spiritual director to countless priests, and consecrated both religious men and women and lay people. Despite this active and demanding ministry, Romero tried to maintain the same spiritual practices he had learned in the seminary: an hour of meditation upon awakening; the Liturgy of the Hours; daily mass; fasting on Wednesdays and Fridays; taking the discipline on Fridays; weekly confession; and his own monthly spiritual direction. As if this were not enough, each evening he presided at a Holy Hour in the presence of the Blessed Sacrament, which included a homily and rosary.

We get the picture: Romero *dominated* the diocese and himself until his ouster in 1966. He followed the prescriptions of prayer, yet the fruit of his prayer did not demonstrate a personal relationship with God, nor yield a genuine compassion for others, or create community, or give evidence of conversion of his attitudes and behaviors. As an ecclesial administrator, Romero achieved esteem in the eyes of his superiors in Rome. He was advanced because he had an impermeable loyalty and obedience to the magisterium. Romero ascribed to clericalism (the culture of the day), which breeds a sense of entitlement, superiority, privilege, and exclusion, and creates a notion of the Church as autonomous and self-sufficient, an empire unto itself. Clericalism is predicated upon a notion of priesthood that claims an ontological change at ordination, setting the priest apart from the rest of the baptized.[6] Enter the *grace of conversion* through a threshold Romero never predicted—his humanity.

After his painful departure from San Miguel, Romero made a life-altering retreat at the Franciscan Retreat House, Planes de Randeros in Mexico. While there, he visited his Opus Dei spiritual director, Father Juan Izquierdo, and a psychiatrist, Dr. Dárdano, with whom Romero had an established

---

[6] See George Wilson, SJ, *Clericalism, The Death of Priesthood* (Collegeville, MN: Liturgical Press, 2008).

relationship.[7] This was a seminal retreat for Romero for several reasons. First, at 48 years of age, on the threshold of midlife, he was experiencing repressed issues of sexuality, feelings of a lack of intimacy, and painful loneliness. Second, Vatican II called the Church to renewal and reframed the identity and vocation of priesthood, dismantling the trappings of clericalism. This was a deeply threatening prospect for Romero, whose whole identity as priest was secure in his isolated, clerical role as a traditional Tridentine priest. Third, after 25 years of active priesthood, Romero felt physically and mentally exhausted, depleted by the demands of his responsibilities and the challenges of administration. Fourth, he acknowledged his rigidity and demanding attitude, which provoked animosity in the priests, together with his frustration regarding his inability to dominate his temperament. Romero presented these troubling traits, along with an intensification of fear, anxiety, conflict with others, agitation, obsession with perfection, depression, and a lack of flexibility, to these two men. Father Izquierdo told him he was scrupulous. Dr. Dárdano diagnosed him as an obsessive-compulsive perfectionist (today the *Diagnostic and Statistical Manual V*[8] categorizes this presenting cluster of issues under Obsessive Compulsive Personality Disorder, hereafter referred to as OCPD).

Clinical researchers generally describe scrupulosity as an anxiety disorder provoked primarily by fear and intolerance of uncertainty. For religious persons, boundaries between normal religious behavior and obsessive-compulsive symptoms are blurred. People who suffer from scrupulosity focus on seeing sin where there is none. They dramatically overreact to falling short of the impossibly high standards they set for themselves, focus on minor details of religion to the exclusion of the major areas, and take religious behavior to the extreme. Sufferers are tortured by the intensity of their doubts about their goodness and they believe, therefore, that they are simply bad. In most instances they internalize that they are not loveable or capable of being loved.

In response to these disturbing thoughts, victims of scrupulosity try to calm themselves by using a host of compulsions. Their discomfort makes it

---

[7] As rector of the seminary, Romero would have referred seminarians for assessment or mental health care to Dr. Dárdano.

[8] American Psychiatric Association. *Diagnostic and Statistical Manual of Mental Disorders,* Fifth Edition (Washington, DC: American Psychiatric Association, 2013).

difficult to dismiss their thoughts, which become sticky and hard to chase away. The persistence of these thoughts, and the frequency and anxious intensity with which they return, turn those irrational thoughts into obsessions. Victims feel they must get rid of the obsession at any cost, and the result is a compulsion.

The 1966 diagnosis provided Romero with an explanation for his behaviors and equipped him with a language with which he could *begin* to understand the complexity of the features of OCPD particular to him. While an intellectual comprehension of the disorder was a critical step, Romero had yet to do any therapeutic work that would help him integrate knowledge with experience. That work was on his horizon.

Romero was appointed secretary general for the Salvadoran National Bishops' Conference, then the executive secretary to the Central American Bishops' Secretariat. In 1970 Archbishop Chávez y González petitioned Rome, and on April 21, 1970, Romero received a phone call from the Apostolic Nuncio notifying him of Pope Paul VI's desire that Romero be consecrated bishop. Romero, unquestioning of the authority of the Holy See, obediently accepted, and in preparation for his consecration as bishop, he made a retreat. While on this retreat, he wrote in his spiritual journal, "I desire to distinguish myself for this: to be a bishop with the heart of Jesus."[9] As bishop, Romero intuited he would lead as Jesus led. God was just calling forth this type of leadership, which was new even to Romero, and over time God would clarify and empower.

Times of transition are times of fragility; they evoke precarity, a threat of being harmed. Grief over personal loss gets tangled in the web of anxiety over the uncertainty of the future and one's place in that future. Romero was in the thick of transition. Vatican II retrieved the theology (mystical and doctrinal), low Christology (Christ present in the people and reality), and ecclesiology (Church as the People of God) that characterized the early

---

[9] *Spiritual Notebook I*, as cited in Delgado, *Oscar A. Romero: Biografía*, June 8, 1970. Romero's Spiritual Notebooks (Journals) I, II, and III are journals of his retreats. Special Collections, John T. Richardson Library, De Paul University, Chicago, IL.

Christian era. This challenged his scholastic theology,[10] high Christology,[11] and notion of Church as Institution.[12] While Romero respected the governing authority of the Council, he resisted its implementation in Latin America.[13]

For Romero, prayer and life were still separated. So were Church and state. *Gaudium et Spes* (the Pastoral Constitution on Church in the Modern World) posed a very real threat to him because it brought forward Catholic social teaching and emphasized the dignity of the human person, a shared community of humanity, economic development, and fostering peace and avoidance of war. His identity as priest was shaken to its foundation. *Presbyterorum Ordinis* (the *Decree on the Ministry and Life of Priests*) stressed the priest's identity as one of the baptized, and his role in serving Christ's Mystical Body. This shattered clericalism and a way of life Romero had found refuge in.

Romero moved from San Miguel to San Salvador, the center of civil and political tension and violence. He shifted from pastor to administrator whose every decision would be scrutinized in the public eye, a definite threat for someone who feared criticism. Theologically and pastorally he differed with Archbishop Chávez, who wholeheartedly supported implementation of Medellín;[14] this put an additional strain on his relationship with Chávez. Romero, by virtue of his new office, was thrust into the political and ecclesial

[10] Scholastic theology is a method and system of rational speculation applied to theology for the purpose of analyzing, illustrating, and showing forth the beauty and the suitability of the mysteries of the Christian Faith. This method of applying to the contents of Revelation the logical forms of rational discussion was called "the dialectic method of theology." Dialectic denotes primarily the art of inference or argument.

[11] High Christology is the study of Jesus Christ, by looking at him as, first, the divine son of God, and then moving downward to the view of him as a human.

[12] As institution, the Church is defined primarily in terms of its visible structure, especially the rights and powers of its hierarchy. In this model there is no representation or democracy but a hierarchical structure.

[13] Immediately after Romero's consecration (June 21, 1970), a Pastoral Week was held in San Salvador to discuss implementation of the General Conference of Latin American Bishops, which was held in Medellín, Colombia, in September 1968. The Medellín Conference gave new vitality to the need for justice and meeting the civil and human needs of the poor under siege in Latin American countries.

[14] The General Conference of Latin American Bishops (CELAM) was held in Medellín, Colombia, in 1968 to further the agenda of the first CELAM meeting in Rio de Janeiro in 1955 and to discuss various applications of Vatican II to the Latin American Church. The Medellín Conference gave a new vitality to responding to the need for justice and the spiritual needs of the poor in Latin America.

spotlight, a definite hazard to this introverted academic. He was placed in a position he neither desired nor was prepared to undertake. To compound all of this, Romero still had not bridged his knowledge of his OCPD with his lived experience. Trying to hold all of these factors in tension proved too much for him, and once again he found himself in Cuernavaca, Mexico, where he underwent three months of psychoanalysis.[15]

Romero was on the threshold from controlling his external world to exploring his inner psychological and spiritual world. He crossed the bridge. While on retreat following the psychoanalysis, Romero came to three key insights that shed light on his personality and how his personality was influenced by his family of origin. First, he acknowledged his immaturity when he vowed celibacy and his lack of an integrated understanding of chastity. Formed by Augustine's Manicheism, the unhealthy dualism of matter and spirit, Romero was taught that intense human desires (matter = sin) are not of God (spirit = grace) and therefore must be dominated. Atonement soteriology justified this brand of holiness.[16] Second, he recognized his psychological wounding as a child reared in a household with a domineering father. His unconscious transference of the adult-child relationship onto other adults led to fears of intimacy, disallowing healthy friendships. He realized his seminary formation and clericalism reinforced the parent-child dynamic. Third, Romero recognized how fear unconsciously dominated his life. Fear of failure provoked unimaginable shame, which led him to interpret any failure as *I am a failure*. There was fear of self-criticism and extrinsic authority that reinforced his disvalue. There was fear of not *being* enough: the temptation to reduce or, worse, dismiss the Incarnation and the inherent dignity of the human being. These fears lead to the dehumanization of workaholism and perpetuates perfectionism. Fear, he noted, generated his rigidity, immaturity, stubbornness, irrational attitudes and behaviors, harshness, and demanding attitudes.

---

[15] November 1971 to February 1972.

[16] Demonstrated best by the spirituality of Pope John Paul II, who effected the spiritual formation of seminarians and consecrated religious congregations founded by him in the past three decades, Atonement Soteriology, based upon 2 Cor 5:21, is the belief that the more one shares in the passion of Christ, the more one is saved. This soteriology has been used to justify unbalanced physical mortification, which masquerades self-hatred (anorexia); the distrust of human sexuality, which can lead to sexual deviancy and/or addiction to pornography, and prohibits pastoral collaboration; and a distorted view of God as One who designed and desires human suffering as a prerequisite to relationship with God.

Romero made significant progress in those three months. He acknowledged how the psychoanalytic treatment supplemented his understanding of theology, ethics, and spirituality. Psychoanalysis clarified a cause for his condition, gave definition to his personality disorder and its consequences, and challenged his ecclesially defined self-concept. It also provided a new context with which to understand a complex personality, inviting him to accept his humanity as a gift. He noted the dimensions of his personality and his soul, which, though distinct, intersected and affected each other. Certainly, the grace of conversion mediated through his own humanity, the shifting landscape of the Church, the heightened political tensions in El Salvador, and a call to ecclesial leadership shifted Romero from living in fear-based precarity to hope-filled vulnerability.

The Grace of Vulnerability

Conversion radically changes a person. In Romero's case, a lifetime governed by fear, control, and dominance—self-dominance, ecclesial dominance, and political dominance—had created a person of vulnerability. As will soon be evident, Romero's vulnerability empowered him to be himself with God, and a profound intimacy grew between them. Vulnerability facilitated a clarity to see the truth about his ecclesial and civil structures, as well as an unrelenting tenacity for human rights and justice. Vulnerability blew Romero's inner life open; it was also a catalyst in transforming his anthropology (the question of being human), his teleology (the purpose of being human), and his ethics (the question of how to live as human beings). It is this vital, constant grace of vulnerability that distinguishes holiness in a bridge-building theology.

Vulnerability, as I use it here, is capacious.[17] For the Christian, it involves intentionally choosing to cooperate with grace in our human condition to grow into our God-given capacity to mature into the likeness of the Son of God. In essence it involves taking responsibility for growing into the

---

[17] Here I draw on James Keenan, SJ, "Vulnerable to Radical Hospitality," an address given at Fairfield University, Fairfield, Connecticut, on October 3, 2019. Capaciousness: the ability to grow. This usage suggests the ability to grow psychologically and spiritually by being aware of and relinquishing one's biases and allowing oneself to be affected by the lives of others who struggle. See also James Keenan, SJ, "Vulnerability and Hierarchicalism," in *Melita Theologica, Journal of the Faculty of Theology, University of Malta* 68/2 (2018), 129-142.

fullness of our humanity *and* our divinity. The Trinity models vulnerability. Each is poised one *toward the other* in mutual love: a love that seeks to relate to the other, and desires to know the other and experience the other's life. It is a love that disposes each to accept and respect the other; a love that is supportive, communal, and embracing; a love that is vigilant, attentive, discerning, and responsible for the other. God chose to be vulnerable in the Incarnation. Jesus elected to be vulnerable to God and the claims God made on him. Romero followed suit and elected to conform himself more completely to Jesus.

Romero took discipleship seriously and followed with integrity and without compromise. Psychoanalysis and a deepening intimacy with Christ expanded his understanding of the human condition and the work of grace in creation. Electing to be "a bishop with the heart of Jesus," Romero declared his intention to align himself more completely with Jesus, his values and mission. Little by little Romero confronted and renounced clericalism and ecclesial colonialism, and the Salvadoran oligarchy and dictatorial government they bankrolled. Slowly he extracted himself from ideologies and systems contrary to the Gospel, Catholic social teaching, Vatican II, and Medellín. In choosing vulnerability, our saint became the mission—and a bridge. What happened in him can happen in us!

Archbishop Oscar Romero: A Bridge Toward Others

Romero's spirituality was Ignatian to the core. Other than the minor seminary (staffed by the Salesian Fathers), his theological and spiritual formation took place with the Jesuits. In 1954-55 he made the *Spiritual Exercises* of St. Ignatius—a 30-day retreat, and his retreat journals[18] are replete with references to the *Exercises.* He had several Jesuit spiritual directors and confessors throughout his life who guided, challenged, and supported him. He even chose, from the *Spiritual Exercises*, his episcopal motto, *Sentir con la Iglasia* ("to be of one mind in thinking with the Church").[19]

---

[18] Special Collections, John T. Richardson Library, De Paul University, Chicago, IL.

[19] David L. Fleming, SJ, *Draw Me Into Your Friendship: The Spiritual Exercises–A Literal Translation and a Contemporary Reading* (St. Louis, MO: The Institute of Jesuit Sources, 1966), 352-370.

The *Exercises* prescribe a cumulative and progressive process that facilitates an encounter with the grace of conversion. This influenced Romero's prayer and, by association, his psychological healing. Meditation challenged him to reflect on the particular manifestations of grace and sin experienced in the unique circumstances of his life, as he articulated following his psychoanalysis. Ignatian contemplation, using active imagination to place oneself in direct proximity to Jesus in a Gospel scene, predisposed him to personal encounters with the Word and invited him to make a choice to love and to follow Jesus more closely with added self-generosity. Discernment challenged him to grow beyond his narrow, seminary-taught conceptions of God and helped him develop a mind and heart more open to the Mystery of God present in the midst of life.

Heading into his years of ecclesial leadership, the *Exercises* provided a different framework for Romero's purpose of prayer. Whereas previously he prayed to know the will of God and the grace to do it, his prayer became mutual and relational—contemplative, mystical in fact.[20] On the first day of a retreat prior to his episcopal ordination in June 1970, Romero wrote, "After several hectic days of work and fatigue, I feel the gentleness and intimacy of Jesus. How I would like to grow in this important, intimate relationship."[21]

Continuing to reflect on Romero's desire to "be a bishop with the heart of Jesus," we witness the fruits of his therapeutic and spiritual work.[22] This kind of leader is well-practiced in self-transcendence and magnanimity, and is disposed *toward others*. Cognizant of being healed and freed from the constraints of his OCPD and clericalism and empowered by the grace of his own conversion and the grace of his office, Romero's ultimate purpose shifted. His purpose was no longer to serve the Church; rather it was to serve God *in* the Church. This was radically different. So too was his disposition; vulnerability replaced domination.

---

[20] I use mystical in the Ignatian sense of the Fourth Week of the *Spiritual Exercises* where one prays the "Contemplation to Gain Love." In this exercise, one prays to receive the grace to see as God sees, to hear as God hears, to respond as God respond as God responds, to love as God loves. There is no doubt Romero received that grace, given the changes in his life.

[21] James Brockman, "The Spiritual Journey of Oscar Romero," *Spirituality Today* 42 (1990), 313.

[22] Romero's *Spiritual Journal I*, Retreats, January 13, 1966, November 1968 and February 16, 1972. Special Collections, John T. Richardson Library, De Paul University, Chicago, IL.

James Keegan, SJ, insightfully noted, "… to be neighbor is to be vulnerable."[23] There is an existing mutuality—first seeing in Christ the one who is vulnerable for us that we might be saved, then to go and do likewise. Keegan goes on:

> … vulnerability is the fundamental capacity within the human condition to appreciate the challenges that others may experience; it is the capacity to recognize, respond or hear the need of the other. It is based upon our capacity for mutual recognition to appreciate within ourselves what others might hear, feel, sense or experience in any precarious situation.[24]

Moral Theologian Enda McDonagh takes Keenan's insight to a higher level. "It is in this loving recognition and acceptance of the other that one first becomes vulnerable to the holy."[25] McDonagh continues:

> This human letting be, in its accepting and enabling sense, renders each human vulnerable to the holy, to the immediate sacredness of every human being, including the self as other, and to the sacred character if the universe itself as created by reflecting and even participating in the holiness of God.[26]

Contemplation creates a natural bridge between the intimacy one has with God and the intimacy one has with others. As one grows to love God with all one's mind, heart, and soul, one begins to see and love oneself and others as God does. From this mutual exchange flows acts of kindness, self-generosity, and love. It was this "crossing over" that generated growth in Romero's vulnerability, which continued to blossom during his years as bishop in Santiago.

On October 15, 1974, Romero was named bishop of the young rural diocese of Santiago de Maria. Because the priests of the diocese held

---

[23] Keegan, 7.

[25] Enda McDonagh, *Vulnerable to the Holy in Faith, Morality and the Arts* (Dublin, Ireland: The Columba Press, 2004), 16.

Romero's predecessor in contempt because they felt he was self-absorbed, accomplished little in the diocese, and was preoccupied with members of the intellectual elite and wealth, they generally affirmed and appreciated Romero's pastoral style. "The new bishop, by his actions, demonstrates that he is a bishop of the *campesinos*, with a sense of the people, especially the poor."[27] The priests also sensed a growth and maturity in Romero, which they respected:

> He was no longer the Romero of San Miguel, full of fear of the young priests. Now he was open to them, lovingly embracing the details of their lives which touched his heart, especially those who were the weakest.[28]

While obviously changed, Romero was still blind to the magnitude of the repression in El Salvador and to his own political inclinations. Because some of the oligarchs were close friends, he refused to believe their participation in and responsibility for the bloodshed in El Salvador. He supported government policies and denied the government's involvement in the widespread disappearances of persons, torture, and murder. In contrast, he held politicalized priests, the Salvadoran Jesuits and Liberation theologians—whom he accused of compromising the mission of the Church—responsible for endangering the lives of innocent people.

Romero's myopia began to dissipate when, on June 21, 1975, the National Guard terrorized and massacred the villagers in Las Tres Calles, a small rural village in his diocese. Guardsmen shot and hacked to death six men from the Astorga family, then proceeded to ransack homes in search of weapons. These dead *campesinos* were catechists and were taken violently from their homes, brutalized, tortured, and killed. Upon hearing this news, Romero went to Las Tres Calles to console the families of the victims and to celebrate liturgy with them, condemning the massacre in his homily as a violation of human rights. Still unable to see beyond his own prejudices, Romero maintained that the military and government were not responsible for these crimes.

---

[27] Jesús Delgado, *Oscar A. Romero: Biografía* (Madrid: Ediciones Paulinas, 1986), 62. Also see Zacharias Diez and Juan Macho, *En Santiago de María Me Topé con la Miseria: Dos Años de la Vida de Monseñor Romero (1975-1977) ¿Años del Cambio?* (Costa Rica: n.p., 1994).

The massacre of Las Tres Calles enabled Romero to see a bit more clearly the source of violence in the country. His personal experience of the massacre helped him confront more directly the reality of the brutal military violence and its indiscriminate targeting of many innocent people. This contributed to the chipping away of Romero's emotional attachments to his powerful friends, yet he still was not free enough to respond with the full authority of his office.

What finally helped Romero recognize the remainder of his political biases was when the military opened fire on unarmed students protesting the government's occupation of Santa Ana University on July 30, 1975. The fatalities numbered 40. The incident led Romero to a serious study of the Medellín documents while he was simultaneously studying *On Evangelization in the Modern World*.[29] In this encyclical, Romero found papal affirmation of what was taking place in his diocese: the Church's mission of evangelization must, if it is to be authentic, be concerned with the material needs of all people and be engaged in the struggle for human liberation from forces that contribute to the oppression of human beings. Romero came to see the apostolic exhortation as a key source of inspiration for the Medellín documents.

Romero's change continued. As bishop he came closer to the brutality of El Salvador's military. His own experience with psychological intervention offered him a new lens with which to place human limitations in perspective, widening his Christian understanding of the human person. Romero's life experience as priest and bishop, the theology and direction of Vatican II and Medellín, the growing threat of an increasingly violent repression and destructive civil war, and escalating persecution of Christians active in the struggle for social justice conspired to chip away his former assumptions. As all of this whirled around him, Romero became interiorly more understanding and supportive of his priests and protective of the defenseless people under his care. Gradually exposed to life struggles from the perspective of the poor, Romero began to recognize the causes of the poverty, suffering, and repression around him, and the deeply Christian motives of so many of those struggling for a better world. Romero's continued exposure to others' precarity and suffering expanded his vulnerability and brought forward his prophetic charism and a personal experience of the Paschal Mystery.

As the sixth Archbishop of El Salvador, Romero was prepared to lead as

---

[29] *Evangelii Nuntiandi* is an apostolic exhortation issued December 8, 1975, by Pope Paul VI.

Jesus led, regardless of personal cost.[30] He led with vulnerability—a Christian ethic—modeling how Christians ought to live.[31] He came to recognize the poor, suffering Christ in the faces, lives, and circumstances of the people he called "my brothers and sisters." His homilies, speeches, and pastoral letters indicate that he began to see Christ incarnate in the suffering poor. As his Christology shifted so did his ecclesiology, and in opting for the poor, he became like Bartolomé de las Casas centuries before, a defender of God, a defender of the poor.[32]

Romero's compassion increased as he listened to heartbreaking stories of widows, mothers, and daughters as they described episodes of fathers, husbands, brothers, and sons taken from their homes, tortured, mutilated, or killed in front of them, or abducted in the middle of the night, never to be heard from again. He listened to accounts of women brutally gang-raped by soldiers and pregnant women whose breasts were cut off or whose bellies were cut open and the infants ripped from their bodies, then used as target practice. He listened to *campesinos* tell how the military decimated their entire village with fire to terrify them, displacing them in the mountains. In Jon Sobrino's view, people came to Romero when lands were taken from them; their only recourse was Romero, whom they trusted to advocate for them.

> It was not that they came to him simply as a friend, seeking consolation. They came to him as a protector who was in duty bound to put

---

[30] Romero was consecrated Bishop on February 22, 1977.

[31] Reflecting on Emmanuel Levinas' ethical demands that imposes itself upon us against our will, Judith Butler writes, "We are, despite ourselves, open to this imposition, and though it overrides our will, it shows us that the claims that others make upon us are part of our very sensibilities, our receptivity, and our answerability. We are, in other words, called upon, and this is only possible because we are in some sense vulnerable to claims that we cannot anticipate in advance and for which there is no adequate preparation. For Levinas, there is no other way to understand the ethical reality; ethical obligation not only depends upon our vulnerability to the claims of others but establishes us as creatures who are fundamentally defined by that ethical relationship." "Precarious Life, Vulnerability, and the Ethics of Cohabitation," in *Journal of Speculative Philosophy* 26 (2012), 141.

[32] Bartolomé de las Casas, *Devastation of the Indies: A Brief Account,* trans. Herma Briffault (Baltimore: Johns Hopkins University, 1992); *In Defense of the Indians: The Defense of the Most Reverend Lord, Dom Fray Bartolomé de Las Casas, the Order of Preachers, Late Bishop of Chiapa, Against the Persecutors and Slanderers of the People of the New World Discovered Across the Sea* (DeKalb: Northern Illinois University, 1992); and *Witness: Writings of Bartolomé de Las Casas* (New York: Orbis, 1992). See also Jon Sobrino, SJ, *Archbishop Romero: Memories and Reflections.* Robert Barr, trans. (Maryknoll, NY: Orbis, 1990), 16.

the full weight of his episcopal authority at the service of the poor and oppressed.[33]

As a vulnerable bishop, Romero experienced Christ in the people who participated in the paschal mystery through their own baptism, suffering, and martyrdom. It is no wonder that in his first pastoral letter as Archbishop, *The Easter Church*, Romero developed the Council's theme of the paschal mystery as a paradigm for the Church and its mission, describing the Church of El Salvador as experiencing its own "paschal hour," that final moment of transformation on the cross, that passing from death to life. It was also, he pointed out, a time of the superabundant power of faith, hope, and love of the risen Christ. Romero wrote:

> The church is the body of Christ. Through baptism all those who belong to it live out that paschal tension, that "passage" from death to life, that "crossing over" that never ends and is called conversion, that continual demand upon us to destroy whatever is sin and to bring into being ever more powerfully all that is life, renewal, holiness, justice.[34]

Formed in Ignatian Spirituality, Romero understood discipleship to mean relationship with the Trinity, and a very human progressive growth into the likeness of the Son of God.[35] His lifetime of struggle to identify with the person, mission, ethics; and a personal experience of the suffering, death, and resurrection of Jesus is what produces the saint. That is the mission—and the bridge.[36]

[33] Ibid., 72.

[34] "The Easter Church," First Pastoral Letter of Archbishop Romero, Easter Sunday, April 10, 1977, in *Voice of the Voiceless: Four Pastoral Letters and Other Statements*. Michael Walsh, trans. (Maryknoll, NY: Orbis, 1985), 57.

[35] This soteriology has foundations in Irenaeus of Lyon's "Progression into God." See Damian Zynda, *Archbishop Oscar Romero: A Disciple who Revealed the Glory of God* (Scranton, PA: University of Scranton Press, 2010), for a thorough treatment of Romero's progression through an Irenaean hermeneutic.

[36] Whereas Pope John Paul II exemplified Atonement Soteriology, Pope Francis (Jesuit) exemplifies Discipleship Soteriology.

CHAPTER ELEVEN

Archbishop Oscar Romero and the Crucified People: A Bridge to Pope Francis

Robert Lassalle-Klein, PhD

Has any one of us wept because of this situation and others like it? Has any one of us grieved for the death of these brothers and sisters? Has any one of us wept for these people who were on the boat? For the young mothers carrying their babies? For these men who were looking for a means of supporting their families?[1]

—*Pope Francis at the Island of Lampedusa*

THIS CHAPTER ARGUES THAT the episcopacy of Archbishop Oscar Romero provides an important bridge for understanding the papacy of Pope Francis. What follows will examine significant historical and spiritual parallels in their journeys as Latin American Church leaders and prelates, many of which appear in comments by Francis on Romero as a model for bishops today. In support of this claim, the following four points are important.

---

[1] Pope Francis, "Homily of Holy Father Francis, 'Arena' sports camp, Salina Quarter, Monday, July 8, 2013." http://www.vatican.va/content/francesco/en/homilies/2013/documents/papa-francesco_20130708_omelia-lampedusa.html. Accessed 12-14-19. Also, "Pope on Lampedusa: 'The Globalization of Indifference'," http://www.vatican.va/content/francesco/en/homilies/2013/documents/papa-francesco_20130708_omelia-lampedusa.html.

First, the episcopacy of Archbishop Romero is defined by its contrast to his early years in Church leadership. Those years were characterized by suspicion and lack of public support for fellow priests and religious who confronted government violations of human rights in response to the 1968 preferential option for the poor by the Latin American bishops at Medellín, Colombia.[2] Francis has expressed a similar need to come to terms with early "faults and sins,"[3] which he says produced important growth and changes in his approach to leadership. Second, it was only after Romero's appointment as archbishop and the assassination of one of his priests, Fr. Rutilio Grande, SJ, who was also a friend, that he began to see public denunciations of violations of human rights as part of his episcopal call. In a similar way, Francis has acknowledged a "great interior crisis" provoked by his "authoritarian... manner of making decisions [which] led me to have serious problems and to be accused of being ultraconservative" while Jesuit provincial superior (1973-1979) during the "Dirty War" in Argentina (1976-1983).[4] Biographers point to the 1976 case of Frs. Orlando Yorio and Francisco Jalics, who resigned from the Jesuits rather than accede to Romero's order to give up their dangerous pastoral work in a Buenos Aires slum, which Fr. Yorio believed left them vulnerable to kidnapping and torture by the regime.[5] Third, Romero came to see himself in a special way as bishop of the crucified people of El Salvador through whom he experienced a transformative mystical encounter with God. Francis' self-understanding as pastor of the poor and rejected around the globe, especially migrants and refugees, reflects similar sensibilities owing, at least in part, to the influence of Archbishop Romero. Fourth, echoes of all the above are found in speeches and writings where Pope Francis explicitly promotes Archbishop Oscar Romero as an episcopal model for himself and for bishops around the world.

[2] Second General Conference of Latin American Bishops, "Document on Poverty in the Church" (2), in *The Church in the Present-Day Transformation of Latin America in the Light of the Council: II Conclusions* (Washington, DC: Division for Latin America–United States Catholic Conference, 1973).

[3] Antonio Spadaro, SJ, "A Big Heart Open to God: An Interview with Pope Francis," *America Magazine*, September 30, 2013. https://www.americamagazine.org/faith/2013/09/30/big-heart-open-god-interview-pope-francis. Accessed online 1-21-20.

[4] Ibid.

[5] William Neuman, "'Dirty War' Victim Rejects Pope's Connection to Kidnapping," *New York Times*, March 21, 2013. https://www.nytimes.com/2013/03/22/world/americas/jesuit-priest-rejects-popes-connection-to-kidnapping.html. Accessed 1-23-20.

Resistance to Medellín's Interpretation of Vatican II

In a 2013 interview with *America* magazine, Pope Francis was asked what he had learned from his experience as Jesuit Provincial Superior (1973-1979) during the "Dirty War" in Argentina (1976-1983) and how this might influence his approach to "governing the universal church."[6] Francis responded, "To be honest... my style of government as a Jesuit at the beginning had many faults.... My authoritarian and quick manner of making decisions led me to have serious problems and to be accused of being ultraconservative." He concluded, "Over time I learned many things. The Lord has allowed this growth in knowledge of government through my faults and my sins." He says this is reflected in his emphasis as pope on consistories of cardinals and synods of bishops as "important places" for "real and active" consultation, concluding, "I do not want token consultations, but real consultations." He has asserted that he now believes "we always need time to lay the foundations for real, effective change. And this is the time of discernment," which he says must be done "in the presence of the Lord, looking at the signs, [and] listening to the things that happen, the feeling of the people, especially the poor."

The episcopacy of Oscar Romero is likewise defined by its contrast to early mistakes grounded in rigidity, which informed his perception as an ultraconservative. Before becoming archbishop, Oscar Romero held what one author calls a traditionalist "quasi-corporatist" ecclesiology. The Church's role in society was to be that of a unifying social institution promoting what Medellín called "a sociocultural process" in which "all of the sectors of society... should, because of justice and brotherhood, transcend antagonisms in order to become agents of national and continental development."[7] Bishop Romero's commitment to this view of the Church as unifier and social glue, along with other more personal factors, had concrete outcomes. It rendered him deeply suspicious of pastoral approaches pushing the Church toward prophetic denunciations of state-sponsored violence against reformist groups mobilizing civil society in support of social change.

As a result, Romero only reluctantly accepted Medellín's interpretation of Vatican II as a primarily pastoral council whose signature mandate to

[6] Ibid.

[7] Second General Conference of Latin American Bishops, "Document on Justice," 13.

the bishops of Latin America in the Pastoral Constitution on the Church in the Modern World (*Gaudium et Spes*) was "reading the signs of the times and... interpreting them in light of the Gospel" (GS, 4). His reluctance can be seen in his struggle to reconcile himself as bishop to Medellín's assertion that the most pressing problem for the Church in the modern world was not the doctrinal atheism of communism or the agnosticism of secularism, but rather the pastoral challenge of responding to the "deafening cry [that] pours from the throats of millions of men and women asking their pastors for a liberation that reaches them from nowhere else."[8]

Romero served as auxiliary to Archbishop Chávez y González of San Salvador from 1970 to 1974. The views outlined above are captured in his public statements and writings from this period as editor of the diocesan newspaper, *Orientación*. His writings consistently characterize more activist views of the Church inspired by Medellín as politically naive distortions of Catholic social teaching politicizing the role of the Church in Salvadoran society. On October 15, 1974, Romero was named bishop of Santiago de María in Usulutan. His final editorial in *Orientación* one week later laments what he sees as "the possible loss of faith... among notable individuals from the church itself," which he associates with "hysterical and histrionic postures of demagogic revolutionism" that "foster disorder and do not offer... solutions."[9] He asserts in contrast that, as editor, he has always "respected the authorities" and emphasized "evangelization" (which we can understand as doctrine) over "human promotion" (focused on the pastoral concerns of Medellín). Comparing himself to his opponents, he writes:

What we do regret... is the explicitly worldly, violent and uncontrolled conduct of those who have tried to make use of religion to destroy the spiritual basis of religion.... For our part, we have preferred to adhere to that which is certain, to cling with fear and trembling to the Rock of Peter, to seek assurance in the shade of the church's teachings, and to put our ears to the lips of the pope instead of leaping

---

[8] Ibid., "Document on Poverty in the Church," 2.

[9] Zacarías Diez and Juan Macho, "En Santiago de María me topé con la miseria," *Dos años de la vida de Monseñor Romero (1975-1976), Años de cambio?* (San Salvador: Imprenta Criterio, del arzobispado de San Salvador, 1995), 48-49.

like reckless and foolhardy acrobats to the speculations of impudent thinkers of social movements of dubious origin.... .[10]

Brockman says that Romero saw his episcopal appointment as vindication by Rome of his views on the proper role of the Church in society expressed in *Orientación* when he writes:

> This trust of the pope in its editor must also be interpreted as the most solemn backing of the church's magisterium for the ideology that has inspired the paper's pages under this editorship. This silent approval from so high a source constitutes the best reward and satisfaction for all of us who work together for this ideal, at the same time that it determines the route to follow.[11]

Given his criticisms of Medellín and its proponents, it is notable that Romero identifies the teaching magisterium of the Church with Rome while failing to even mention Medellín as an authentic expression of Vatican II.

Two incidents from this period capture Romero's reluctant evolution toward what Ignacio Ellacuría, SJ, describes as his "theoretical" acceptance of Medellín. On June 21, 1975, at 1:00 a.m., members of the National Guard entered the village of Tres Calles, ransacking the houses of five *campesinos* while looking for weapons, and murdered the unarmed men in front of their families. Passionist fathers Zacarias Diez and Juan Macho recall that they and other local priests told Romero, "We must do something, Bishop,"[12] proposing several forms of public response.

> "But Monseñor was on another wavelength and didn't think like us," they recall. Instead, Romero wrote an anguished personal letter to his friend, President Colonel Arturo Armando Molina, and a summary of the events for the Salvadoran bishops. Looking back the priests say,

[10] Ibid., 48; and María López Vigil, *Oscar Romero: Memories in Mosaic* (Washington, DC: Ecumenical Program on Central America and the Caribbean, 2000), 59.

[11] Ibid.; and López Vigil, *Oscar Romero*, 59. Diez and Macho, 59.

[12] Diez and Macho, 146-49; James R. Brockman, *Romero: A Life* (Maryknoll, NY: Orbis Books, 1989), 61.

"It is true; he did something: it was an energetic protest and a strong denouncement." On the other hand, however, "it was not public, it was private, since he still believed that denunciations from authority to authority were more effective."[13]

A second incident involved one of the Church's peasant training centers, which Romero characterizes "as *centers of subversion*"[14] in a confidential November 1975 memo for the Pontifical Commission on Latin America. Earlier that year the Papal Nuncio had expressed suspicions about the center in Los Naranjos, and Romero was considering whether to close or reorient the project when one of its priests joined the occupation of the San Salvador cathedral following the July 30, 1975, student massacre.[15] Shortly thereafter, on August 16, the center director, Fr. Juan Macho, was refused entry at the airport into El Salvador and forced to return to Madrid after being told by migration, "Look, you have a lot of problems in Jiquilisco [your parish].... The order is that you cannot get off the plane."[16] Romero again wrote to Molina, this time defending Fr. Macho's "priestly actions... [as] the director of the Los Naranjos Center for Campesino Development."[17] The letter was successful, and Fr. Macho was allowed to return, but the center was temporarily closed and an interim director installed.[18]

Four months later Romero left for the October 20-22, 1975, meeting of the aforementioned Pontifical Commission in Rome. There Romero presented his "very confidential" memo outlining "Three Factors in the Priests' Political Movement in El Salvador."[19] These included the Jesuits of Central America, the "Social Secretariat" and "Justice and Peace Commission" of the Archdiocese, and "groups of priests, religious orders, and *committed Christians*" who "spread their ideas in... [Church-sponsored] peasant development centers... identified by the government as 'centers of subversion.'"

[13] Robert Lassalle-Klein, *Blood and Ink: Ignacio Ellacuría, Jon Sobrino, and the Jesuit Martyrs of the University of Central America* (Maryknoll, NY: Orbis Books, 2014), 241.

[14] Brockman, *Romero*, 61.

[15] Brockman, *Romero*, 59.

[16] Diez and Macho, 72; Brockman, 59.

[17] Diez and Macho, 72.

[18] Brockman, *Romero*, 59.

[19] Diez and Macho, 49-53.

Shortly after Romero's return in early December, he invited Bishop Marco René Revelo, head of the catechetical commission and auxiliary bishop of Santa Ana, to meet with him and the priests of Los Naranjos. Not surprisingly, Revelo and Romero concluded that certain classes had "manipulated" the documents of Medellín and distorted Catholic social teaching in a way that confused the politicized catechists.[20] On the other hand, however, it was the beginning of a dialogue with the Passionists, which produced an agreement that work would continue, while courses taught by center staff would be shifted to parishes so that Romero and the local priests could oversee the process.[21] The government, the nuncio, and the priests from the center were all satisfied, and Fr. Macho became both director of the center and vicar for the diocese, where he began working closely with Romero. The net result was that "from that day forward Romero became more focused on better understanding Medellín." In the view of the Passionists, a breakthrough had been achieved as "an outcome of the Los Naranjos affair" because "the experience finally opened his mind to Medellín, since until then it had been closed by suspicions and doubts to the teaching of such an important document."[22] That same month, Pope Paul VI published *Evangelii Nuntiandi* (December 8, 1975), linking evangelization in the modern world to powerful denunciations of poverty and oppression such as those found in the documents of Medellín.

All of these factors, then, led Romero to reconsider the previously unquestioned priority he had assigned to maintaining good relations between the Church and the government in the face of state-sponsored violence against his people. Instead, as with Jorge Bergolio, Romero's early problems in Church leadership led him to both consult more carefully with his clergy and to assume a more active role in defending their efforts to implement Medellín's discernment that God was calling the Latin American Church to support and defend the poor. Errors of the past became a bridge to the future.

An Episcopal Style Grounded in Medellín

An important biographer of Pope Francis observes that, while Provincial Superior of the Jesuits during the brutal fascist dictatorship in Argentina, "he

---

[20] Jesús Delgado, *Oscar A. Romero, Biografía* (San Salvador: UCA Editores, 1986), 65.

[21] Brockman, *Romero*, 60; the agreement appears in Diez and Macho, 129-34.

[22] Delgado, *Oscar A. Romero*, 66; Diez and Macho, 120.

felt he could not speak out because he had seen priests and bishops killed for doing so. His job, he felt, was to protect his Jesuits, and he took comfort in the fact that all of them made it through the period alive."[23] Another observes, "Bergoglio was no hero. He was no outspoken opponent of the regime, no prophet, and no icon of human rights. He was... a leader of an institution whose interests he needed to protect."[24] Commentators point to the young superior's insistence that his former professors, Frs. Orlando Yorio and Francisco Jalics, leave their dangerous pastoral work in a Buenos Aires slum, which provoked their request to leave the order. Fr. Forio asserts that their dismissal left them unprotected when it was finalized just days before their 1976 kidnapping and torture by the regime.[25] Francis explains that:

...the superior general of the Jesuits... Father Pedro Arrupe, told them they had to choose between the community they were living in and the Company of Jesus, and ordered them to move. As they persisted... they asked to leave the Company. It was a long, internal process that lasted more than a year... [and] was not a hasty decision of mine.[26]

Francis nonetheless speaks of a "great interior crisis" provoked by his "authoritarian... manner of making decisions [which] led me to have serious problems and to be accused of being ultraconservative." He says that reflection on this period produced important changes reflected in the substance and style of his leadership as pope.[27]

[23] Raymond A. Schroth, SJ, "Readings: The Real Bergoglio," *America*, August 27, 2013. Book review of Paul Vallely, *Pope Francis: Untying the Knots* (London and New York: Bloomsbury Academic, 2013).

[24] Andrew Sullivan, "What Is the Meaning of Pope Francis?" *Deep Dish*, December 17, 2013. http://dish.andrewsullivan.com/deepdish/longform/untier-of-knots/. Accessed 1-21-20.

[25] William Neuman, "'Dirty War' Victim Rejects Pope's Connection to Kidnapping," *New York Times*, March 21, 2013. https://www.nytimes.com/2013/03/22/world/americas/jesuit-priest-rejects-popes-connection-to-kidnapping.html. Accessed 1-23-20.

[26] Francesca Ambrifetti and Sergio Rubin, *Pope Francis: His Life in His Own Words* (New York: G.P. Putnam's Sons, 2010, 2013), 203.

[27] Spadaro, "A Big Open Heart to God."

Similar dynamics are found in the story of Oscar Romero. Five weeks after his appointment as archbishop, one of his priests and a friend, Fr. Rutilio Grande, SJ, was assassinated for his efforts to evangelize the peasants of Aguilares, El Salvador, with the message of Medellín. Almost immediately, Romero embraced public denunciations of violations of human rights as part of his episcopal call and began to develop an episcopal approach organized around the preferential option for the poor. There are disagreements among his friends and followers regarding the exact nature of the timing of what occurred, but all agree that a significant change took place in regards to his role as a public voice for Medellín's challenge to the Latin American Church and to society. Archbishop Gregory Rosa Chávez, a close associate of Archbishop Romero who worked with him in communications and interviewed the archbishop weekly on the diocesan radio station, YSAX,[28] offers an important perspective. He insists that Archbishop Romero did not have a sudden conversion, but rather experienced a gradual evolution toward a decision to take a public position on the abuse of human rights. In support of this theory Chávez cites the documentary by a Swiss journalist who spent a week with Romero during the final phase of his life. Rosa Chávez says that the journalist asks, "Have you been converted, Monseñor Romero?" and Romero responds, "I wouldn't say *converted*. Rather, it's been a gradual evolution that led to a decision to respond to the situation in the country as a pastor."[29]

How, then, are we to explain that it was only after his appointment as archbishop and the assassination of Fr. Rutilio Grande that Romero began to take full responsibility for defending his people against state-sponsored terror? It was only then that he developed an episcopal agenda grounded in Medellín's call "for conversion on the part of the whole Church to a preferential option for the poor... aimed at their integral liberation."[30] The answer to this question has important bearing on the nature of Romero's influence on Pope Francis.

---

[28] Brockman, *Romero*, 116.

[29] Interview of Bishop Gregorio Rosa Chávez by Robert Lassalle-Klein, San Salvador, November 12, 2009.

[30] Third General Conference of Latin American Bishops, *Puebla: Evangelization at Present and in the Future of Latin America: Conclusions* (London: St. Paul and CIIR, 1980); cited in Donal Dorr, *Option for the Poor: A Hundred Years of Vatican Social Teaching*, rev. and enlarged ed. (Maryknoll, NY: Orbis Books, 1983), 210.

Archbishop Rosa Chávez asserts, "There are two theories about the conversion of Monseñor Romero—the theory of the Jesuits and our own theory. The Jesuits say he was converted thanks to Rutilio. But we say that he was already in a process of conversion."[31] Laying out the ambiguity here, Rosa Chávez explains:

> Before being named archbishop he was bishop in a poor rural area where he met many *campesinos*, while always questioning, 'What is God asking of me?' On the other hand, he was very close friends with Rutilio Grande, and Fr. Grande's death affected him deeply. They were very similar as pastors.

Monsignor Ricardo Urioste, vicar general of the diocese of San Salvador under Romero, similarly asserts, "I don't think the killing of Rutilio Grande provoked the conversion of Monseñor Romero."[32] As evidence of Romero's prior concern for the poor, Urioste cites an incident in 1976 when Romero, as bishop of the diocese of Santiago de Maria, "opened his bishop's house to the poor." James Brockman's biography of Oscar Romero recounts the details of this incident, noting that the bishop criticized the "selfishness" of the coffee growers for denying a "just wage" to the harvesters, forcing them to spend cold nights sleeping in the public square of Santiago de María during the harvest. In response, Romero opened the cathedral rectory, the diocesan offices, and a hall for clergy meetings in the bishop's residence so that "hundreds of workers thus had at least a roof over their heads at night and shelter from the cold."[33] Brockman asserts, however, that while Romero "did what he could to alleviate the hardships of the harvesters," on the other hand, he offered "no solution for the injustice beyond wishing that the landowners were not so selfish and fraudulent." Brockman states that public interventions of this sort would have to wait until "after he became archbishop" and the death of Rutilio Grande when, like the *campesinos* of Aguilares, "he would come

---

[31] Interview with Bishop Gregorio Rosa Chávez.

[32] Speech and interview with Monsignor Ricardo Urioste by Robert Lassalle-Klein, Santa Clara University, April 28, 2010.

[33] Brockman, *Romero*, 56.

to recognize that the oppressed must organize in order to pressure for their rights, and he would vigorously defend the rights of their organizations."

I have argued elsewhere that the Jesuits, Bishop Rosa Chávez, and Monsignor Urioste are all partially correct in that their claims address different pieces of the puzzle of the transformation or "conversion" of Archbishop Romero. Clearly, Romero's embrace of Medellín's call to a preferential option for the poor may be properly described in his own words, cited by Archbishop Rosa Chávez, as "a gradual evolution that led to a decision to respond to the situation in the country as a pastor."[34] On the other hand, the archbishop himself distinguishes the "gradual evolution" of his option for the poor from his later "decision to respond to the situation in the country as a pastor." Here the archbishop differentiates his own early evolution toward a preferential option for the poor from his later decision to publicly denounce the situation in the country.

Romero himself recalls, "Father Grande's death and the death of other priests impelled me to take an energetic attitude before the government."[35] He says, "because of Father Grande's death I made a statement that I would not attend any official acts until this situation [of who had killed Grande] was clarified." As a result, "A rupture was produced, not by me with the government but [by] the government itself because of its attitude." For this reason, I have suggested that we should distinguish Romero's *personal conversion* from his later *political conversion.*[36]

Using the language of conversion developed by Donald Gelpi, SJ,[37] I would argue that we can properly distinguish Romero's gradual decision to assume personal responsibility for the suffering of the poor (his *personal conversion*) from his decision following the assassination of Rutilio Grande and other priests. After the assassination, he took public responsibility before the government for their violations of the human rights of his people (his *socio-political conversion*). Setting aside the language of conversion for a moment, however, perhaps all parties can agree that, following the death of

[34] Interview of Bishop Gregorio Rosa Chávez.

[35] Letter from the bishops of El Salvador to Cardinal Amleto Cicognani, August 24, 1964 (San Salvador: Archives of the Society of Jesus of Central America). Copy in the UCA El Salvador file. Cited in Beirne, *Jesuit Education and Social Change*, 73.

[36] Lassalle-Klein, *Blood and Ink*, 111-12.

[37] Donald Gelpi, SJ, *The Gracing of Human Experience: Rethinking the Relationship between Nature and Grace* (Collegeville, MN: Liturgical Press/Michael Glazier, 2001), 292-293 and 297-301.

Rutilio Grande, Romero began to take greater responsibility as archbishop for the systematic and ongoing violations of human rights by the government and others through public denouncements of this "situation in the country." Further, for the first time he began to develop an episcopal agenda explicitly focused on drawing the Church close to the poor and the defense El Salvador's many victims of state-sponsored violence. This way of being a bishop is the pattern we find in the pontificate of Pope Francis.

The Crucified People as Bridge to God

Many commentators identify synodality and the preferential option for the poor as defining marks of the papacy of Francis. I would argue that Francis' self-understanding as pastor of those who are poor and rejected around the globe, especially migrants and refugees, should be added to the list. There can be little doubt that the life and ministry of Archbishop Romero serves as a model and inspiration for the conviction of Pope Francis that the prelate encounters God in a special way through his role as bishop and pastor of the poor and marginalized.

Eight months after Romero's assassination, Ignacio Ellacuría published an article entitled "Archbishop Romero, Sent by God to Save his People."[38] Here Ellacuría outlines three stages or developments in Romero's three-year ministry as archbishop (1977-1980), which is useful for our purpose. He distinguishes Romero's initial embrace of Medellín from what followed and asserts, "Through this initial conversion, which was nothing but the start of something that could have ended there, Monseñor Romero... [was just] beginning a profound conversion of his mission." He says, "It is this mission, and his fidelity to it, that finally transforms him... into a fundamental factor in the history of salvation of El Salvador."[39] And he concludes that Romero:

> ... recognized in this people... the voice of God himself... he saw
> in the crucified people the God of salvation [and]... he understood

---

[38] Ignacio Ellacuría, "Monseñor Romero, un enviado de Dios para salvar a su pueblo," *Escritos teológicos,* III (San Salvador: UCA Editores, 2002), 93-100; reprinted from *Sal Terrae* 811 (1980), 825-32; and *ECA* 19 (1990), 5-10.

[39] Ibid., 97.

their struggles for liberation as the path toward a new earth and a new heaven.

Ellacuría's first point is that, before becoming archbishop:

> Monseñor Romero... was considered an opponent of... Medellín. In-
> terested mainly in orthodoxy, he was wary of... the theology of lib-
> eration and... attacked those who denounced the country's structural
> injustice as infected with Marxism.[40]

But things changed when "the assassination of Fr. Grande, the first of the priest martyrs he was called to bury, shook his conscience [so that] the veils hiding the truth were torn away." Romero asserts that the authenticity of Fr. Grande's priestly ministry, and his love for the rural peasants of Aguilares, revealed to him "what it meant to be apostle in El Salvador today; it meant being a prophet and a martyr."[41] Ellacuría says that Fr. Grande's ministry showed Romero that Medellín's preferential option for the poor implied solidarity with the struggles of Latin America's poor majorities for liberation from poverty, military rule, and state-sponsored violence. And Ellacuría asserts that this inspired Archbishop Romero to take his first tentative steps as a prophetic voice against state-sponsored repression.

Ellacuría's second point is that this was just "the beginning of a profound conversion of his mission." He says, "It is this mission, and his fidelity to it, that finally transforms him... into a fundamental factor in the history of salvation of El Salvador."[42] Ellacuría says that the "preferential option for the oppressed" changed from a merely "theoretical" question to a challenge to "faithfulness to the gospel" and his ability "to see the historical Jesus in this oppressed people." As a result, Archbishop Romero started doing things that led him down a path that he followed:

> ... to its ultimate consequences when he recognized in this people
> without a voice the voice of God himself, when he saw in the crucified

[40] Ibid., 95.

[41] Ibid., 96.

[42] Ibid., 97.

people the God of salvation, [and] when he understood their struggles for liberation as the path toward a new earth and a new heaven.

Thus, the crucified people became the holy ground for his encounter with God.

Third, Ellacuría asserts that Romero's ministry came to embody "the salvation of the historical process that is being realized in El Salvador."[43] Ellacuría asserts that Archbishop Romero "never tired of repeating that political processes, however pure and idealistic, are not enough to bring humanity's liberation."[44] Recalling St. Augustine's claim that "in order to be human one must be *more* than human," Ellacuría asserts that, for Archbishop Romero, "history that... tries to be only human, quickly ceases to be so." He explains this is why Romero "never stopped calling [us] to transcendence" in homilies about "the word of God, [and] the action of God in breaking through human limits."

In response, Ellacuaría says, "The people opened themselves to Christian transcendence." Day by day, "the word, the life, [and] the example of Monseñor Romero made the Christian message credible to ever larger sectors of the Salvadoran people [as]... he opened up to an ever increasing and more pure kind of hope."[45] Ellacuría says that Romero "saw more light than darkness" in El Salvador's tortured political process, and he spoke "in favor of the oppressed" while avoiding "identification *with*" any particular political party or solution.[46] As a result, the Salvadoran people "received from Monseñor Romero a new strength to hope, to struggle in hope, [and] to offer their lives in heroic sacrifices full of meaning" so that "their struggles for liberation acquired through him a transcendent meaning...."[47]

In this way Archbishop Romero "became an exceptional example of how the power of the gospel can become a transformative historical force."[48] Ellacuría says that Romero lives on as an historical force not merely because "there are many who remember him," or because "he removed the blindfold that kept them from recognizing the truth of the gospel" unfolding before them. Rather, Archbishop Romero also remains a force "because there

[43] Ibid., 100.

[44] Ibid., 98-99.

[45] Ibid., 99-100.

[46] Ibid., 100.

[47] Ibid.

[48] Ibid.

are many who are disposed to follow his steps, knowing that Monseñor Romero was an exemplary follower of Jesus of Nazareth in the last three years of his public life."

I would argue that Pope Francis is an example of just such a person. In what follows I will examine some ways in which the words and actions of Pope Francis reflect the influence of Archbishop Romero's episcopacy, and I will suggest that Romero's encounter with God as bishop and pastor of the crucified people serves as a kind of spiritual guidepost and inspiration for the papacy of Pope Francis.

Archbishop Romero: Model for the Vatican II Bishop

This section will briefly examine aspects of the speeches and publications of Pope Francis promoting Archbishop Oscar Romero as a model for the Vatican II bishop committed to God's preferential option for the poor. Five examples will support this claim. The conclusion will suggest that Romero's influence is being universalized for the Church as elements of Francis' self-understanding as pope, who sees himself as called to be bishop and pastor to both migrants and refugees, and the communities that must decide whether to receive them.

First, the vigorous support by Pope Francis for the beatification and canonization of Archbishop Romero clearly highlights the pope's interest in Romero as a model for Christian discipleship and the Vatican II bishop. In announcing that Romero would be canonized with Pope Paul VI, the Vatican News cites Julian Filochowski, who declares that it was Paul VI "who implemented the Second Vatican Council, while the archbishop was 'the first martyr of the Council,' assassinated for implementing its teaching on the preferential option for the poor."[49] Expanding on this point, John Thiede, SJ, rightly asserts, "The beatification of Oscar Romero opens the door for an expansion of the definition of martyrdom... [since] throughout the text Romero is referred to as a Martyr."[50] And through various words and actions,

---

[49] Philippa Hitchen, "Oscar Romero to be Recognised as Saint of Universal Church," *Vatican News*, May 18, 2018, 19, 17. https://www.vaticannews.va/en/vatican-city/news/2018-05/archbishop-romero-canonisation-paul-vi-filochowski.html. Accessed 1-20-20.

[50] John Thiede, SJ, *Remembering Oscar Romero and the Martyrs of El Salvador* (Washington, DC: Lexington Books, 2017), 109.

Francis leaves little doubt regarding his position on the *questione dispu-tatae*, whether assassination at the hands of Christians for the preferential option for the poor meets the traditional qualifications for martyrdom as a witness to the faith who is killed in *odium fidei*. Indeed, the Associated Press reports that, during the ceremony celebrating Romero's canonization, Francis wore "the blood-stained rope belt that Romero wore when he was gunned down."[51]

Second, Pope Francis cites Romero as a model for contemporary bish-ops. In his January 24, 2019, talk to the bishops of Central America,[52] Francis highlights "Saint Oscar Romero, whom I recently had the privilege of canonizing," describing "his life and his teachings [as]... a source of in-spiration for our Churches and, in a special way, for us as bishops." He says Romero's way of living out his episcopal motto, "thinking with the Church," should serve as "an active and life-giving witness for us, who are likewise called to the daily martyrdom of serving our people." Echoing *Gaudium et Spes*, Francis says:

> Romero showed us that the pastor, in order to seek and discover the Lord, must learn to listen to the heartbeat of his people. He must smell the "odor" of the sheep, the men and women of today, until he is steeped in their joys and hopes, their sorrows and their anxieties.

Referencing Romero's homilies, he asserts that bishops must understand that "God saves in history, in the life of each person... and this is also his own history, from which he comes forth to meet us." He says that bishops must understand, like Romero, that "young people are the face of Christ for us, and... we cannot reach Christ by descending from above, but by rising up from below." And finally, referencing the impact of the assassination of Fr. Rutilio Grande on Archbishop Romero, he says that Romero's response

[51] Camila Domonoske, "Oscar Romero, Pope Paul VI Elevated to Sainthood," National Public Radio, October 14, 2018, 10:39 a.m. ET. https://www.npr.org/2018/10/14/657277667/oscar-romero-pope-paul-vi-elevated-to-sainthood. Accessed 1-20-20.

[52] Pope Francis, "Apostolic Journey of His Holiness Pope Francis to Panama on the Occasion of the 34th World Youth Day, Meeting with Central American Bishops (SEDAC), Address of His Holiness," Church of San Francisco de Asis (Panama), Thursday, January 24, 2019. http://www.vatican.va/content/francesco/en/speeches/2019/january/documents/papa-francesco_20190124_panama-vescovi-centroamericani.html. Accessed 1-20-20.

should likewise "serve as a yardstick... to help us measure our own hearts as bishops and ask, 'How much does the life of my priests affect me?'"

Third, Francis shares Romero's interpretation of the preferential option for the poor as Medellín's discernment of God's will for the Church, which he embraces as a defining mark of his episcopacy. In his first apostolic exhortation, *Evangelii Gaudium*, Francis takes the typically Latin American position that, "For the Church, the option for the poor is primarily a theological category rather than a cultural, sociological, political or philosophical one," meaning that God is the one who shows the poor "his first mercy." He says this has important "consequences for the faith life of all Christians, since we are called to have 'this mind... which was in Jesus Christ' (*Phil* 2:5)." Most importantly, he insists that the Church is called by God to make its own:

> ... option for the poor which is understood as a "special form of primacy in the exercise of Christian charity... implicit in our Christian faith in a God who became poor for us, so as to enrich us with his poverty."

Fourth, Francis embraces the mystical dimension of Romero's belief that he is called to be the bishop of the crucified people of El Salvador through whom God has chosen to offer salvation. For example, Francis says in *Evangelii Gaudium*, "This is why I want a Church which is poor and for the poor. They have much to teach us. Not only do they share in the *sensus fidei*, but in their difficulties they know the suffering Christ" (#198). For Francis, the option for the poor is not just an ethical norm; rather, it is a privileged place, holy ground for the encounter with Christ. Accordingly, "The new evangelization is an invitation to acknowledge the saving power at work in their lives and to put them at the center of the Church's pilgrim way." He concludes:

> We are called to find Christ in them, to lend our voice to their causes, but also to be their friends, to listen to them, to speak for them and to embrace the mysterious wisdom which God wishes to share with us through them.

Fifth and finally, Francis historicizes Romero's sense of call to be the bishop of the crucified people through his advocacy for migrants. He insists,

"It is essential to draw near to new forms of poverty and vulnerability, in which we are called to recognize the suffering Christ" (#210). He asserts, "Migrants present a particular challenge for me, since I am the pastor of a Church without frontiers, a Church which considers herself mother to all." He treats dispossessed migrants and refugees as a defining sign of the times and symbols of poverty and marginalization. He views them as the historical embodiment of the suffering servant Christ, whose innocence exposes the guilt of those who would snatch away their lives for personal gain. He asserts that he and his fellow bishops are called to be their pastors. And he believes that God comes to meet and to save humanity in a special way through the bridge of solidarity with the hopes, dreams, and struggles of those who strive to provide life for their families.

In all of these ways, then, Archbishop Oscar Romero provides an important bridge for understanding the papacy of Pope Francis, which I have argued draws inspiration from aspects of Romero's leadership of the Church of El Salvador (1977-1980). First, both the episcopacy of Archbishop Romero and the papacy of Francis are defined by contrast to their early years in Church leadership. Both are shaped by regrets for past failures to build consensus with their fellow priests and religious and to adequately defend their attempts to live out God's preferential option for the poor. Second, each came to see vigorous public denunciations of violations of human rights as part of their episcopal call following the torture and/or death of fellow priests and religious under their pastoral care. Third, both came to see themselves called by God to serve as bishop and pastor to the poorest and most persecuted people, through whom each speaks of a transformative mystical encounter with God. And finally, through his words and actions, Pope Francis seems to regard Archbishop Romero as a kind of spiritual guidepost for episcopal leadership in the universal Church, and a model for the Vatican II bishop committed to God's preferential option for the poor, who listens to his people and his clergy with an open heart.

PART IV

Bridge Theology: Forming Bridge Builders in the Classroom

CHAPTER TWELVE

The Bridge of Solidarity: Faith-Based Advocacy for Undocumented Students

ANA GRANDE, MA

IN THE 1980S AND 1990S, anti-immigrant sentiment surged in the state of California, caused by friction from the increased migration of people from Central America who were perceived as a threat to the state's economic instability. In addition to the escalating socio-political persecution of immigrants, ballot measures such as Proposition 187[1] and 209[2] added to anti-immigrant sentiment. The struggles of the undocumented community continue in many areas of society today and are deeply felt in undocumented students' pursuit of public higher education or embarking upon their career of choice. This chapter explores how faith communities can be a bridge of solidarity for those motivated by their faith. This solidarity will engage the migrants in our midst who live without documents. This chapter will outline the historical legislative obstacles that undocumented students have endured in their pursuit of higher education. These include the struggle to pass the California Dream Act, the elation following the Deferred Action

---

[1] A 1994 California ballot measure denying immigrants public education, health care, and other social services within the state.

[2] California measure in 1996 amending the state constitution considering sex, gender, or ethnicity as bases for public college and university admission.

for Childhood Arrivals (DACA), and the Church's accompaniment of those that continue to live on the margins of society.

History and Background

During the 1980s, Blessed Sacrament Church, located in Hollywood, California, participated in the sanctuary movement of the time.[3] Utilizing the former convent and renaming it Casa Rutilio Grande, it embraced refugees arriving from war-torn countries in Central America. Casa Grande established English as a Second Language (ESL) classes for new immigrants to help them better acculturate to American society, and empowered the migrants and their allies to use Cardinal Joseph Cardijn's See-Judge-Act social analysis methodology.[4] Cardijn's method of social analysis provided the context to place real issues into conversation with the social justice documents of the Catholic Church. Together, immigrants and advocates would analyze the political policies or happenings of that day, judge them according to scripture and the social justice teachings of the Church, and act accordingly. Action was always the hardest part of the analysis. Although many saw the social injustices of public policies, and compared those with scripture, the actions that followed by members of Blessed Sacrament Church were often the opposite of those followed by citizens in the community at large. Examples of these would be the sanctuary movement versus deportation and an open admission policy in our parish school versus the denial of admission to public schools for undocumented children. These actions illustrated the core components of Catholic social teaching when parish community members treated immigrant strangers with kindness, compassion, and dignity. Outside the church grounds these same immigrants were met with reproach, discrimination, hatred, and frustration.

By the time Proposition 187 became a ballot measure, the communities of faith in Los Angeles had developed core groups of leaders to educate the community at-large about the proposition and its adverse effects. From homilies to house meetings and community forums the priests, sisters, and laity of Blessed Sacrament worked for justice. However, over the years this

---

[3] During the 1980s and early 1990s several Catholic parishes served as immigrant sanctuaries.

[4] See-Judge-Act social analysis is also known as the Cardijn method after Cardinal Joseph Cardijn, founder of the Young Christian Workers Movement.

spirit of justice and hospitality evaporated from parish communities. Other social and political issues began to take precedence over issues of welcome, hospitality, and settlement of immigrants in American society. Although the hierarchy of the Church has not diminished their focus on social justice issues for undocumented immigrant individuals and families, the laity of the Church are seldom inspired to implement the social justice teachings and documents of the Church regarding immigration and welcoming the stranger. New laws did help some.

Federal laws were passed to decrease the anguish of migrant families. First was the Immigration and Control Act (IRCA) signed by President Reagan in 1986. This was followed by the Illegal Immigration Reform and Immigrant Reform Act (IIRIRA) in 1996 signed by Bill Clinton. Both sets of laws, while filling a void in the status of millions of undocumented individuals, also diminished the need for the laity to continue advocating for the rights of migrants. The social consensus became that immigration reform would eventually take care of itself. By 2008, no immigration reform had been passed and, at that time, over 11 million undocumented individuals and their families were left to live in the shadows and on the margins of our nation.

Activism led me to the position of Campaign Director for PowerPAC.[5] In 2008, students, along with PowerPAC, were able to achieve real progress with their advocacy and formulate a statewide coalition in support of the California Dream Act.[6] Undocumented students, commonly known as DREAMers, are also known as the 1.5 generation.[7] As part of the 1.5 generation, these students have grown up in the American culture.[8] Speaking English, attending public schools, and enrolling in public higher education institutions, this 1.5 generation was still not able to obtain institutional financial aid to continue their education. The need for faith-based advocacy

[5] PowerPAC, a political action committee based in San Francisco and Los Angeles seeking to build coalitions of students of color, empowering them through the civic and democratic process. www.powerpac.org.

[6] PowerPAC, along with students, created the Power and Unity statewide coalition in support of Senate Bill 1301 (Cedillo), which is explained in detail in Chapter 2.

[7] These children, born abroad yet brought at an early age to live in the United States by their parents, have some association with their countries of origin, but their primary identification is with the United States.

[8] The 1.5 generation are children that arrived in the U.S. prior to their 14th birthday.

remains as imperative as it was two decades ago. The document, *In Solidarity*, is a reminder for the Church and particularly for parish communities to see, judge, and act according to their own social justice and intellectual tradition, which commenced over a century ago.[9]

DREAMers

The history of undocumented students in Los Angeles is for the most part unrecognized. Many have been in this country their entire lives and have attended K-12 education in public schools in the United States.[10] According to the Urban Institute, approximately 65,000 undocumented students graduate from United States high schools each year. Of this number, 25,000 undocumented youth reside in California.[11] Prior to 1985, the 1.5 generation was unknown to the higher educational and state legislative system in California.[12] Regardless of their years in California, the University of California, California State University, and California community colleges denied undocumented students in-state tuition solely based on their immigration status. Five intrepid students challenged the definition of California residency in the University of California systems, which ultimately created an unprecedented movement for undocumented students in the state of California.

Two interconnected issues, education and immigration, were addressed in 1985 with *Leticia A. vs. Board of Regents of the University of California*. This rarely known case was a challenge put forth by five undocumented students in the state of California to obtain in-state tuition.[13] The case itself determined the eligibility of undocumented students to receive in-state tuition and clarified the inconsistent definitions of California resident status for the University of California and California State University system. In 1991, after six years of deliberation, the Alameda court ruled

[9] The first social justice encyclical, *Rerum Novarum*, was written by Pope Leo XXII in 1891.

[10] http://www.ailf.org/ipc/policybrief/policybrief_2007_dream.pdf.

[11] http://www.nilc.org/immlawpolicy/DREAM/DREAM_Demographics.pdf.

[12] *Leticia A. v. Board of Regents of the University of California* brought to light the struggle of undocumented students in the state.

[13] http://info.sen.ca.gov/pub/01-02/bill/asm/ab_0501-0550/ab_540_cfa_20010502_124759_asm_comm.html.

that undocumented students qualified for in-state tuition as defined by the University of California and California State University.[14] In *Leticia A. vs. Board of Regents of the University of California,* the Alameda County Superior Court held that the policy of determining residency based on terms other than those applied to United States citizens was unconstitutional pursuant to the California Constitution.[15] The judged cited *Plyer vs. Dole,*[16] the 1984 ruling that allowed undocumented students to obtain primary through high school public education, to justify their ruling in the *Leticia A* case. The court ruling was short-lived; a disgruntled University of California employee challenged the *Leticia A.* decision.

Without funds or greater community support, DREAMers struggled between two choices: (1) to pay international fees, which tripled their in-state tuition or (2) to drop out of higher education. DREAMers, the 1.5 generation, sought help from legislators to redefine California residency and obtain in-state tuition. Legislators eager to step in and author proposals were Assembly member Richard Polanco and Senator Martha Escutia. Both brought attention to the plight of undocumented students but failed in their attempts to pass legislation proposing in-state tuition.

AB540: 1998-2001

In 1998 California Assembly member Marco Antonio Firebaugh revitalized the legislative process for undocumented students to receive in-state tuition. After numerous failures, a new measure was proposed in 2001. The measure tried to remove the criteria excluding students in the process of obtaining citizenship and became inclusive of all students—both those from out of state and the undocumented. Assembly Bill 540, commonly known as AB540, was signed into law in October 2001 by Governor Gray Davis. The legislation permitted any student, regardless of immigration status, to pay in-state tuition

[14] Rodolfo F. Acuña, *Anything but Mexican: Chicanos in Contemporary Los Angeles* (New York: Verso, 1996), 126.

[15] Laura Yates, *Plyler v. Doe* and the Rights of Undocumented Immigrants to Higher Education: Should Undocumented Students be Eligible for In-state College Tuition Pay? *Washington University Law Quarterly,* Summer, 2004. 82 Wash. U. L. Q. 585.

[16] Plyler v. Doe, 457 U.S. 202 (1984).

at the University of California, the California State University, and California community colleges as long as they met the following requirements:[17]

1. Attended a California high school for three or more years

2. Graduated from a California high school or attained the equivalent of a high school diploma

3. Registered at a California higher education institution within one year of high school graduation

4. Filed or in the process of filing an affidavit required by individual institutions stating the student would apply for legal residency as soon as it was permitted

5. Were not a non-immigrant holding a valid non-immigrant visa

In addition, students who were residents of other states such as Oregon and Nevada and met the requirements through AB540 also benefitted from this legislation. According to the University of California's Office of the President, approximately 90% of AB540 students were documented, 5% were in transition, and 1% were undocumented.[18] Upon the passage of AB540, the reality of undocumented students in California came to light. An analysis by the state of California estimated that there were about 3,500 college students enrolled in California State University and the California community colleges who were eligible for non-resident tuition waivers according to AB540.[19] In California, where approximately 26.2%[20] of residents are foreign born (the highest in the nation), AB540 came at a much needed time as the 1.5 generation graduated from high school.

---

[17] University of California, Center for Higher Education Policy Analysis, 2006. *The College and Financial Aid Guide for: AB540 Undocumented Immigrant Students*. (Los Angeles: University of Southern California).

[18] University of California, Office of the President, 2007. *AB540 Annual Report*. California: http://www.ucop.edu/sas/sfs/docs/ab540_annualrpt_2007.pdf.

[19] Urban Institute.

[20] University of Southern California, School of Policy, Planning, and Development, February 2005. *California Demographic Futures: Projections to 2030, by Immigrant Generations, Nativity, and Time of Arrival in U.S.* Los Angeles: http://www.usc.edu/schools/sppd/research/popdynamics/pdf/CDFFULLreport2005.pdf.

The California DREAM Act

Advocacy on behalf of undocumented students did not cease with the passing of AB540. In fact, it continued for years. AB540's sole responsibility was to redefine California's in-state tuition to be inclusive of undocumented and out-of-state students. With this legislative gain came a new challenge, both personal and legislative, for undocumented students. Although undocumented students obtained in-state tuition, they still faced a personal financial challenge inhibiting their pursuit of higher education. Socially, undocumented student advocates established private scholarship funds to aid students;[21] legislatively, they promoted dialogue and political challenges in the state. Legislative proposals surfaced between 2002 and 2011 but were defeated at the governors' desks (both Republican and Democrat) each year. Statistics about the undocumented students' economic contribution and liabilities were developed to promote dialogue with legislators. Additionally, new collaborative partnerships were created as a catalyst for an unprecedented movement.

Senator Gil Cedillo first introduced Senate Bill (SB) 160, the California Dream Act, in 2005. The proposal allowed AB540 undocumented students to obtain institutional and state financial aid. Year after year, Senator Cedillo tenaciously reintroduced the bill. After continued vetoes throughout the years, Senator Cedillo and the students changed their strategy, recognizing that the only way to achieve momentum was to form a coalition of progressive and eager community organizations: the Power and Unity Coalition.[22] The Power and Unity Coalition would organize and advocate for the California Dream Act from 2008 through the bill's passage in 2011. This coalition garnered support from diverse sectors of society including business, community organizations, media, students, educators, parents, and faith-based institutions. All were invited to support, own, and advocate for the Dream Act.

Startled by its ability to bring interested parties to the table and discuss the different strategies they were to embark upon, the coalition lacked a strong partner in its advocacy efforts—the Catholic Church. Why was the involvement of the Catholic Church, its leaders and laity, of vast importance? Simply put, both Governor Arnold Schwarzenegger and Governor Jerry Brown were Catholic. Moreover, DREAMers were mainly cultural Catholics

---

[21] Scholarship funds were established through several nonprofits such as MALDEF.

[22] The office of Senator Gil Cedillo joined PowerPAC.org to form the Power and Unity Coalition.

who had not been embraced by their communities and felt abandoned by their faith during this hardship.

Solidarity: Bridging Catholic Social Justice and Lived Reality

Acknowledging the teachings of Catholic social thought is the first step to understanding the connection between social justice issues and the Roman Catholic Church. The tradition of Catholic social teaching began with a groundbreaking papal encyclical over 120 years ago.[23] Catholic social thought is considered an intellectual tradition within the Church that is essential for the Church's mission to the world. It explains and guides a Christian perspective on the contemporary social events and issues confronting our time.[24] Each subsequent encyclical addressed the gap between rich and poor nations and guided both Christians and policymakers to arrive at a Gospel understanding of social issues.[25] A call to embody a commitment of faith, values, and ethics is the core of social justice teachings, emphasizing faith-based action that enacts justice.[26] Authentic Catholic social teaching can be imagined as a "three-legged stool." Each leg of the stool represents scholarship in Church teachings, tradition, the lived experience of the people of God, and scripture.[27] Unfortunately, Catholic social teaching still remained outside the mainstream of ordinary parish life.[28] Members of the Church hierarchy wrote and published important documents intending to guide parishioners into a deeper understanding of their mission in the world. Unfortunately, these teachings were not usually communicated to the faithful, and thus were rarely lived out. As a result of this lack of awareness of Catholic social teachings at the local level, these teachings remained obscure to mainstream Catholics at the time.

---

[23] The first social justice encyclical, *Rerum Novarum*, was written by Pope Leo XIII in 1891.

[24] Peter J. Henriot, Edward P. DeBerri, and Michael J. Shultheis, *Catholic Social Teaching: Our Best Kept Secret.* (Maryknoll, NY: Orbis Books, 1999), 5.

[25] Ibid., 8.

[26] Ibid., 6.

[27] Teachings include papal encyclicals and document published by the United States Conference of Catholic Bishops.

[28] Henriot, 3.

However, resources such as the Gospel of Luke, the papal encyclical *Gaudium et Spes*, and the USCCB document *Stranger No Longer, Together In a Journey of Hope*, encouraged the advocacy and activism of parishes throughout California between 2008 and 2011. These documents judged through the lens of faith and Catholic social tradition, empowering students and their families to reconnect with their faith at a personal level, bestowing a sense of dignity and love of others. These documents, once shared with the students, their parents, communities, and allies, became a forceful act of love toward one another, enabling these students to risk their identities and proclaim, "undocumented and unafraid."

Scripture

The interconnectedness of scripture and the intellectual thought of the Roman Catholic Church allows the gospels to speak to current times and contexts. Scripture has become the new touchstone for Catholic social teaching.[29] The scriptural leg of the three-legged stool provides a historical context, setting the stage for a better frame of reference in today's struggle for justice. Contextualizing the California Dream Act within the Catholic social teaching framework, the Gospel of Luke 10:30 explains the general public's rejection of undocumented students, "the other," and calls forth the acceptance of "the other" that will bring everyone into communion with each other.

The Gospel according to Luke is a historical narrative bestowing value on the present time, as opposed to the other gospels that emphasize the end of time.[30] This difference in emphasis in the Gospel of Luke calls for everyone to act as Jesus did, but now, in the present. Unlike other canonical gospels, Luke has a focus on women, conversion, and acceptance. Parallel to the California Dream Act, the Gospel of Luke is consistent with advocacy efforts needed for undocumented students. The Gospel of Luke, particularly in the parable of the Good Samaritan, alludes to the need for being a neighbor, regardless of class or laws.

[29] Ibid., 20.

[30] Daniel J. Harrington, *Sacra Pagina: The Gospel of Luke* (Collegeville, MN: Liturgical Press, 1991), 21.

Jesus replied, "A man fell victim to robbers as he went down from Jerusalem to Jericho. They stripped and beat him and went off leaving him half dead. A priest happened to be going down the road, but when he saw him, he passed by on the opposite side. Likewise, a Levite came to the place, and when he saw him, he passed by on the opposite side. But a Samaritan traveler who came upon him moved with compassion at the sight. He approached the victim, poured oil and wine over his wounds and bandaged them. Then he lifted him up on his own animal, took him to an inn and cared for him. The next day he took out two silver coins and gave then to the innkeeper with the instructions, "Take care of him. If you spend more than what I have given you, I shall repay you on my way back," Which of three, in your opinion, was neighbor to the robbers' victim?" He answered, "The one who treated him with mercy." Jesus said to him, "Go and do likewise."[31]

Throughout the Gospel of Luke, specifically in the parable of the Good Samaritan, the Gospel calls the reader to treat "others" compassionately just as Jesus calls us all to do. It is not about who merits care but rather who needs care. The Gospel emphasizes that regardless of the encounters we may experience, the naked and defenseless must be treated with compassion: "You go and do the same."[32] Compassion becomes the central theme of Luke's Gospel, allowing the reader to grasp the meaning of compassion and the love of God, which extends toward acceptance and conversion. The wealthy converts and all Gentiles were called to be children of God, Jesus-like in word and action. Through their compassion for and solidarity with "the other," they are in right relationship with God. The priests and Levites who symbolically represented the leadership of the people were restricted by purity regulations in their contact with "the others." Conversely, the Samaritan was able to extend hospitality and compassion because he stood outside the prescribed Jewish law. In the Samaritan's compassion for "the other," the bridge to a right relationship with God was crossed. Recall that Samaritans, in the Lucan context, were

[31] Luke 10:29-37.

[32] Harrington, 175.

heretical "Jews" who had intermarried with Israel's historical enemies and were not accepted by the Jewish community. Although Jewish themselves, Samaritans believed in different gods and were outcasts from traditional Jewish communities. Jesus reverses the question from one of legal obligation (Who deserves my love?) to one of mercy-giving (Who needs my love?). The challenge brought forth by the parable of the Good Samaritan asks us: Who is in solidarity with "the other"? This foundation is carried forth and developed in the papal encyclicals, specifically *Gaudium et Spes*, a call for the Church to see the "signs of the times" and actively seek the Kingdom of God in this world.

Catholic Intellectual Tradition[33]

To complement the Gospel of Luke, *Gaudium et Spes* contributes to the analysis of faith-based advocacy. As the second leg of the stool, *Gaudium et Spes* was one of the documents set forth by the Second Vatican Council[34] to clarify the role of the Church in working for the Kingdom of God in a rapidly changing world.[35]

With its emphasis on the progress of the poor and marginalized— "the other"—*Gaudium et Spes* continues the tradition of social justice by approaching problems in the world from the basis of scripture. *Gaudium et Spes* explicitly states that there is need not merely for personal conversion of the mentality and attitudes of people but also for "many reforms" in socioeconomic life itself—that is, in its structures (GS 63.5).[36] The discussion of systematic structures that exacerbate socioeconomic inequalities constantly resurfaces throughout the document. In all aspects of life, including the social and economic, the dignity and vocation of the human person must be

---

[33] In an attempt to remain true to the translation of the documents discussed, the wording will appear gender-specific. However, this does not reflect non-gender, inclusive language.

[34] The Second Vatican Council was called forth by Pope John XXIII "to eradicate the seeds of discord and promote peace and the unity of all humankind." The Second Vatican Council was also the first ecumenical (representative of the entire world) council, with over 2,600 bishops attending. See Richard P. McBrien, *Catholicism* (Minneapolis, MN: Winston Press, 1981). The Second Vatican Council concluded in December 1967.

[35] Henriot, 10.

[36] Donal Dorr, *Option for the poor: A hundred years of Catholic social teaching.* (New York: Orbis Books, 2013), 157.

honored and advanced along with the welfare of society, for human beings are the source, the center, and the purpose of all socioeconomic life (GS 63).[37]

Both the Good Samaritan and *Gaudium et Spes* call the Church to a special obligation that binds us to our neighbor in every person, and of actively willing their good when they cross our path. This is true whether they are a foreign laborer unjustly looked down upon or a hungry person who disturbs our conscience by recalling the voice of the Lord (GS 27.3).[38] The three vital components to being a neighbor and promoting justice for "the other" include: (1) overcoming fear of the unknown and possible threats; (2) reflecting a compassionate outlook; and (3) Jesus-like actions. The justice of which the document speaks is not simply the resolution of political grievances. It extends to the whole economic order.[39] Education and access to education are essential parts of the contemporary economic order. *Gaudium et Spes* and the Good Samaritan call for the Church to prevail amid hostile circumstances in meeting those ends, and in keeping with its proper role, to help its citizens build bridges of solidarity toward "the other" (GS 67.6).[40]

The Gospel of Luke and *Gaudium et Spes* demand consideration for the marginalized, the oppressed, and "the other" as neighbors. It is not enough to be concerned *for* the poor; one must discover what it means to be *with* the poor.[41] Providing undocumented students with equal access to education represents a concern *for* them, yet the papal encyclical reminds each Christian that we are called to be *with* them by advocating for their right to institutional financial aid. Scripture mandates love of neighbor. Every person is our neighbor; active love is necessary (GS 28).[42] The ideal presented in *Gaudium et Spes* of being neighbor to "the other" is marred by the social reality caused by discrimination and fear of the unknown, which perpetuate injustice and un-Jesus-like behavior. Only over the bridge of solidarity can we enter into compassionate relationship with "the other."

---

[37] David J. O'Brien and Thomas A. Shannon, eds. *Catholic social thought: The documentary heritage.* (New York: Orbis Books, 2000).

[38] Ibid.

[39] Dorr, 154.

[40] O'Brien.

[41] Dorr, 167.

[42] Henriot, 89.

Through *Gaudium et Spes* the Church reflected on its own call to help humanity gain a deeper insight into its full destiny, so that it can fashion the world to better serve human dignity, search for a fraternity that is universal and more deeply rooted, and meet the urgent needs of our age with a unified effort born of love (GS 91.2).[43] Tailored to the signs of the times within their own regions, regional bishops have responded to *Gaudium et Spes* and, faithful to the Gospel, to matters within their territories. There are two episcopal letters that emphasize the bridge of solidarity to be neighbors to "the other," and uphold their dignity through compassion and respect. *Strangers No Longer: Together in a Journey of Hope*, co-authored by Mexican and North American bishops, is consistent with the Good Samaritan's acts of compassion, understanding, and respect while overcoming fear and—at times—laws.

Being neighbor to "the other" is to be *of service* to "the other," just like the Good Samaritan in Luke's Gospel; and to be *with* "the other" in service is to achieve a community in communion with one another.[44] *Strangers No Longer* welcomes the presence of immigrants within their parish communities and calls for just treatment of the immigrant community by parishes, public officials, and the community at large. Furthermore, *Strangers No Longer* reflects on the social justice teachings of the Catholic Church and scripture to enlighten the Church in the treatment and solidarity of immigrants in the United States and Mexico. We judge ourselves as a community of faith by the way we treat the most vulnerable among us. The Catholic Church's proposed treatment of migrants challenges the consciences of elected officials, policymakers, law enforcement officers, residents of border communities, and providers of legal aid and social services, many of whom share our Catholic faith.[45] Sharing the responsibility of caring for "the other" becomes the central message of *Strangers No Longer*, justifying the right to migrate, the right to protect borders, and the right to treat "the other" with dignity.

When any country of origin hinders the growth or endangers the dignity of its people, this usually results in the migration of people to other countries. This can destabilize the social order and family structure for many individuals. Communities of faith are called to minister to and work toward changes in both church and society. They must confront structures that impede the

---

[43] O'Brien, 211.

[44] A sacrament within the Church—"communion"—but can also mean "united" or "in solidarity."

[45] Ibid., 6.

immigrant from exercising their dignity and living as children of God.[46] To accept "the other" as part of the parish community makes the immigrant no longer a stranger but a friend, a family member, a dignified human being.

Undocumented students need to be embraced by the Church as members of parishes and communities of faith. These episcopal letters also convey that advocating for the educational rights of undocumented students is both a pastoral concern and a public policy issue.[47] Conversion to understand and accept "the other" is part of the process of accompanying "the other," whereas the process of conversion deals with confronting attitudes of cultural superiority, indifference, and racism. It is no longer acceptable to treat migrants as foreboding aliens, terrorists, or economic threats, but rather as persons with dignity and rights, revealing the presence of Christ, and recognizing students as bearers of deep cultural values and rich faith traditions.[48]

Once established communities begin to acknowledge and affirm the gifts and contributions of "the others," a spirit of welcome develops and enlivens an entire community. This is the conversion for which *Strangers No Longer* highlights the need. This leads to a bridge of solidarity *with* "the other," especially in times of oppression caused by societal and civic factors. As leaven in society, pastoral agents who constantly seek this type of conversion can be instruments of peace and justice to promote systemic change by making legislators and other government officials aware of what they see in the community.[49]

Conversion happens on two levels, beginning with the individual pastoral agent and moving into civic and societal institutions. Undocumented students long to be part of a society that accepts them regardless of their legal status. Parishes can serve as a bridge for this type of solidarity between students, society, and government. Collaborating and bringing dialogue to the table, parishes can increase the awareness of the needs of undocumented students in the area of education. Ministering to undocumented students no longer affects the community solely within parish walls but is a prevalent call to minister with them outside parish boundaries. To echo the plight of undocumented students within the parish community leads the community

[46] Ibid., 9.

[47] Ibid., 40.

[48] Ibid., 40.

[49] Ibid., 43.

of faith into conversion and communion with them. Thus, the community becomes a bridge that leads to solidarity.

The Lived Experience of Faith-Based Advocacy

By lived experience, the Church advocates for a comprehensive immigration reform that is inclusive of families, as well as cultural and labor backgrounds. The United States Conference of Catholic Bishops urged elected officials to pass immigration reform in light of the gospels and Catholic social teachings that construe a moral and ethical framework for such legislation.[50] The California Catholic Conference of Bishops has advocated each year for the passage of the California Dream Act,[51] but it is the small churches and parishes that have failed to advocate for undocumented students. This lack of participation is seldom deliberate. A lack of information and a true interest in the subject hinders faith-based advocacy for undocumented students. To advocate for undocumented students in their quest for equal access to education is the first phase of a three-phase cycle: conversion; communion; and solidarity, which the gospels and Catholic Social teachings emphasize. *Conversion* through Christ, *communion* with Christ, and *solidarity* in Christ are the basic principles found in the literary contexts of the Lucan Gospel, *Gaudium et Spes*, and the episcopal letters published by the United States Conference of Bishops.

Building Bridges of Solidarity

To be in solidarity is a response in reflection, attitude, and action toward the Gospels, Christian tradition, and lived experience. Through the development of consciousness, the reflection and response of the individual and community builds a bridge of solidarity with our neighbor, "the other." Solidarity is an action that is benevolent in spirit, heart, and mind from which consciousness has developed. It is an action necessary to connect worship and the practice of justice.[52] Gutierrez uses the word "worship" to mean

---

[50] J. Kevin Appleby, "Toward Immigration Reform," *America* (americamagazine.org), (March 19, 2007), 196, 10.

[51] http://www.istillhaveadream.org/SB1TheCaliforniaDreamActProposal.pdf, 12.

[52] Gustavo Gutierrez, *The God of Life* (New York: Orbis Books, 1989), 45.

public prayer; however, within the scope of this chapter, "worship" includes the notion of private prayer. In the bishops' call to have a faith that enacts justice, the individuals and parish communities are asked to bridge their reflection and response to the needs of "the other." The newfound consciousness and conversion must be further developed throughout the parish communities, overflowing to the general public for the benefit of "the other."

The Los Angeles Archdiocese estimates that there are approximately 1 million Catholics[53] in its geographic boundaries. Of these 1 million Catholics, 10-15% are undocumented youth.[54] Historically, parishes have been neighbors to immigrants, through parish-based programs such as *Justice for Immigrants*[55] that advocate a dignified treatment of immigrants and comprehensive immigration reform. This model of solidarity can be adopted for the advocacy of undocumented students. Undocumented students already fit the context and platform developed by *Justice for Immigrants.*

Solidarity with immigrants requires a journey on the bridge of the love of Christ.[56] Advocacy on behalf of undocumented students as a response to the Gospels and social justice tradition can be empowering for students and the community at large, allowing them to be in communion with the spirit of Christ. Thus, advocacy is an ecclesial response to new pastoral needs of undocumented students, leading them toward the transformation of their migration experience not only as an opportunity to grow in Christian life, but also as an occasion for new evangelization and mission.[57] Like actions of the Samaritan who went to the inn and cared for the injured traveler, this act dignifies undocumented students. The injured traveler is no longer an injured man ignored by the Levite and priest. Jesus made the Samaritan, who was looked upon as an unholy outcast and foreigner, the model of solidarity because he came to the aid of an injured man who was a stranger to him.[58] Parishes are called to do the same—to dignify the presence of undocumented students within their parishes and communities. Upon the conversion and

[53] John Orr, *Religion and Multiethnicity in Los Angeles.* Center for Religion and Civic Culture, University of Southern California, 1999.

[54] Instituto Fe y Vida: http://www.feyvida.org/research/fastfacts.html.

[55] http://www.justiceforimmigrants.org/parishes.html.

[56] *Erga Migrates Caritas Christi*, Vatican City, 2004.

[57] Ibid., 3.

[58] California Catholic Conference of Bishops' Statement on Immigration Reform, March 21, 2006.

communion process, parishes and individuals are transformed into innkeepers, becoming a bridge in the realization of solidarity. As innkeepers, the parish community lives out the call of the bishops to welcome the stranger among them and act on behalf of their well-being.

These innkeepers responding to the bishops' call are asked to extend a welcome and convey hospitality toward "the others." By engaging other parishioners in the process of conversion, communion, and solidarity, the parish can be a bridge of solidarity to the heart and mind. As innkeepers, the parish is challenged to an ethical and moral dialogue on behalf of the injured traveler, responding and justifying their actions through the tradition of the Church. The response and justification of actions are found in *Gaudium et Spes* and *Strangers No Longer: Together in a Journey of Hope*. Each of these documents calls the Church to act according to the signs of the times. A never-ending cycle of conversion, communion, and solidarity can therefore be perpetuated by the actions of the innkeepers. These innkeepers are the Church, the common folk who bridge time and space, while caring for those who are most vulnerable.

Conclusion

The Church should be a bridge to ethical and moral principles that emphasize the words and actions of Jesus. From the vantage point of solidarity, the way individuals begin to view "the other" and God changes dramatically. Solidarity with undocumented students provides believers with Gospel values lived in everyday life. Undocumented students seek to dignify their lives through educational development. Education is a vital need to further advance one's life today. The California Dream Act did not solve every problem, but it served as a stepping-stone for undocumented students within the state to progress educationally and economically in the community they call home. They need communities of faith to stand in solidarity with them. Communities of faith are called by their traditions to be a bridge to solidarity with undocumented students.

CHAPTER THIRTEEN

The Practical Theological Journey of Participatory Action Research: Building the Bridge Between the Classroom and the Field

CLAUDIA H. HERRERA-MONTERO, PhD

> *Ultimately, one carries out participatory action research with fear and trembling because it depends on God's Kairos and the movement of the Spirit.*
>
> —*Elizabeth Conde-Frazier*[1]

IN THE MINISTERIAL JOURNEY of the university setting, led and empowered by the Spirit, one encounters human faces, with living stories, full of joy, hope, and struggle. One learns to prayerfully reflect and *listen to the heartbeat* of the community and to the people's journey. In *Evangelii Gaudium* (Joy of the Gospel), Pope Francis talks about the Church as "first and foremost a people advancing on its pilgrim way towards God."[2] Then

---

[1] Elizabeth Conde-Frazier, "Participatory Action Research," in *The Wiley-Blackwell Companion to Practical Theology*, ed. Bonnie J. Miller-McLemore (Malden, MA: Wiley-Blackwell Publishing Press, 2012), 240.

[2] Ibid.

he continues: "As the Church seeks to experience a profound missionary renewal, there is a kind of evangelization which falls to each of us as a daily responsibility."[3] This missionary renewal is lived out person-to-person in everyday life:

> This is the informal preaching which takes place in the middle of a conversation; personal dialogue, when the other person speaks and shares his or her joys, hopes and concerns for loved ones, or so many other heartfelt needs.[4]

In practical theology, this personal dialogue is critical in order to produce new bridges of relationships with creation.

Attending to *Lo Cotidiano* (the Everyday)

Practical theology directs particular attention to the everyday and the reality of the world. This process happens in the ordinary and moves from "informal" to "formal" attending,[5] exhorting the theological enterprise to become:

> ...a way of life, where it enters our dwelling in the world... and in which we [theologians] continually "answer and respond" to the call and vocation of apprenticeship and discipleship in God's ways.[6]

The virtue of "practical wisdom," that helps practical theology to discern and reflect on one's vocation—the encounter between *our dwelling in the world* and the crying of the world—correlates with the *interpretive* and the *normative* tasks in practical theology that help the theologian to listen and to interpret the world through the practices of everyday life.

---

[3] Ibid., 127.

[4] Ibid.

[5] Richard R. Osmer, *Practical Theology: An Introduction* (Grand Rapids, MI: Eerdmans, 2008), 37-39.

[6] Terry A. Veling, *Practical Theology: "On Earth As It Is in Heaven"* (Maryknoll, NY: Orbis, 2005), 16.

Ada María Isasi-Díaz drew upon hermeneutics of suspicion that assert the descriptive, hermeneutical, and epistemological significance of *lo cotidiano,* everyday experience and practice of the people.[7]

This perspective shifts practical theology to explore the everyday not as a static vision of daily life, but as an *incarnational practice* defined as the lived experience that dwells with God's purpose in the world. Orlando O. Espín refers to *lo cotidiano* as "the real life that is lived, lived and experienced, by real people, in the everyday."[8] *Lo cotidiano* is lived not in abstract concepts of reality, but is *incarnational* as it reveals God's purpose in human flesh and its dwelling in the world. *Lo cotidiano,* as lived experience, is more than a colloquial and sometimes abstract term addressed (*con lucha*) beyond the Latina/o audience. For the purpose of this work, *lo cotidiano* is explored as a methodological frame, defined as participation, embodiment and lived practice or lived experience in the everyday, and a *locus theologicus* in the practical theological enterprise.

Overview of Participatory Action Research

There are different perspectives about the historical roots of participatory action research. For the purpose and interest of this work, there will be a brief notation of the development of this methodology beginning in South America. Kathryn Herr and Gary L. Anderson note:

> ... the work of Miles Horton and John Gaventa of the Highlinder Center served as an early inspiration for Participatory Action Research in North America, but it was the appearance of Paulo Freire's *Pedagogy of the Oppressed* in English in 1970 that galvanized critical research in the U.S.[9]

---

[7] Kathleen A. Cahalan and Gordon S. Mikoski, *Opening the Field of Practical Theology: An Introduction* (Lanham, MD: Rowman & Littlefield, 2014), 160.

[8] Orlando O. Espín, *Idol and Grace: On Traditioning and Subversive Hope* (Maryknoll, NY: Orbis Books, 2014), 114.

[9] Kathryn Herr and Gary L. Anderson, *The Action Research Dissertation: A Guide for Students and Faculty* (Thousand Oaks, CA: SAGE, 2005), 15.

During the last four decades, "participatory research has been done all over Latin America and the rest of the third world. The first World symposium of Action Research was held in Cartagena, Colombia in 1977,"[10] almost a decade after Medellín.

Paulo Freire focused on working with illiterate communities in Brazil as a way of social action. He proposed a methodology where illiterate adults or *campesinos* (rural agricultural workers) in Latin America become active participants and collaborators in the articulation of their own needs, struggles, and hopes, and therefore became agents for social change. Herr and Anderson note that this research identifies *generative themes* or *issues of vital importance* with a dual purpose: "(a) to help participants (usually adults) to acquire literacy and (b) to help them engage in social critique and social action."[11] In their work *We Make the Road by Walking*, Myles Horton and Paulo Freire present an introduction to a dialogue between both authors on the dynamics of education and literacy projects. The following is an example of some of the dialogues in which both authors metaphorically articulate the process of pedagogy using both practical and theoretical examples:

> *Myles*: Well now, when we talk about this kind of background, it's mainly the things that would help people understand where I came from in terms of my ideas and my thinking, what they are rooted in. Is that the idea?
>
> *Paulo*: Yes. Everything you recognize as something important. I think that even though we need to have some outline, *I am sure that we make the road by walking*.[12]... You're saying that in order to start, it should be necessary to start.

---

[10] Ibid.

[11] Ibid.

[12] The phrase "we make the road by walking" is an adaptation of a proverb by the Spanish poet Antonio Machado, in which one line reads "*se hace camino al andar*" or "you make the way as you go." See Antonio Machado, *Selected Poems*, trans. Alan S. Trueblood (Cambridge: Harvard University Press, 1982), 143; Myles Horton and Paulo Freire, *We Make the Road by Walking: Conversations on Education and Social Change* (Philadelphia, PA: Temple University Press, 1990), 6-7.

220   *Claudia H. Herrera-Montero*

Myles: I've never figured out another way to start.

Paulo: The question for me is how it is possible for us, in the process of making the road, to be clear and to clarify our own *making* of the road...It's necessary. But I am not worried... because I think that they will come out of the conversation.

Myles: Not knowing what you had in mind, Paulo. I've been thinking about some of the things I'd like not so much to get into the book but to get out of this conversation... I'd like to get your reaction. There will be a lot of questions in the back of my mind as we go through this conversation... I see this thing as just unfolding as we go along... The conversation should be rooted and just keep moving along. I think we'll run out of time before we run out of ideas.[13]

This conversation serves as a metaphor for the flexible dynamic of the methodology of participatory action, accounting for the openness of the collaborators to the external circumstances of time and place, as well as how both the participants and the researcher are mutually attentive to new insights that emerge along the course of the research. McTaggart notes, "Collaboration is fundamental to the idea of action research."[14] This dynamic differs from conventional research, as it offers a methodology that gives flexibility to the use of different methods and new dialogue among participants throughout the research. In the process of listening and discernment, one does not fully anticipate final results or answers within ordinary time and space. Rather, based on primary observations, the faithful disciple is called to prophetically grasp meaning, reflect, imagine—even carrying trembling and the uncertainty that brings *la lucha* to survive—and seeks to transform the theological enterprise.

Conde-Frazier notes that practical theology focused on justice "requires living in the borderland between God and the people. It creates a prophetic space where we do not announce or denounce but help to bring about alternative practices for more humane living."[15] Prophetic space, response, or

[13] Ibid.

[14] Robin McTaggart, "Participatory Action Research: Issues in Theory and Practice," *Educational Action Research* 2.3 (1994), 314, http://dx.doi.org/10.1080/0965079940020302.

[15] Conde-Frazier, "Participatory Action Research," 241.

voices indicate the movement of the spirit to reflect, respond, and call out in action to the good news of salvation. *Lo cotidiano* is prophetic, then, as "a way of approaching theology as a space where God encounters those who are oppressed at the very place of their suffering."[16] It anticipates hope for the future, recalls the news of salvation, and brings new insight and knowledge. In the process of listening:

> ... one learns to observe, collect data, analyze or make meaning from the data, think critically, imagine, and synthesize data in order to come up with insight and action. Insight is wisdom and understanding from the inside and the power to see deeply. Critical thinking is making connections and seeing implications. Imagination is looking at what form to give to the wisdom we have derived. How does it shape the world differently? Action comes as we organize our thinking to see the causes of reality. Our actions are then informed by critical reflection.[17]

The world is shaped differently when humanity fully participates in the articulation of its own historical project in dialogue with divine purpose. The practice of engaging people in the articulations of their own struggles and hopes is what Conde-Frazier calls "incarnational research."[18] This process opens the space for dialogue and theological reflection between the researcher and the people. It calls us to reflect on people's lived experiences in the world, to listen prophetically to God's purpose and revelation through those lived experiences, to imagine God's revelation through new insights, and to raise new questions that move us to action.

Participatory Action with College-Age Students in South Florida

My social location as a practical theologian, drawing from the spiritual and cultural wells of the Catholic and U.S. Latino/a experience, shapes my understanding and lenses as a practical theologian, and the way I write and interpret

[16] Ibid., 235.

[17] Ibid.

[18] Ibid.

theology and the world. It has also moved me to mentor college-age students from a contextual lens beyond the classroom setting. Working as a Church leader and educator in South Florida, I have had the opportunity to serve a unique and diverse student body. St. Thomas University, a majority-minority Catholic institution in the Archdiocese of Miami, located in Miami Gardens, Florida, serves students from Hispanic-Latino/a and Caribbean descent. The uniqueness of this social location has allowed me to reflect on the importance of affirming these students' identity through narrative and oral stories. When students are empowered to name their particular social location and claim that particularity as a starting point for their reflection, they are able to make meaningful connections between their lives, with all that is part of them, and their vocation in the world. Finding their call and identity, *who they are* and *where they come from*, empowers them to embrace, reimagine, and create new ways to exercise their leadership in the world.

Participation-Action in Immokalee, Florida

My classroom work incorporates the practice of theological method and methodology that aims to inspire engaged learning beyond the classroom. I utilize practical theology's methodology of participatory action research in order to engage college-age students as active agents of change in society. This is a way of bridging the classroom with underrepresented and vulnerable communities, specifically the migrant farm-working community in Immokalee, Florida. Immokalee is a large town in Collier County, Florida, home to the largest farm-worker community in Florida; the majority of the population from Mexico, Guatemala, and Haiti.[19] It is known as the largest producer region of tomatoes in Florida and a place that has witnessed the cry of the migrant community for more humane labor and wage conditions.

    The first stage of engaged learning is *Listening to the Sources*. This phase focuses on learning and researching the reality of the migrant farm-worker community in Immokalee and the agricultural system in South Florida. This research piece was implemented before we traveled to Immokalee. The students were assigned readings on Catholic social teaching regarding human dignity and the rights of workers and families. In the past year, I incorporated an in-depth reading and reflection on Pope Francis' *Encyclical on the*

[19] See: Coalition of Immokalee Workers (CIW), in http://www.ciw-online.org.

Environment and Human Ecology (Laudato Si). In addition, this research piece was combined with other learning techniques such as presentations by guest speakers who are community organizing leaders.

The second phase is called the participatory or *encuentro* phase. *Encuentro* is directly associated with the culture of *encounter* and is therefore a bridge-building learning technique that invites students to encounter the living experience of the most vulnerable. This is the service learning or participation-action experience in Immokalee that is part of the class curriculum. This phase proposes "incarnational research"[20] because it listens to and enters deeply into the lived experiences of the people in God's *kairos*. "One learns to observe, collect data, analyze, or make meaning from the data, think critically, imagine and synthetize data in order to come up with insight and action."[21] This process also intends to articulate the "values, symbols, ideas and other conceptual vehicles that elevate [the students] to discover, rediscover or uncover a hidden meaning or truth connecting [them] to God"[22] and others in order to understand the reality of a community in need. In the process of listening and discernment, students do not fully anticipate final results or answers within ordinary time and space. Rather, the faithful disciple, as an active agent of change in the world, based on primary observations, is called to prophetically grasp meaning, reflect, imagine, and seek to transform the theological enterprise by bringing out concrete actions.

Theological Reflection on an Immersion for Justice and Peace: Bridging the Classroom and the Field

This section describes the experiences of St. Thomas University students that attended an immersion with the farm-worker community in Immokalee as part of a religious studies course. The course incorporates engaged learning as part of the teaching and learning pedagogy. Some of the practices and reflections shared by the students in the context of a five-day immersion in Immokalee are helpful here. In this case, the Journey to Emmaus was used

---

[20] Conde-Frazier, "Participatory Action Research," 241.

[21] Ibid.

[22] Jeanette Rodriguez, "Mestiza Spirituality: Community, Ritual, and Justice." *Theological Studies* 65.2 (June 2004), 319.

as a theological reference and was utilized as part of theological reflection at the beginning and end of each day.

> **First Day: "Walk and invite"**... And it happened that while they were conversing and debating, Jesus himself drew near and walked with them, but their eyes were prevented from recognizing him.... (Luke 24: 15-16)... But they urged him, "Stay with us, for it is nearly evening and the day is almost over." So he went in to stay with them (Luke 24:29).[23]

On the first day, Christian scripture presents the experience of the apostles on the road to Emmaus to a group of students embarking on a five-day immersion in a low-income migrant community in Immokalee. The immersion started with attendance at Mass at a local parish in Immokalee, followed by settling into a homeless shelter in the town center of Immokalee. Some of the preliminary impressions were:

> "Going to this local Mass was eye opening for me. Church is the center of people's hope, center of the community. I was impacted by the children."

> "I realized that we come here with some sources that they do not have."

> "I appreciate everything that I have...."

> "They do not have anything; they just have God...."

> "I was impacted by the faces of all the people here... I can see the struggle in their faces."

> "They are trying to make sense of what happened with their lives and figure out how these things can happen while they build relationships with people in order to have clarity and discover God in it."

> **Second Day: "Recognize."** And it happened that while he was with them at table, he took bread, said the blessing, broke it and gave it to

---

[23] *The New American Bible*, revised edition.

them. With that their eyes were opened, and they recognize him, but he vanished from their sight (Luke 24:30-31).

On the second day, students considered how Christian scripture teaches us that we are on a journey in which we meet the stranger, and in the stranger we recognize and encounter Christ. On the second day, students had the opportunity to encounter different social contexts: (1) a visit to the local elementary school (*Redland Christian Migrant Association*) in order to volunteer with the kids; (2) a meeting with the CIW (*The Coalition of Immokalee Workers*) to learn about their work in the local community; and (3) volunteer work with the local shelter soup kitchen. During night reflection, the group shared a meal together and concluded with theological reflection. Two students sang in Creole and another student read Scripture in Spanish. We remembered those who bring food to our table and offered our prayer in memory of the farm-workers. The students from the group were respectful, reflective, and open to breaking bread with the community of the shelter.

Third Day: "Feel." Were not our hearts burning within us while he spoke to us on the way and opened the scripture to us? (Luke 24:32).

On the third day, the group traveled to Fort Myers in order to visit the CIW's Florida Modern-Day Slavery Museum and participate in an intercollegiate march for farm-worker rights.[24] Some of the students were able to speak with community organizers about local issues that affect their wages. On the night of reflection a guest speaker from the CIW came to our shelter to talk about his personal experience as an active leader in the Coalition. The students had the opportunity to exchange dialogue, ask questions, and raise concerns. In participation action, it is critical that conversation partners articulate reflections together in order to generate new themes and come up with concrete action. In the process of listening:

---

[24] The Florida Modern-Day Slavery Museum "is a cargo truck, outfitted as a replica of the trucks involved in a recent slavery operation (U.S. v Navarrete, 2008), accompanied by displays on the history and evolution of slavery in Florida." http://www.ciw-online.org/freedom_march/museum.html.

... *insight* is wisdom and understanding from the inside and the power to see deeply. *Critical thinking* is making connections and seeing implications. *Imagination* is looking at what form to give to the wisdom we have derived. How does it shape the world differently? *Action* comes as we organize our thinking to see the causes of reality. Our actions are then informed by critical reflection.[25]

The world is shaped differently when humanity fully participates in the articulation of its own historical project in dialogue with divine purpose. The practice of listening to people describe their own struggles and hopes is what Conde-Frazier calls "*incarnational research.*"[26] This process opens the space for dialogue and theological reflection. It calls us to reflect on people's lived experiences in the world, to listen prophetically to God's purpose and revelation through those lived experiences, to imagine God's revelation through new insights, and to raise new questions that move us to action.

During the last three days, the group encountered new and different experiences that are part of the ordinary life of the people in Immokalee, but very new to each student. By engaging the reality of Immokalee, students "multiply their horizons of meaning and enable them to adjust the lenses through which they view the world, themselves, God and the things of God."[27] These are some of the reflections shared by the students:

"I feel connected with the people... We are really committed to them."

"I feel uncomfortable about the reality of beds at night."

"I feel respect for the people of Immokalee."

"I feel confused: How could people do that to them? How can a human being be exploited by other human beings?"

"I feel a confirmation of what I had in mind and a human face with who I relate it... ."

[25] Ibid.

[26] Ibid.

[27] Mark William Radecke, "Service-Learning and the Spiritual Formation of College Students" *Word & World* (2006), 291.

Fourth Day: "Become One." So they set out at once and returned to Jerusalem where they found gathered together the eleven and those with them who were saying, the Lord has been truly raised and has appeared to Simon! (Luke 23: 33-34).

On the fourth day the journey started at 4:00 a.m. The students woke up and walked from the shelter to the main parking lot where farmworkers wait for a truck with the hopes of being chosen for a day of work in the fields. Some of the students greeted the workers in Spanish and Haitian Creole. A profound experience for me, of being an educator and theologian, was seeing the students connecting with their roots and feeling comfortable speaking with the people in Immokalee in their language of origin, the language of their families. Following this opportunity, the group set out to volunteer with Habitat for Humanity.

That very same night, the students felt the need to give away their pillows and donate them to the residents sleeping on the floor outside of our shelter. One of the students said, "At least we had pillows and sleeping bags while we stayed there, the guys sleeping next to us do not have anything." There was a breakthrough of the Spirit in human time and there was no longer ordinary time, but *Kairos* time working in the ordinary life. Rebecca Chopp notes, "This time does not blend the borders of the self as much as it calls all borders into question."[28] In this prophetic space, God reveals to the people in *kairotic* time through ordinary people and ordinary life, which becomes a vital source of theology; a *locus theologicus*.

Fifth Day: "Share." So they set out at once and returned to Jerusalem... (Luke 23: 33-34).... Then the two recounted what had taken place on the way and how he was made known to them in the breaking of the bread (Luke 23:35).

Scripture teaches that once the Apostles recognized Jesus during the breaking of the bread and the reading of scriptures, they set out at once and returned to Jerusalem to gather with the community and proclaim the good

[28] Rebecca Chopp, *The Power to Speak: Feminism, Language, God* (Eugene, OR: Wipf and Stock, 1991), 291.

news of salvation. On the fifth day, the group packed and returned to Miami. I noticed how difficult it was for them to say good-bye, as we felt connected with the people in the shelter. We realized how much they gave us, instead of us to them. We came emptied and broken and returned filled with the Spirit and ready to do the important work in the world.

The students on this trip "expected to change the world." They returned to campus realizing that instead their world had been changed. One student named Maria associated the story of Emmaus with a migrant worker who arrives at a strange place and encounters a community that supports him/her—in this case, the CIW. She said, "Even they are not sure what is going on, they go to the meetings and they trust in a coalition that fights for their rights, which is their hope." Maria explained that this story is about solidarity and becoming one community: "We are in a journey of helping each other and, sharing our stories with the group during the trip, spending time together, eating together, sleeping together and praying together." In addition, Maria spoke about her experience in volunteering with the kindergarten kids. She said:

> I saw hope and happiness in the face of those kids who perhaps are
> in the midst of a struggle that I cannot see... but my heart felt so
> good when I was with them to the point that it was hard for me to
> say goodbye. It was hope in the midst of the despair of the migrant
> community of Immokalee.

On the other hand, Rosa considered that the experiences lived there helped her fully understand what is going on in Immokalee. Comparing her experience with Scripture, she said, "You can hear all the stories about what the people in Immokalee are going through but until you experience being there, you don't fully understand." For example, she talked about passing out the sandwiches at night to the people in the shelter and seeing their faces when they received them was to fully understand their hunger. During our time in Immokalee we encountered suffering, struggle, and injustice; moreover, we shared not only smiles but joys and stories with the kids in the schools, with the people in the homeless shelter, and with the farm-workers.

When the students returned from the immersion, they were required to develop a project correlating their reflections between their service-learning and class content. What is noteworthy is that the majority of students expressed their interest in continuing service-learning work in local communities. By listening to the narratives and lived experiences of active participants in the theological reflection, in this case college-age students serving in Immokalee, *participation* recognizes "the value of including [the people] as essential in the generation of useful knowledge"[29] towards change, transformation, and therefore *action* that "is informed by critical reflection,"[30] in the theological exercise. The act of recognizing participants within the framework of *lo cotidiano*, or the everyday, meets the challenge of exploring daily life as more than mere abstract concept and grasps *the lived experiences* of the people whose articulation of their own lives is critical for the task of practical theology. This type of theology is a discipline with the world as its field of study, a world where bridges are built in the encounter with the needs of others.

---

[29] Elizabeth Conde-Frazier, "Participatory Action Research: Practical Theology for Social Justice," *Religious Education*, 101, 3 (Summer 2006), 321.

[30] Ibid., in *The Wiley-Blackwell Companion to Practical Theology*, ed. Bonnie J. Miller-McLemore (Malden, MA: Wiley-Blackwell Publishing Press, 2012), 234.

Bibliography

Cahalan, Kathleen A. and Gordon S. Mikoski. *Opening the Field of Practical Theology: An Introduction*. Lanham, MD: Rowman & Littlefield, 2014.

Chopp, Rebecca S. *The Power to Speak: Feminism, Language, God*. Eugene, OR: Wipf and Stock, 1991.

Coalition of Immokalee Workers (CIW), in http://www.ciw-online.org

Conde-Frazier, Elizabeth. "Participatory Action Research." In *The Wiley-Blackwell Companion to Practical Theology*, edited by Bonnie J. Miller-McLemore. Malden, MA: Wiley-Blackwell Press, 2012, 234-243.

—. "Participatory Action Research: Practical Theology for Social Justice." *Religious Education* 101, 3 (Summer 2006), 321-329.

Espín, Orlando O. *Idol and Grace: On Traditioning and Subversive Hope*. Maryknoll, NY: Orbis Books, 2014.

—. Introduction to *The Wiley Blackwell Companion to Latino/a Theology*. Edited by Orlando O. Espín. Malden, MA: Wiley Blackwell, 2015.

Francis. *Evangelii Gaudium*. http://www.vatican.va/content/francesco/en/apost_exhortations/documents/papa-francesco_esortazione-ap_20131124_evang elii-gaudium.html. Accessed June 1, 2016.

Freire, Paulo. *Pedagogy of the City*. Translated by Donaldo Macedo. New York, NY: Continuum, 1993.

—. *Pedagogy of the Oppressed*. Translated by Myra Bergman Ramos. New York, NY: Continuum, 2003.

Gadamer, Hans-Georg. *Truth and Method*. Translated by Joel Weinsheirmer and Donald G. Marshall, New York, NY: Continuum, 2011.

Gutiérrez, Gustavo. *A Theology of Liberation: History, Politics and Salvation*. Translated and Edited by Sister Caridad Inda and John Eagleson. Maryknoll, NY: Orbis Books, 1973.

—. *A Theology of Liberation: History, Politics and Salvation, 15th Anniversary Edition with a New Introduction by the Author*. Translated and edited by Sister Caridad Inda and John Eagleson. Maryknoll, NY: Orbis Books, 1988.

Heitink, Gerben. *Practical Theology: History, Theory, Action Domains*. Translated by Reinder Bruinsma. Grand Rapids, MI: Eerdmans, 1999.

Herr, Kathryn and Gary L. Anderson. *The Action Research Dissertation: A Guide for Students and Faculty*. Thousand Oaks, CA: SAGE Publications, 2005.

Horton, Myles and Paulo Freire. *We Make the Road by Walking: Conversations on Education and Social Change*. Philadelphia, PA: Temple University Press, 1990.

Isasi-Díaz, Ada María and Yolanda Tarango. *Hispanic Women: Prophetic Voice in the Church*. Minneapolis, MN: Fortress Press, 1988.

Isasi-Díaz, Ada María. *En La Lucha. In the Struggle: A Hispanic Women's Liberation Theology*. Minneapolis, MN: Fortress Press, 1993.

—. *La Lucha Continues: Mujerista Theology*. Maryknoll, NY: Orbis Books, 2004.

—. "Lo Cotidiano: A Key Element of Mujerista Theology." *Journal of Hispanic/Latino Theology*, 10, 1 (August 2002), 5-17.

—. *Mujerista Theology: A Theology for the Twenty-First Century*. Maryknoll, NY: Orbis Books, 1996.

McTaggart, Robin. "Participatory Action Research: Issues in Theory and Practice." *Educational Action Research* 2, no. 3 (1994): 313-337. http://dx.doi.org/10.1080/0965079940020302

Nanko-Fernández, Carmen. "Lo Cotidiano as Locus Theologicus." In *The Wiley Blackwell Companion to Latino/a Theology*, edited by Orlando O. Espín. Malden, MA: Wiley Blackwell, 2015, 15-33.

Osmer, Richard R. *Practical Theology: An Introduction.* Grand Rapids, MI: Eerdmans, 2008.

Radecke, Mark William. "Service-Learning and the Spiritual Formation of College Students." *Word & World* 26, 3 (Summer 2006), 289-298.

Reason, Peter and Hilary Bradbury. *Handbook of Action Research: Participative Inquiry and Practice.* Thousand Oaks, CA: Sage, 2008.

Rodriguez, Jeanette. "Mestiza Spirituality: Community, Ritual, and Justice." *Theological Studies* 65, 2 (June 2004), 317-339.

Sanoff, Henry. *Community Participation Methods in Design and Planning.* New York, NY: John Wiley and Sons, 2000.

Swinton, John and Harriet Mowat. *Practical Theology and Qualitative Research.* London: SCM Press, 2006.

Veling, Terry A. *Practical Theology: "On Earth as it is in Heaven."* Maryknoll, NY: Orbis, 2005.

Whiteheads, James D. and Evelyn Eaton. *Method in Ministry: Theological Reflection and Christian Ministry.* Lanham, MD: Sheed & Ward, 1995.

CHAPTER FOURTEEN

Building Bridges Between Universities and Their Neighbors: The Jesuit Commitment to Community-Engaged Teaching and Learning

Daniel X. Walsh, MSW, MPA

Introduction

In 1560, Juan Alfonso de Polanco wrote to fellow Jesuit Diego Lainez that:

> …generally speaking, there are [in the Society] two ways of helping our neighbors: one in the colleges through the education of youth in letters, learning, and Christian life, and the second in every place to help every kind of person.[1]

From its inception, the educational ministry of the Society of Jesus was rooted in engaging the world: in helping our neighbors.

[1] John O'Malley, *The First Jesuits* (Cambridge, MA: Harvard University Press, 1993), 200.

Similarly, in 1636, Puritan missionary John Eliot wrote: "If we nourish not learning, both church and commonwealth will sink."[2] Early on in American history there were clear links between the role of higher education and the public good. Over time, American higher education has undergone a dynamic movement that has returned to this original civic and public purpose.

In 2017, much later than either of these events, Creighton University, a Jesuit institution located in the Midwestern United States, created an office of academic service-learning to coordinate and promote students' curricular engagement in the community and foster global citizenship perspectives. This initiative was intended to build bridges between the common strategies of civic and community engagement in higher education with the unique charisms of Jesuit education.

Both public higher education and Jesuit higher education have calls for engaging and benefitting the community, especially through service-learning pedagogy. What appears to be distinct, however, is the way in which Jesuit values and pedagogy, service-learning experiences, and a social justice perspective converge to form students who engage the world.

This chapter will examine civic and community engagement through the lenses of public and Jesuit education to better understand the critical contributions that Catholic education offers to our healthy civic and democratic society and the development of educated, engaged citizens. A study of Creighton University's service-learning program will further illustrate efforts to integrate community engagement with a perspective that builds bridges from faith toward justice.

Helping Our Neighbors in Jesuit Education

Engaging society was woven into Jesuit education from its beginning. The early Jesuits founded the Society of Jesus in order to dedicate themselves to the service of their neighbors.[3] Their commitment to service moved Jesuits to adapt themselves to persons, places, and times, which unexpectedly led to the founding of the first Jesuit schools (which had not been one of their initial objectives). However, the early Jesuits (as illustrated in Polanco's 1560

---

[2] Ernest Boyer, "The Scholarship of Engagement," *Journal of Public Service & Outreach* 1.1 (1996), 11.

[3] "The Promotion of Justice in the Universities of the Society," *Promotio Iustitiae*, 116 (2014), 7.

letter to Lainez), offered educational opportunities as one of the best ways they could serve the societies of their time.[4]

Jesuit higher education institutions throughout their 500-year history have been noted for their ability to adopt changing pedagogical techniques. This history stretches from the *Ratio Studiorum*, to the more recent interest in service-learning and global learning.[5] Specifically, the Society's education ministry since the 16th century has been characterized by the Ledesma-Kolvenbach educational paradigm, namely utility, justice, humanism, and faith.[6] This education process at Jesuit universities has always including challenging the preconceived notions of students and pushing them to rethink long-held conceptions of the world.[7] Challenging student perceptions of the world is vital to the overarching meaning and purpose of a modern Jesuit higher education focusing on justice.[8]

Justice in Jesuit Higher Education

Justice is a principle that promotes the common good. It enables students to contribute to the "proper governance of public affairs and the appropriate formulation of laws."[9] Contemporary society was heavily influenced by democracies that demanded a new kind of graduate from Jesuit institutions, "responsible citizens who participate in public affairs, promote equal opportunity, and commit themselves to working together for the common good."[10]

A commitment to justice and promotion of responsible citizenship characterize the long tradition of community engagement (helping others) of the Society from the beginning. These are consistent with recent developments within the Catholic Church. The World Synod of Catholic Bishops convened in 1971 and issued the document "Justice in the World," declaring

---

[4] Ibid.

[5] James J. Fleming, "The Emerging Role of Service Learning at Jesuit Universities," *Explore: A Quarterly Examination of Catholic Identity and Ignatian Character in Jesuit Higher Education* (1999), 2.

[6] "The Promotion of Justice in the Universities of the Society," *Promotio Iustitiae*, 8.

[7] Fleming, "The Emerging Role of Service Learning at Jesuit Universities," 1.

[8] Ibid., 2.

[9] "The Promotion of Justice in the Universities of the Society," *Promotio Iustitiae*, 9.

[10] Ibid.

that "action on behalf of justice and participation in the transformation of the world fully appear to us as a constitutive dimension of the preaching of the Gospel."[11]

Consistent with this history, in 1975 the Society began integrating justice into its mission more explicitly. The Society stated that that the promotion of justice was essential to the Jesuit mission in Decree 4 of General Congregation 32 (GC 32): "The mission of the Society of Jesus today is the service of faith, of which the promotion of justice is an absolute requirement."[12] This Decree, which emphasized the option for service to the poor, moved Jesuit institutions toward more effective accompaniment of and service to the poor. Between 1983 and 2008, the Society further refined this commitment to justice. GC 33 endorsed the option for justice in its first decree; GC 34 made an even more extensive endorsement in its restatement of the Society's mission in Decrees 2 through 5; and GC 35 confirmed once again the Society's mission as expressed in GC 32 and reflected on it in the light of the theological concept of reconciliation.[13]

Speaking Truths

In 2001, in a speech at Santa Clara University entitled, "The Service of Faith and the Promotion of Justice in American Jesuit Higher Education," Rev. Peter-Hans Kolvenbach, SJ, argued that the promotion of justice has a central place in Jesuit higher education. Reflecting on the 25th anniversary of GC 32, Kolvenbach contended that fostering the virtue of justice in our students was not enough, because St. Ignatius wanted love to be expressed not only in words but also in deeds. We must therefore raise our Jesuit educational standard to "educate the whole person of solidarity for the real world."[14]

For Kolvenbach, the means of achieving this type of education was experiential:

---

[11] World Synod of Bishops, *Justice in the World* (1971), 2.

[12] General Congregation 32, Decree 4 (1975), https://jesuitportal.bc.edu/research/general-congregations/general-congregation-32/.

[13] "The Promotion of Justice in the Universities of the Society," *Promotio Iustitiae*, 10-11.

[14] Peter-Hans, Kolvenbach, SJ, "The Service of Faith and the Promotion of Justice in American Jesuit Higher Education," in *A Jesuit Education Reader*, ed. George W. Traub, SJ (Chicago, IL: Loyola Press, 2008), 155.

When the heart is touched by direct experience, the mind may be challenged to change. Personal involvement with innocent suffering, with the injustice others suffer, is the catalyst for solidarity which then gives rise to intellectual inquiry and moral reflection.[15]

Experiential education allows:

> ... the gritty reality of this world into their lives, so they can learn to feel it, think about it critically, respond to its suffering and engage it constructively. They should learn to perceive, think, judge, choose and act for the rights of others, especially the disadvantaged and the oppressed.[16]

As students begin to locate their learning outside of the classroom and from the perspectives of the poor and marginalized, they may begin to understand and practice solidarity.

The call for engaging in the work of solidary was not limited to students. Kolvenbach highlighted the essential functions of faculty in their teaching and learning—we cannot expect students to develop a commitment to justice if they themselves are not also committed to it:

> ... our professors' commitment to faith and justice entails a most significant shift in viewpoint and choice of values. Adopting the point of view of those who suffer injustice, our professors seek the truth and share their search and its results with our students.[17]

Father Ignacio Martín-Báro, SJ, one of the Jesuits martyred in El Salvador, noted that, "the more active, critical, community-oriented, and dialectical that a pedagogical method is, the greater chance it will have of being able to affect consciousness."[18] Thus, pedagogical methods employed by faculty are critical to the goals of justice and solidarity so that students are able to build bridges from the teachings of the Catholic faith and the realities that are unjust.

[15] Ibid.

[16] Ibid.

[17] Ibid., 157.

[18] Fleming, "The Emerging Role of Service Learning at Jesuit Universities," 2.

To be truly successful, the service of faith and promotion of justice in higher education must be a project undertaken by the entire institution. Since GC 32 Decree 4, Jesuit institutions of higher learning have incorporated this perspective into the formation of their students; communicated it to both teaching and non-teaching staff; become involved in the social issues of their countries; urged their students to carry out research among the poor and from their perspective; and organized university projects in accord with the demands of this mission.[19]

This institution-wide project explicitly integrates the option for the poor. Ignacio Ellacuría noted that:

> A Christian university must take into account the Gospel preference for the poor. This does not mean that only the poor study at the university; it does not mean that the university should abdicate its mission of academic excellence—excellence needed in order to solve complex social problems. It does mean that the university should be present intellectually where it is needed: to provide science for those who have no science; to provide skills for the unskilled; to be a voice for those who do not possess the academic qualifications to promote and legitimate their rights.[20]

Indeed, the Catholic Jesuit university must speak to the wider world, engaging in a broader project called the *proyección social* (social projection), an expression from Ellacuría. Dean Brackley, SJ, writes that *social projection* includes all those means by which the university projects the truth it discovers, the critique, and concrete proposals for solutions directly into the social world outside the campus in order to help shape social consciousness.[21] For Ellacuría, this truth was framed by the option for the poor in Catholic social teaching, linking the university to the vision of St. Ignatius in the Spiritual Exercises:

[19] "The Promotion of Justice in the Universities of the Society," 1.

[20] Ignacio Ellacuría, SJ, "The Task of a Christian University," Convocation address at the University of Santa Clara, June 12, 1982, quoted in Peter-Hans Kolvenbach, SJ, "The Service of Faith and the Promotion of Justice in American Jesuit Higher Education," 155.

[21] Dean Brackley, SJ, "Higher Standards," in *A Jesuit Education Reader*, ed. George W. Traub, SJ (Chicago, IL: Loyola Press, 2008), 193.

Ask yourselves the three question Ignatius of Loyola put to himself
as he stood in front of a crucified world: What have I done for Christ
in this world? What am I doing now? And above all, what should I
do? The answers lie both in your academic responsibility and in your
personal responsibility.[22]

The idea of *social projection* later appears in *Ex Corde Ecclesiae*, Pope John
Paul II's apostolic constitution on Catholic colleges and universities:

A Catholic University, as any University, is immersed in human society; as an extension of its service to the Church, and always within its
proper competence, it is called on to become an ever more effective
instrument of cultural progress for individuals as well as for society.
Included among its research activities, therefore, will be a study of
serious contemporary problems in areas such as the dignity of human life, *the promotion of justice for all*, the quality of personal and
family life, the protection of nature, the search for peace and political
stability, a more just sharing in the world's resources, and a new economic and political order that will better serve the human community
at a national and international level. University research will seek to
discover the roots and causes of the serious problems of our time.... .

If need be, a Catholic University must have the courage to speak uncomfortable truths which do not please public opinion, but which are
necessary to safeguard the authentic good of society (32).[23]

In addition to John Paul II's call for intentional solidarity on behalf of Catholic Universities, GC 36 further developed *social projection*, inviting the
Society to focus on the work of universities as contributors to the mission of
justice, but also reconciliation:

---

[22] Ignacio Ellacuría, "The Task of a Christian University," quoted in Thomas P. Rausch,
Educating for Faith and Justice: Catholic Higher Education Today (Collegeville, MN:
Liturgical, 2010), 50.

[23] John Paul II, *Ex Corde Ecclesiae*, encyclical letter, sec. 32.

Our educational apostolates at all levels and our centers for communication and social research should help form men and women committed to reconciliation, who can confront obstacles to reconciliation
and come up with solutions. The intellectual apostolate should be
strengthened so that it can help in the transformation of our cultures
and societies.[24]

Superior General Arturo Sosa, SJ, explained that reconciliation is:

... a message of hope based on a deep conviction of how the Holy
Trinity acts throughout human history. The Society of Jesus was born
and finds its own identity as a bridge builder in the work of reconciliation that comes by way of establishing *social justice*.[25]

The Society's commitment to higher education allows it to contribute to this
reconciliation so that people might live full lives. "Having life abundantly"
Sosa says, "means becoming part of and entering deeply into the span of
peoples and cultures that make up humanity. It involves delving into those
deep, complex and large-scale social changes that are taking place in our
world."[26] Universities are a means to help students learn how to promote
justice by more deeply engaging in the world through social projection, with
the larger goal of reconciliation.

Scholarship of Engagement

One major development in the history of public purpose in higher education was the work of Boyer, who in 1996 coined the term "scholarship of
engagement." Boyer writes:

... universities and colleges remain... one of the greatest hopes for intellectual and civic progress in this country. I'm convinced that for
this hope to be fulfilled, the academy must become a more vigorous

---

[24] GC 36, Dec. 1, no. 34.

[25] Arturo Sosa, SJ, "The University as a Source of Reconciled Life" (Speech, World Meeting of
Jesuit Universities, Spain, July 10, 2018), 3.

[26] Ibid., 1.

partner in the search for answers to our most pressing social, civic, economic, and moral problems, and must reaffirm its historic commitment to what I call the scholarship of engagement.[27]

The broad lexicon found in public higher education includes related but slightly distinct terms: community engagement; civic engagement; and engaged scholarship. These nevertheless fall under the broader umbrella of engagement, and their core meanings can be applied to Boyer's scholarship of engagement as it relates to students, faculty, the institution, and the community.[28] A term that often appears linked to these terms in faith-based institutions, including Jesuit institutions, is social justice. While civic engagement is inherent in the purpose and mission of faith-based institutions, they often incorporate social justice that draws heavily on biblical traditions and is tied to their advocacy for value-based liberal education to nurture students' critical thinking and to develop and engage a commitment to addressing social programs.[29]

Justice in Service-Learning

At the nexus of justice in Jesuit higher education and community engagement in public higher education, a movement towards service-learning for student formation began. Service-learning emerged in the late 1960s to capture the spirit and essence of efforts to build bridges between experiential learning and traditional academics.[30] Up until that time in America, higher learning focused on knowledge generation through experimentation and research, which was transferred to students didactically through lectures and readings.[31] The community only served as a place to apply that new knowledge acquired from classroom learning. The term *service-learning* was created

[27] Boyer, *Scholarship of Engagement*, 11.

[28] Welch, *Engaging Higher Education*, 38.

[29] John Eby, "Civic Engagement in Faith-Based Institutions," 2010, quoted in Marshall Welch, *Engaging Higher Education: Purpose, Platforms, and Programs for Community Engagement*, 16.

[30] Timothy Stanton et al., *Service-Learning: A Movement's Pioneers Reflect on Its Origins, Practice, and Future* (San Francisco, CA: Jossey-Bass, 1999), quoted in Marshall Welch, *Engaging Higher Education: Purpose, Platforms, and Programs for Community Engagement*, 25.

[31] Fleming, "The Emerging Role of Service Learning at Jesuit Universities" (Spring 1999), 3.

because they "were looking for something with a value connotation that would link action with a value of reflection on that action."[32]

Jacoby defined service-learning as:

> ... a form of experiential education in which students engage in activities that address human and community needs together with structured opportunities intentionally designed to promote student learning and development. Reflection and reciprocity are key concepts of service learning.[33]

Beginning in this time period, service-learning became the primary means for promoting civic learning among university students.

In light of both the critical issues of the world and the Jesuit mission in higher education:

> ... service-learning offers a potent and engaged pedagogy consonant with the long and successful history of Jesuit education, consistent with the central tenets of Ignatian spirituality and compatible with the Jesuit focus on educating students for a just society.[34]

This method isn't necessarily new as reflection on experience has always been part of Jesuit pedagogy. According to John English, SJ, "the *Ratio Studiorum* was just a technique to move people through experience to reflection, to articulating, to interpreting, and to deciding."[35]

Justice Learning Process

Service-learning involves more than just action and reflection. In the public conception of service-learning, there is a generally agreed upon process involving

---

[32] Timothy Stanton et al., as quoted in Marshall Welch, 25.

[33] Barbara Jacoby, *Service-learning in Higher Education: Concepts and Practices* (San Francisco, CA: Jossey-Bass, 1996) 5, quoted in Welch, Marshall, *Engaging Higher Education: Purpose, Platforms, and Programs for Community Engagement*, 25.

[34] Fleming, "Emerging Role of Service-Learning," 2.

[35] As cited in Fleming, 4.

inventory, preparation, action, reflection, and evaluation.[36] Students begin the process by identifying community needs and assets. Next, students prepare to engage the community through learning about the community and their own biases, why they are doing this work and, critically, how issues of power and privilege can affect the experience. Student action in the community explicitly bridges course learning objectives with community-identified priorities (this may mean direct or indirect service). Students reflect on their experiences throughout this process, but especially after the community actions in terms of personal insights, community issues, and the academic objectives of the course. Finally, learning is assessed through course assignments, projects, and discussions that relate to the community experience. Community partners provide feedback on whether there was an impact through the collaboration.

Ignatian pedagogy offers a rich interpretation of this community-based learning structure. After Vatican II and GC 32, Ignatian charisms including *care of the whole person, men and women for and with others, magis, and finding God in all things* were explicitly articulated as Ignatian pedagogical philosophies in the International Commission for Apostolate of Jesuit Education (ICAJE) in 1986.[37] Central to Ignatian pedagogy that cultivates the justice outcome is the recursive process of experience, reflection, and action.[38] These dynamics occur within the learner and their environment, so the context of the student, with regard to disposition and readiness, is also taken into consideration. Additionally, after action, the student is expected to be evaluated or evaluate the process of experience, reflection, and action.

As a specific teaching framework, the Ignatian Pedagogical Paradigm is founded on the belief that banking information is insufficient for student learning. In this framework, transformational experiences build bridges between students' learning on cognitive, emotional, and behavioral levels.[39] It is

---

[36] *Note:* Adapted from Center for Experiential Learning, *Components of successful service-learning courses,* Loyola University Chicago (n.d.), https://www.luc.edu/experiential/service-learning/Basics_faculty.shtml.

[37] Heidi Streetman, "Jesuit Values, Ignatian Pedagogy, and Service Learning: Catalysts for Transcendence and Transformation Via Action Research," *Jesuit Higher Education: A Journal,* 4. 1 (2015), 37.

[38] Ibid., 39.

[39] "Ignatian Pedagogy," Georgetown University (n.d.), https://commons.georgetown.edu/teaching/design/ignatian-pedagogy/.

hoped that students participating in this type of learning context will develop a deeper understanding of self and the world through service to that world.

Broadly articulated, the Ignatian pedagogical paradigm starts with "context," considering the *cura personalis* (care of the whole person) of the students themselves. In the "experience" that follows, students engage course material and community action in a way that fully involves them. The process continues as the student engages in a process of "reflection" on the experiences and the reactions it caused: cognitive and emotional; personal; societal; and behavioral. Differentiated from the traditional service-learning process, the Ignatian pedagogical paradigm is meant to build a bridge toward a final phase of action. This real education will lead the student to take actions, large and small, to create a better world for all, and particularly those most in need.[40] Finally, IPP also includes evaluation of student learning through the process, especially through continued reflection and discernment.[41]

Service-learning therefore takes on a distinct character in Jesuit higher education. In this framework:

> ... educating for citizenship that is committed to justice involves helping students understand that a university degree means not only specialized training but also taking on social responsibility as a vital part of one's professional career. Along with their studies, students acquire new civic duties. Basically, it is a matter of endowing students with values that go beyond gaining money, fame, and success, and instead forming leaders concerned for society and the world.[42]

Arturo Sosa, SJ, adds to this goal of Ignatian pedagogy:

> Seeing ourselves as world citizens should be one of the outcomes of studying or working in a Jesuit university. It is an essential element in the kind of humanity that Jesuit education seeks to support and foster. We must also make it possible for our students to hear the call to serve society as a personal commitment. Direct involvement in the

---

[40] Ibid.

[41] Ibid.

[42] "The Promotion of Justice in the Universities of the Society," *Promotio Iustitiae*, 17.

political sphere means putting oneself at the service of reconciliation and justice—something both necessary and complex.[43]

Community engagement and service-learning have evolved in parallel between institutions of the Society and American public institutions, but a key specialization is this focus on justice. What follows is a case study of how justice has been infused into service-learning and community engagement at a Jesuit university.

Helping Our Neighbors at Creighton University

Creighton University, a Jesuit university located in the United States, has recently undertaken institutional efforts to bridge experiential learning with justice education. Creighton's mission as a Catholic and Jesuit institution is committed to building bridges between the service of faith and the promotion of justice. The university mission states the social aims of the institution from the beginning: "As comprehensive, Creighton's education embraces several colleges and professional schools and is directed to the intellectual, social, spiritual, physical and recreational aspects of students' lives and to the promotion of justice." The mission speaks of core value of service to others:

> Creighton exists for students and learning. Members of the Creighton community are challenged to reflect on transcendent values, including their relationship with God, in an atmosphere of freedom of inquiry, belief and religious worship. Service to others, the importance of family life, the inalienable worth of each individual and appreciation of ethnic and cultural diversity are core values of Creighton.[44]

As a Jesuit institution, Creighton also operationalizes some of the justice-oriented characteristics of Jesuit education, including "Women and Men for and with Others: Sharing gifts, pursuing justice, and having concern for the poor and marginalized" and "Forming and Educating Agents of Change:

---

[43] Arturo Sosa, SJ, "The University as a Source of Reconciled Life" (Speech, World Meeting of Jesuit Universities, Spain, July 10, 2018), 8.

[44] See https://www.creighton.edu/about/mission.

Teaching behaviors that reflect critical thought and responsible action on moral and ethical issues."[45] Until recently, there has not been an intentional, institution-wide effort to promote and coordinate curricular engagement with the community aimed at these outcomes.

Office of Academic Service-Learning

Academic service-learning (AcSL) courses at Creighton University closely align with this justice mission. The Office of Academic Service-Learning (OASL) was established in 2017 by a presidential initiative, echoing multiple requests from faculty and administrators over the past years to develop a system to support faculty as they engage the community through their courses. OASL connects academic courses with community partners to enhance academic learning, meet community-identified needs, and foster global perspectives through engagement and reflection. Influenced by traditional definitions of the term,[46] OASL defines AcSL as:

> ... an experiential educational strategy that integrates community service into academic courses so that learning is enhanced and community partners receive concrete benefits. Students study, serve and reflect on their experience in order to deepen their appropriation of knowledge.[47]

Reflections on Experience

Whether service-learning has bridged the gap between the traditional public benefit approach to higher education and the justice orientation of Jesuit institutions at Creighton University remains to be seen, but we've gleaned several insights, nevertheless.

Faculty teaching service-learning courses that explicitly link social justice outcomes to the community experiences noted the changes observed in students. As one professor reflected:

[45] Ibid.

[46] See Sigmon, 1967; Jacoby, 1996.

[47] See https://www.creighton.edu/geo/academicservicelearning/.

Teaching service-learning courses is the most rewarding work I do because it educates and transforms the whole student in the process of serving the larger society. For that reason, it is also the most difficult work I do. Transforming students' lives requires challenging them to develop new skill sets, new dispositions regarding the purpose of learning, and self-confidence. The self-confidence component is absolutely critical. The current college student population across America is beset by insecurities, anxieties, and a sense of hopelessness. Much of this is due to an inability to feel empowered to participate in shaping their own futures. Service-learning research and action initially aggravates their state of anxiety, but if students are pedagogically developed through assignments that develop skills with which to engage the world productively, their fears can be transformed to hope. When their academic formation includes assignments that enhance their self-confidence, they are more willing to seek opportunities to work with and for others. While the most obvious goal is to serve the needs of the larger society, a necessary step in the process is serving the educational and emotional needs of students who can become partners with others in promoting hope and furthering justice.[48]

Here we see service-learning challenging students' perspectives, motivating them to seek more opportunities for community-based work, and forming them from a justice perspective.

"We don't learn from experience," John Dewey famously stated, "but from the reflection on that experience."[49] Students, in reflecting on their experiences of justice-focused service-learning, may begin to make connections among systems causing oppression and seek solutions. As a goal, students are not only called to *know* about justice, but to *do* justice. As one student reflected about her service-learning experience:

Service-learning projects contribute to larger goals of the environmental justice movement in many ways. The most important way that I have seen service-learning projects contribute to environmental

---

[48] Anonymous Creighton faculty member, email to author, 2019.

[49] John Dewey, *Experience & Education* (New York, NY: Kappa Delta Pi, 1938).

justice is helping with an education in awareness. Before this class, I had never heard the term environmental justice. I had always been concerned with the environment, but never knew there was a term to encompass my thoughts. I learned through this class and my experience at the lead screening that environmental justice is so important and that all people should be educated on this topic. The environment and the human race are so much more tied together than most people realize. This needs to change so that we can continue to work towards environmental justice for all. Our society tends to leave individual communities behind like we have in the past such as communities effected by lead. Service-learning projects bring awareness to communities that would not have as much attention put towards them as they should. This service-learning project made me want to make a change and act on what I learned. I believe that lead-screening should help our society learn that no one should be exposed to lead because there is such an easy change we can make and need to make.

This service-learning project has helped me learn and grow in so many ways. I have learned about the community, myself, and how I fit into the greater Omaha community. This service-learning has motivated me to teach others and share my knowledge to make sure that everyone is educated and can live their healthiest and best lives. Health initiatives and education will help the lead problem in Omaha and hopefully one day fix this problem completely. This class has motivated me to advocate for kids and others affected by lead to help in the prevention of lead poisoning and to keep our society safer.[50]

In both reflections, we can see the individual civic commitments sought by traditional American public education in words such as "serving society," developing "self-confidence," and "bringing awareness to communities." But we also see the beginnings of something deeper: "transforming lives," and having a goal not just of promoting democracy but of "promoting hope and furthering justice." As the student above reflected, the service-learning project changed not only her attitudes and thinking, but also her behaviors: "[it] made me want to make a change and act on what I learned."

[50] Anonymous Creighton student; reflection provided to author by faculty member, 2020.

Conclusion

On the larger mission of a Catholic university, Pope Francis said that "research and study ought to be integrated with personal and community life, with missionary commitment, with fraternal charity and sharing with the poor, with care of the interior life in relationship with the Lord."[51] This kind of education has both a civic and a social systems focus. In order to educate for citizenship that is committed to justice, professors need to help students understand that a university degree means not only specialized training but also taking on social responsibility as a vital part of one's professional career.[52]

At Creighton University, we continue to grow in closer alignment with the ideals set forth by the long, rich history of Ignatian tradition as it relates to helping our neighbors, the service of faith and promotion of justice, *social projection*, and more recently to reconciliation. The infusion of these charisms into service-learning pedagogy distinguishes it from similar public higher education initiatives. At the same time, years of research on service-learning and civic engagement from the public perspective offer many truths that benefit the Jesuit vision for higher education.

Because the real measure of our Jesuit Universities is who our students become,[53] we need our students to be equipped to critically reflect on the complex problems that concern humanity, to speak truths that unmask social prejudice and discrimination, to participate in public debates, and to be open to other ways of thinking.[54] Such an attitude builds bridges between academic dialogue and community action.

---

[51] Pope Francis, "Address of Pope Francis to the Community of the Pontifical Gregorian University, Together with Members of the Pontifical Biblical Institute and the Pontifical Oriental Institute," speech at Paul VI Audience Hall, Rome, April 10, 2014.

[52] "The Promotion of Justice in the Universities of the Society," *Promotio Iustitiae*, 23.

[53] See n. 14.

[54] See n. 52.

Bibliography

Components of successful service-learning courses, Loyola University Chicago (n.d.), https://www.luc.edu/experiential/service-learning/Basics_faculty.shtml.

Community Engagement, Brown University Swearer Center, 2016. https://www.brown.edu/swearer/carnegie/about.

"The Promotion of Justice in the Universities of the Society," *Promotio Iustitiae*, 116 (2014), 7.

Boyer, Ernest, "The Scholarship of Engagement," *Journal of Public Service & Outreach* 1, 1 (1996).

Brackley, Dean, SJ, "Higher Standards," in *A Jesuit Education Reader*, ed. George W. Traub, SJ (Chicago, IL: Loyola Press, 2008), 193.

Cuban, S. & Anderson, J., "Where's the Justice in Service-Learning? Institutionalizing Service-Learning from a Social Justice Perspective at a Jesuit University," *Equity & Excellence in Education*, 40, 2 (2007), 145.

Dewey, John, *Experience & Education* (New York, NY: Kappa Delta Pi, 1938).

Eby, John, "Civic Engagement in Faith-Based Institutions." In *Handbook of Engaged Scholarship: Contemporary Landscapes, Future Directions*, edited by H.E. Fitzgerald, C. Burack, and S.D. Seifer. (East Lansing, MI: Michigan State University Press, 2010), 165-180.

Ellacuría, Ignacio, "The Task of a Christian University," Convocation address at the University of Santa Clara, CA, June 12, 1982.

Fleming, James J., "The Emerging Role of Service Learning at Jesuit Universities," *Explore: A Quarterly Examination of Catholic Identity and Ignatian Character in Jesuit Higher Education* (1999).

Jacoby, Barbara, *Service-learning in Higher Education: Concepts and Practices* (San Francisco, CA: Jossey-Bass, 1996).

Pope Francis, "Address of Pope Francis to the Community of the Pontifical Gregorian University, Together with Members of the Pontifical Biblical Institute and the Pontifical Oriental Institute." Speech at Paul VI Audience Hall, Rome, April 10, 2014.

Pope John Paul II, *Ex Corde Ecclesiae*, encyclical letter.

Kolvenbach, Peter-Hans, SJ, "The Service of Faith and the Promotion of Justice in American Jesuit Higher Education," in *A Jesuit Education Reader*, edited by George W. Traub, SJ (Chicago, IL: Loyola Press, 2008), 155.

Mitchell, Tania, "Traditional vs. Critical Service-Learning: Engaging the Literature to Differentiate Two Models," *Michigan Journal of Community Service Learning* 14, 2 (2008), 51.

O'Malley, John, *The First Jesuits* (Cambridge, MA: Harvard University Press, 1993), 200.

Rausch, Thomas P., *Educating for Faith and Justice: Catholic Higher Education Today* (Collegeville, MN: Liturgical Press, 2010), 50.

Society of Jesus, *General Congregation* (1975) , 32.

Sosa, Arturo, SJ, "The University as a source of reconciled life." Speech at the World Meeting of Jesuit Universities, Spain, July 10, 2018, 3.

Stanton, Timothy, Dwight E. Giles, and Nadinne I. Cruz, *Service-Learning: A Movement's Pioneers Reflect on Its Origins, Practice, and Future* (San Francisco, CA: Jossey-Bass, Inc., 1999).

Welch, Marshall, *Engaging Higher Education: Purpose, Platforms, and Programs for Community Engagement* (Sterling, VA: Stylus, 2016).

World Synod of Bishops. Justice in the World (1971).

Bridging Faith and Action: The Case of Catholic Charities and Cardijn's See-Judge-Act Methodology

BRIAN R. CORBIN, PhD
Executive Vice President, Member Services, Catholic Charities USA

THROUGHOUT ITS HISTORY, THE national Catholic Charities movement has applied Cardinal Joseph Cardijn's See-Judge-Act methodology by reflecting on its experience and analyzing the world around it (see), connecting back to its theological roots (judge), and planning appropriate responses (act) to improve the lives of those served and to promote justice.[1] This approach enables an arm of the Church to engage in real-time responses to the needs of vulnerable, marginalized, and hurt persons, families, and communities. In effect, Cardijn's methodology bridges faith and action for the Church through the explicit work of Catholic Charities, which responds to the "least" brothers and sisters of Jesus (Matt 25:40). This bridging of faith and action through orthopraxis—consistent with the Latin American Church

---

[1] United States Conference of Catholic Bishops, *Catechism of the Catholic Church* (No. 5-109), Washington, DC: USCCB Publishing, 2000. Number 2423. http://www.scborromeo.org/ccc/p3s2c2a7.htm#2423.

experience—shapes the response of local Catholic Charities agencies and its national ministry, attuned to the "signs of the times."[2]

I. Experience

Strategic planning for services and organizational structures remains a fixture of "reading the signs of the times" for Catholic Charities agencies locally and nationally. Reverend J. Bryan Hehir identifies several distinct moments of Catholic Charities' collective utilization of Cardijn's See-Judge-Act method: creating its Charter in 1910; its Cadre Report in 1972; its VISION 2000 process in 1996; and its Campaign to Reduce Poverty in 2010. The method continues now during its New Moment process.[3]

In recent decades, many Catholic Charities agencies adapted the theologically based social analysis work of Holland and Henriot, which provides a framework to link faith and action for persons and institutions as envisioned by Cardijn.[4] A first step in this framework is reflection upon Catholic Charities' experience in serving persons through our organization. The *raison d'etre* for Catholic Charities agencies is the claim that the "poor belong to us" in so far as we listen to and care for those most in need.[5] The lived experiences of those who come to us for help provide the experiential aspect of analysis for our work. Our responses, however, require constant renewal because programs and services change their effectiveness, social reality uncovers new needs, and governmental shifts prioritize modalities. Catholic Charities' claim that the "poor belong to us" becomes clear when one understands that it is an organization integral to the Church. We learn from *Deus Caritas Est* that Catholic Charities or "Caritas" is an insepara-

[2] Second Vatican Council, *Gaudium et Spes. Pastoral Constitution of the Church in the Modern World.* 1965. http://www.vatican.va/archive/hist_councils/ii_vatican_council/documents/vat-ii_const_19651207_gaudium-et-spes_en.html.

[3] J. Bryan Hehir (ed.), "Theology, Social Teaching, and Catholic Charities: Three Moments in History." In *Catholic Charities USA: 100 Years at the Intersection of Charity and Justice* (Collegeville, MN: Liturgical Press, 2010), 27-46.

[4] Joseph Holland and Peter Henriot, *Social Analysis: Linking Faith and Justice* (Maryknoll, NY: Orbis Books, 1983).

[5] Dorothy Brown and Elizabeth McKeown, *The Poor Belong to Us: Catholic Charities and American Welfare* (Cambridge, MA: Harvard University Press, 2009).

ble element of the Church (*DCE*, 25).[6] In a follow-up *Motu Proprio*, *On the Service of Charity,* Benedict XVI notes that Catholic Charities organizes love for the Church.[7] Pope Francis taps into this when saying the Church is likened to a "field hospital" responding directly to the needs of those most vulnerable and considered "disposable."[8] Pope Francis brings new vitality to the See-Judge-Act tradition, explicitly used in his encyclicals and apostolic exhortations.

The historical experience of Catholic Charities points to the unique nexus of three elements: social policy; theology; and practice. Catholic Charities must be informed by and live out Catholic ethical, theological, and social teachings regarding the nature of human life and its flourishing. As a religious-based organization operating in the American legal, economic, cultural, and political milieu, Catholic Charities is impacted by various social policies regarding poverty and religious liberty. As a nongovernmental provider of social services, Catholic Charities provides expertise in social work practice and the governance of nonprofit corporations. In turn, these elements—shaped by experience—contour the action of Catholic Charities ministries and services that impact theological reflection, governmental social policy, social work practice, and institutional leadership.

II. See

Experiences based on direct work with persons and communities require Catholic Charities agencies to be open to new responses to emerging issues through "reading the signs of the times." This means stopping and again "seeing" the world repeatedly.

Catholic Charities agencies listen directly to the voices of those most impacted by social programs and services. Staff and governing boards use focus

---

[6] Benedict XVI. *Deus Caritas Est.* Encyclical Letter, 2005. https://w2.vatican.va/content/benedict-xvi/en/encyclicals/documents/hf_ben-xvi_enc_20051225_deus-caritas-est.html

[7] Benedict XVI. *On the Service of Charity.* Apostolic Letter, Motu Proprio. Vatican Press, 2012. https://w2.vatican.va/content/benedict-xvi/en/motu_proprio/documents/hf_ben-xvi_motu-proprio_20121111_caritas.html

[8] Anthony Spadaro, SJ, A Big Heart Open to God: An Interview with Pope Francis. *America,* 2013, 209(8). https://www.americamagazine.org/faith/2013/09/30/big-heart-open-god-interview-pope-francis

groups, surveys, and data analysis to ascertain effectiveness and program viability. Analyses gleaned from the social sciences provide key insights. For instance, Catholic Charities USA launched its Campaign to Reduce Poverty in 2010 and challenged its member agencies to engage with Catholic universities to employ qualitative and quantitative research and evaluation to ascertain best practices that move persons and families out of poverty.[9]

The principle of "subsidiarity" guides Catholic Charities as the hard work of "seeing" locally is critical to respond to the needs of a particular community. [10] To interpret the information at hand, Catholic Charities engages its workers in various "communities of practice" to share their experiences and "see" the world from their local place. As they "read the signs of the times," these practitioners share best practices with Church leaders and policymakers and identify new realities requiring innovative responses. Through sharing such knowledge, Catholic Charities calls others of goodwill to be in solidarity with them as they accompany people who are in need and want to change structures that keep them in poverty.

Of course, for a Church-based institution, "seeing" the world is not a neutral social science experiment. Considering our Catholic social teaching, we must "see" the world in and through the eyes of those who are most vulnerable, and through the eyes of Christ. Catholic Charities relies on its belief that God hears the cry of the widow, orphan, and stranger among us. This perspective leads us to delve deeply into the data to examine more closely the differing needs of those persons most impacted.

III. Judge

Catholic Charities makes "judgments" according to scripture and Catholic social teaching in order to bridge our interpretations about the nature of

---

[9] Catholic Charities USA (CCUSA), *Poverty in America: A Threat to the Common Good.* (Alexandria, VA: Catholic Charities USA, 2006); and CCUSA, *Poverty and Racism: Overlapping Threats to the Common Good* (Alexandria, VA: Catholic Charities USA, 2008).

[10] Pontifical Council for Justice and Peace. *Compendium of the Social Doctrine of the Church* (2005), 185-188. http://www.vatican.va/roman_curia/pontifical_councils/justpeace/documents/rc_pc_justpeace_doc_20060526_compendio-dott-soc_en.html#Origin%20and%20meanin.

integral human development and social justice to our Catholic identity.[11] The scriptures transform us as we model our response on God's revelation through history, culminating in the life and works of Jesus. The Catholic social and moral tradition encompasses papal, synodal, and United States Catholic bishops' teachings and policy positions on poverty-related topics.

Pope Francis, via a video message at the 2014 Catholic Charities USA Annual Gathering, challenged Catholic Charities staff and volunteers to go into the streets to find and serve those persons, families, and communities most in need.[12] He implored Catholic Charities to be "engines" of change that find new ways to alleviate, reduce, and prevent poverty as missionary disciples. This call drives the "judgment" of Catholic Charities staff as they design new programs or engage in community efforts to improve neighborhoods. Thus, theological "judgment," rooted in scripture and tradition, helps Catholic Charities to ask necessary questions when "seeing" the world around us, and then to design new responses—to act.

IV. Act

After theological reflection, Catholic Charities plans appropriate action that works for and with those most impacted. Planning for action in this way is rooted in the threefold mission of Catholic Charities to serve, advocate, and convene, as articulated in the "Cadre Report,"[13] reaffirmed in VISION 2000[14] and the 2017 New Moment.[15]

---

[11] Paul VI introduced the concept of integral human development in his encyclical, *Populorum Progressio*, 1967, 14. http://www.vatican.va//content/paul-vi/en/encyclicals/documents/hf_p-vi_enc_26031967_populorum.html.

See for some applications: Geoff Heinrich, David Leege, and Carrie Miller, *A User's Guide to Integral Human Development (IHD): Practical Guidance for CRS Staff and Partners*. Catholic Relief Services, 2009; Jacquineau Azetsop, SJ (ed.), *Integral Human Development: Challenges to Sustainability and Democracy* (Eugene, OR: Wipf and Stock Publishers, 2019).

[12] Francis, CCUSA Annual Gathering - Pope Francis Address. *YouTube.com*, 2014. https://youtu.be/mzxhS2JbcA0.

[13] National Conference of Catholic Charities (NCCC), *Cadre Study: Toward a Renewed Catholic Charities Movement*. (Washington, DC: Catholic Charities USA, 1972; 1992).

[14] Catholic Charities USA (CCUSA), *VISION 2000*. (Alexandria, VA: Catholic Charities USA), 1996.

[15] Catholic Charities USA (CCUSA), *A New Moment. Envisioning the Ministry of Catholic Charities* (2017-2022). (Alexandria, VA: Catholic Charities USA, 2017).

The Catholic Charities ministry relies on its code of ethics[16] to determine what practices and actions are most appropriate. "Service" empowers individuals and families to move out of poverty. "Advocacy" includes both being a voice for the voiceless in a specific case, such as assisting a family with a utility bill and renegotiating a future payment plan with that utility, and also in promoting justice on economic, political, and social levels. In fact, the 1910 Charter establishing the National Conference of Catholic Charities (NCCC) states that agencies will be "the attorney for the poor."[17] "Convening" provides an opportunity and an obligation to call the Church itself (dioceses, parishes, religious organizations) and others of goodwill to collaborate in social services and advocacy to fight poverty and build a just society. These action plans—to serve, advocate, and convene—lead to new experiences and realities that require rereading the "signs of the times," thus inaugurating a new phase of See-Judge-Act.

V. A New Moment

In 2015, in response to Pope Francis' call for Catholic Charities to serve as an engine for change, Catholic Charities USA initiated a review of its local and nationally focused ministries, utilizing the "See-Judge-Act" methodology. This effort required asking new questions ("see") about the state of the world around us and the services provided by Catholic Charities. This questioning led to a new round of theological "judgments," and ultimately new "actions" of charity and justice.

Catholic Charities centered its theological reflection upon the parable of the Good Samaritan (Lk 10:25-37). The actions of the Good Samaritan were likened to contemporary emergency measures, while those of the innkeeper were equated with Catholic Charities' institutional efforts to provide long-term support and recovery and transform harsh social structures. This reflection led to a refocusing of priorities around sharing innovations in affordable housing, integrated health and nutrition, immigration and refugee

[16] Catholic Charities USA (CCUSA), *Code of Ethics*. (Alexandria, VA: Catholic Charities USA, 2018).

[17] William J. Kerby, Proceedings of the 1910 National Conference of Catholic Charities: An interpretation. In *Foundational Documents*, 2011. (Alexandria, VA: Catholic Charities USA, 1910, 2011).

services, leadership development, and Catholic identity. The ministry further chose to elevate its creative work in social enterprise initiatives, disaster response and resiliency services, and social policy and advocacy. All of these areas, as well as a commitment to foundational ministries such as adoption, foster care, senior services, and others, continue to advance the threefold mission of service, advocacy, and convening.

VI. Some Challenges

Two challenges, at least, emerge from the utilization of Cardijn's See-Judge-Act moral methodology. One challenge is quite pragmatic. When change is required, Catholic Charities leaders seek best practices in organizational development and strategic planning. Many of these tools come from business, military, and government. In and of themselves these are fine, but something is missing when these tools are used in isolation from the basic character of Catholic moral decision making. It is imperative that Catholic Charities leaders integrate Catholic methods when using these other tools for decision making.

A second challenge involves the formation of Catholic Charities leaders as they advance through the ranks, and for other employees as they transfer from secular occupations into executive roles in Church ministry. Such leaders possess transferable skills useful in the world of Catholic-sponsored nonprofit, multi-stakeholder/funder, nongovernmental organizations. Catholic Charities, however, is not just another welfare service provider, but one tethered to the ministry of the local bishop and connected to the global Church. Formation of new leaders and those transferring from other institutional settings remains a critical strategic priority as identified in A New Moment.[18]

Catholic Charities USA's two-track O'Grady Leadership Institutes provide opportunities for training and formation in Catholic identity and methods. The Leadership One track assists new and emerging leaders in reflecting upon and better understanding their roles as leaders in general, with specific attention to their work in Catholic Charities. The Leadership Two track tackles more advanced organizational theory and planning rooted in the Catholic moral and social tradition. The "See, Judge, Act" method explicitly

---

[18] Catholic Charities USA (CCUSA), *A New Moment. Envisioning the Ministry of Catholic Charities (2017-2022).* (Alexandria, VA: Catholic Charities USA, 2017).

undergirds the entire experience, commencing with reflections based on Cardijn's insights and Holland and Henriot's social analysis, and ending with specific action plans once they return home.[19] Catholic Charities USA aims to embed these leadership formation experiences in Cardijn's theoretical construct, though attempting such an enterprise over five days remains daunting and oftentimes only touches the surface.

Conclusion

The authors in this book have explored the nature and scope of theological bridge-building contributions. Insights and challenges abound from this historical and theological work. This Afterword stressed how one major institution of the Church—"Caritas" or Catholic Charities—relies on Cardinal Joseph Cardijn's pastoral contributions. Catholic Charities honors Cardijn by demonstrating how practitioners claim and use See-Judge-Act in its institutional DNA[20] and continue to find ways to explicitly make that method real and true to its roots to bridge faith and action.

[19] Holland and Henriot.

[20] See various essays in J. Bryan Hehir (ed.), *Catholic Charities USA: 100 Years at the Intersection of Charity and Justice* (Collegeville, MN: Liturgical Press, 2010).